SERIES EDITORS:
Stewart R. Clegg &
Ralph Stablein

Edited by
Bert van Hees and
Paul Verweel (eds)

Deframing organization concepts

ADVANCES IN ORGANIZATION STUDIES

Liber & Copenhagen Business School Press

Deframing Organization Concepts
ISBN 91-47-07767-0 (Sweden and Norway)
ISBN 87-630-0180-2 (Rest of the world)
© 2006 Bert van Hees & Paul Verweel (eds) and Liber AB

Publisher's editor: Ola Håkansson
Cover design: Designlaboratoriet
Antarktis ved Dronning Mauds Land.
© Tor Ivan Karlsen/arcticphoto.net
Typeset: LundaText AB

1:1

Printed in Slovenia by
Korotan Ljubljana, Slovenien 2006

Distribution:
Sweden
Liber AB, Baltzarsgatan 4
S-205 10 Malmö, Sweden
tel +46 40-25 86 00, fax +46 40-97 05 50
http://www.liber.se
Kundtjänst tel +46 8-690 93 30, fax +46 8-690 93 01

Denmark
DBK Logistics, Mimersvej 4
DK-4600 Koege, Denmark
phone: +45 3269 7788, fax: +45 3269 7789
www.cbspress.dk

North America
Copenhagen Business School Press
Books International Inc.
P.O. Box 605
Herndon, VA 20172-0605, USA
phone: +1 703 661 1500, toll-free: +1 800 758 3756
fax: +1 703 661 1501

Rest of the World
Marston Book Services, P.O. Box 269
Abingdon, Oxfordshire, OX14 4YN, UK
phone: +44 (0) 1235 465500, fax: +44 (0) 1235 465555
E-mail Direct Customers: direct.order@marston.co.uk
E-mail Booksellers: trade.order@marston.co.uk

Advances in Organization Studies

Series Editors:
Stewart Clegg
Professor, University of Technology, Sidney

Ralph E. Stablein
Professor, University of Otago, New Zealand

Advances in Organization Studies is a channel for cutting edge theoretical and empirical works of high quality, that contributes to the field of organizational studies. The series welcomes thought-provoking ideas, new perspectives and neglected topics from researchers within a wide range of disciplines and geographical locations.

Table of Contents

Preface

Professor Cary L. Cooper

This book provides a unique insight into the old adage "if you always do what you always did – you'll always get what you always got!" In other words, it is important from time to time in the social sciences to reflect on exactly what we are exploring, in this case, the true nature and meaning of our organizational concepts. The Editors in this scholarly volume de-construct the word 'concept' into its constituent elements, something that has rarely taken place in our jargon-loaded world of organizational behavior. They contend that a 'concept' usually includes: (i) one or more terms, or a categorization or labelling system, (ii) an umbrella construct or theory with sub-concepts; (iii) a clear set of relationships between 'the concept' and data, facts, etc., (iv) a way of measuring the relationship between these concepts and facts, either observationally or empirically; (v) a link between concepts which they term hypotheses, which in turn are related to a theory, which can then be tested, and finally, (vi) and these concepts can be related to 'moral values and objectives', or some form of ideology.

They then extend this approach to understanding organizational concepts that are currently significant in the broader organizational behavior literature, such as the 'learning organization', 'self-managing teams', 'organizational culture and climate', 'customer-friendly organizations', 'old and new leadership and contingency approaches', etc. It is in the deframing of these well worn but contemporary concepts that the book comes alive, in exploring the tensions between them and 'real life' behavior and attitudes. These journeys help us to understand the conceptualization of the changing nature of work as we enter the 21st Century.

Worklife in the developed world has moved on dramatically since the 1970s, a period of industrial strife, conflict, and retrenchment. The workplace became the battleground between employers and workers, between the middle and working classes, and between liberal and conservative thinking. This was an era about power and control in many developed countries. Out of the turmoil of the 1970s came the 'enterprise culture' of the 1980s, a decade of privatisations, legislation constraining industrial relations disputes, mergers, strategic alliances, and globalisation, transforming economies into hot-house, free market environments. By the end of the 1980s and into the early 1990s, the sustained recession, the privatising mentality of the public sector and new technology, laid the groundwork for one of the most profound changes in the workplaces of the developed world since the industrial revolution, the 'short term contract' culture. Just as organisations were re-engineering themselves to be more flexible and adaptive by outsourcing many of their functions and creating 'the flexible workforce', employees were expected to be open to continual change, adaptable, and aware that jobs were no longer for life. The psychological contract between employer and employee in terms of 'reasonably permanent employment for work well done' was truly being undermined, as more and more employees no longer regarded their employment as secure and began to realise that their career and futures were in their own hands and not in the human resource departments of the large corporates. Indeed, in an ISR (1995) survey of 400 companies, in 17 countries employing over 8 million workers throughout Europe, the employment security of workers significantly declined between 1985 and 1995: UK, from 70 % in 1985 to 48 % in 1995; Germany from 83 % to 55 %; France, from 64 % to 50 %; the Netherlands, from 73 % to 61 %; Belgium, from 60 % to 54 %; and Italy, from 62 % to 57 %.

The movement towards the 'short term contract' culture has also meant a 'longer hours' culture in many companie (Worrall & Cooper, 2001), greater mobility between employers and more portfolio careers. Indeed, in predicting the nature of future corporate life, many experts argue that most organisations will have only a small core of full time, permanent employees, working from a conventional office (Cooper & Jackson, 1997). They will buy most of the skills they need on a contract basis, either from individuals working at home and linked to the company by computers and modems, or by hiring people on short term contracts to do specific jobs or to carry out specific projects. In this way, companies will be able to maintain the flexibility they need to cope with a rapidly changing world.

This movement will actually give employees more control of their working life, but with substantially less security. Sparrow and Cooper (1998) identified four areas that are affected by changing employment relationships at work: (1) what we want out of work and how we maintain individuality in a world where we face a choice between more intense employment or no employment at all; (2) our relationships with other individuals in a work process that can be altered in terms of social interactions, time patterns, and geographical locations; (3) the co-operative and competitive links between different internal and external constituents of the organisation in their new more flexible form; and (4) the relationships between key stakeholders and institutions such as governments, unions, and managers.

This book helps to highlight some of the most important concepts of our time, linked to the changing workplaces of the future, to deconstruct them and provide a better road map for future theory-building and organizational research. The end of our struggle is to ensure that the workplace of the future achieves its potential, or as Studs Terkel hopefully proclaims in his book WORKING "work should be about a search for daily meaning as well as daily bread, for recognition as well as cash, for astonishment rather than torpor, in short, for a sort of life rather than a Monday through Friday sort of dying".

References

Cooper, C.L. and Jackson, S. (1997). *Creating tomorrow's organizations: a handbook for future research in organizational behavior*. Chichester: John Wiley & Sons.

International Survey Research. (1995). Employee satisfaction: tracking European trends. London: ISR.

Sparrow. P. and Cooper, C.L. (1998). New organizational forms: the strategic relevance of future psychological contract scenarios. *Canadian Journal of Administrative Sciences*, 15, 356–371.

Worrall, L. and Cooper, C.L. (2001). The long working hours culture. *European Business Forum*, 6, 48–53.

Chapter 1

The quality of organisation concepts: meaning, context and development

Bert van Hees and Paul Verweel

Over the last decades a large number of organisation concepts has been introduced in the theory and practice of organisation. The ongoing introduction and variation of concepts like culture, learning, quality, competencies, shareholder value, etc. seems to have become more important than the development of new paradigms, theories, frameworks or the improvement of existing ones. The concepts are developed by business schools, large consultancy agencies and disseminated by publishers, the media, and a large network of management training institutions. They find their way into practice at remarkable speed. It has for example taken hardly a decade for organisation culture to develop into a basic element of the daily language of organisations.

The question is, of course, where this proliferation and variation of concepts is taking us, theoretically and practically. What is the value of these concepts? Do they increase our understanding, have they any analytical power and/or are they of practical use?

This book aims to scrutinize the quality of organisation concepts by deframing them, by checking how concepts have been – and are being – defined and constructed, the quality of the frameworks (theories, paradigms) to which they are connected, the quality of the connection itself, and the application of the concept in practice.

Concepts can have all sorts of deficiencies in their definitions or construction, theoretical connections, analytical possibilities, structure, and can have unjustified applications. Some of these limitations can be overcome by using different concepts (or better: concepts connected to different frameworks) side by side, as Bolman and Deal (1991) do in their 'Deframing organizations' and in this they apply ideas from Morgan's book on *Images of organization* (1986): they use 4 different frames or perspectives on organisation and leadership which help them to examine a situation from multiple vantage points and develop a (more) holistic picture. They use a structural framework (structure), a political (power and coalition), a human resources (growth and collaboration) and a symbolic (meaning and language). Their approach implies a criticism on many an organisation concept which is based on just one framework or perspective. In our book we will see the way in which a concept connects to one (or more) framework(s) (theories, paradigms) as one of the quality criteria.

In this book we will examine a number of concepts in detail: the learning organisation, selfmanaging teams, organisation culture, customer-friendliness, the new manager and the new employee. Before giving summaries of these articles, we will discuss the nature of concepts, their usage and meaning, and we relate this usage to the context of modernity. In modernisation there exists a basic tension between lifeworld and system world and the organisation concepts covered in this book will show various ways to cope with this tension.

As a start, we take a look at the discussion which has taken place on the quality of these concepts.

Taking position

The increase, quality and the functions of organisation concepts have been discussed in several quarters. Authors like Eccles and Nohria (1994), Karsten and Van Veen (1998), Boogaard and Vermeulen (1997), and Ten Bos (2000), have been mainly critical of the development, the proliferation and the value of concepts. For authors like Sennett (2000) and Boogaard and Vermeulen (1997), concepts are mainly constructions of the mind that are part of management rhetoric which have little to contribute to daily practice of organisations. The function and influence of concepts is, in that case, purely political by nature. With the aid of the new concepts, intentionally or unintentionally, suggestions of humanisation (Sennett) or progress (Boogaard and Vermeulen) are made, which, however, cannot be observed in the day-to-day practice of organisation.

In the eyes of Boogaard and Vermeulen they are buzzwords which, under pressure of competition between companies, are meant to reduce the insecurity of managers, and in practice little comes of the promises they bring. Eventually, it is often old wine in new bottles.

Sennett (2000) is pessimistic about the direction in which organisations are developing, and is sceptical about the contribution these new ideas and concepts have to offer for guiding this development. He sees a lot of movement and little progress in the opportunities for development of people in organisations. Concepts like flexibility and client-centeredness, in practice rather increase people's existential insecurity than the opposite, while work and work pressure remain a defining part of existence. In his eyes, not much has come of the great promise of information and computer technology, which was to bring flexibilisation in the interests of the employee, and greater self-realisation within and without the work organisation.

Ten Bos, on the other hand, suggests that scientists and *practioners* make too little use of a number of characteristics of the hypes driving these concepts. Hypes, or fashions create room for creativity, for new insights, observations or paradigms (Ten Bos 2000).

Eccles and Noriah (1994) see an important discrepancy between the language with which the new concepts provide the managers, and the practical actions that should result from these concepts. In their eyes, however, this language is of importance for organisations and actors to (re)position themselves. And even though the implementation of new concepts remains problematic, they do have a mobilising effect.

Karsten and Van Veen (1998) recognise both the fleetingness of thinking in terms of new concepts and the importance of conceptualisation for the *knowledge community* of managers, consultants and scientists. Knowledge communities are organised around certain concepts. They argue that some of the new concepts, and the usage of language they entail, in fact find their way into practice.

Van Veen (2000) points out the lack of generally accepted knowledge concerning management problems, implicating that there is hardly a mechanism for passing on existing insights to new generations of managers. In addition, much of the knowledge is difficult to put into practice, requires interpretation in local contexts, and needs 'creative translation'. Concepts can help to distribute and (re)generate existing knowledge.

In this book we will consider the content and the influence of concepts more closely, and we shall see that there are varying positive and negative, predictable and unpredictable effects to be taken into account.

Force fields and interpretation frames affect what actors see, expect and appreciate, as well as the nature of the effects that occur. The meaning of concepts used in organisational practice does not only depend on theoretical content. On the one hand, actors give their own meaning to a concept, focus on their own ideas concerning value or use, and the results attached to working with a concept. On the other hand, actors operate in a dynamic force field, and in the process become aware of results and meanings that accrue. They make use of their knowledge of the force field, their own interpretive frames and those of others. Concepts can load a situation with a certain outlook and assessment, while at the same time "the logic in words, decisions and actions is constructed after the fact. We reflect on what happened to determine the what, who and why."(Weick 1995). Results remain unnoticed because they belong to the implicit side (background) of the force field, or because they fall outside the interpretation frames. The results and meaning of working with a concept, the advantages and disadvantages and the value this has for an actor, is subject to the influence of processes in the force fields. Thus, an *empowering* concept that describes and promotes the increase in power of employee-actors can be used in a force field or practical context in which circumscribing and restricting possibilities for action of employees is a primary concern, and so lead to framing (or reducing) the thinking on all that could be done with that power (Ten Bos 1998: 70–71).

The divergent nature and meaning of concepts

What is a concept? The word 'concept' is used in various meanings. On the one hand it refers to an idea, an abstraction from observed events, a representation of a variety of facts, it may contain a number of categories. On the other, it can refer to a point of view, a notion, a theoretical framework or: a collection of ideas about the phenomenon. In the latter meaning, a concept refers to a way of understanding, an interpretation framework, a *frame*. Finally, the word can have the meaning of a plan; a draft, a rough sketch. In the literature on organisational concepts, these meanings are used miscellaneously, and the distinction between concept, theory and framework is blurred. Please note that the concept 'image' is likewise multi-faceted.

The nature and content of concepts can diverge substantially. The complexity of a notion can be large or small, there can be more or fewer elements, with many or few interconnections.

One or more of the following elements may be comprised in a concept:

1. one (or more) terms; a concept sometimes contains a categorisation, sometimes only a few labels, whereby the label can be more or less well-defined
2. sometimes there may be a system of concepts, with an umbrella concept (for instance, sociotechnical systems thinking or theory, subsuming the concepts of social system and technical or task system)
3. information on the nature of the relationship between a concept and certain facts, data, observations
4. the link between a concept and the facts referred to, can be created by measurable variables or indicators. These variables or indicators can be given to a greater or lesser extent, as can the links between concepts and variables, between variables and facts
5. a concept can be linked to other concepts and this link or relationship between concepts can be indicated; the link can have the form of (loosely or strictly connected) hypotheses or be less formal. The hypotheses may be connected to a theory, to theoretical foundations and assumptions. This theory can be more or less empirically tested and more or less researched as to its informational content (Opp 2002). The framework (theoretical approach or theory) itself can be sketchy or well-defined,

more or less empirically based, more or less well constructed. So the links between concepts and framework (theory or theoretical approach) can vary from weak to strong.

6. finally, concepts can be related to moral values and objectives, justifications and an ideological programme. Sometimes this moral content is not explicitly indicated, but can be derived from the presentation of the concept: the presentation, arrangements and examples given, can be read so as to make clear what is good and bad, who belongs and who does not, what is desirable and what is not. There can be an implicit message in the concept.

A concept may not only comprise a greater or lesser number of the listed elements (be more or less complex), the quality of the whole can also vary widely. Quality is the degree to which elements are coherent, have been described unambiguously, intersubjectively and empirically, and in which the connections between elements have been logically circumscribed, where references to theories, fitting applications and to research results have been indicated, in such a way that they can be checked, reconstructed, or in certain circumstances, can be repeated. The quality or ambiguity – the reverse of quality – of conceptual elements plays a central role in the use of concepts.

Ambiguity does not only have disadvantages. When concepts are not clearly defined, and leave room for ambiguity, that may be their charm, because it raises questions and is food for thought, while enabling local adaptations of meanings.

Concepts, then, may vary between *low complexity and low quality* to *high complexity (inclusive) and high quality*, with two variants in between, *complex and low quality* and *low complexity and high quality*. Empirical science has a preference for quality, and because of the time and money involved in testing concepts, it will tend to make concessions on the side of complexity. Business sciences, which are closer to daily practice, will more readily employ topical, little-researched concepts, present new relationships in order to do justice to all sorts of developments at a certain cost in quality. In addition, they will sooner give in to the need for presenting concepts with a message or a programme. The task-centred, programmatic and at the same time moralising element can be clearly present in such business concepts, as can be seen for instance in shareholder value models (*Economy and Society*, special issue, February 2000).

Usage and meaning

The concepts are building blocks for 'definitions of reality'. The organisation is an arena of possible definitions of reality and thus of different concepts. The use of concepts is not just a question of the wealth of the description, of ((un)scientific) consistency and possibilities for application, but also a question of power in the organisation, more especially 'definitional power'. The concepts indicate how practice should be regarded, and how it should be changed. The introduction of concepts in organisations is mainly the prerogative of managers and consultants, highly regarded professionals and trainers, who try to transfer their vision of the organisation, management and function of the organisation to employees and clients by means of the introduction of the concepts. Concepts are not only based on theoretical and empirical descriptions (sometimes hardly so) and explanations of practice, but also on normative ideas and guidelines, on commonsense notions, on references to prestigious persons, projects and organisations, who publish their assumptions on how things should be regarded in day-to-day practice, and how they should be managed. Sometimes they bring kitchen-knowledge: tacit knowledge of top cooks in a business kitchen, made public.

Quite a few organisational concepts voice the desire of managers of reducing complexity and coming to grips with worlds of meaning and the frames employed. Other voices and concepts are welcome in the force fields of organisational networks as long as they support the concepts of the dominant coalition. When they do not do so, they are often qualified as resistance to be tackled with weapons like instruction, training, courses, discussions, assessment and mobility (just to mention a few popular weapons).

By means of concepts, voices and views are (dis)covered, or rival notions blocked. They help to create communities of voices and dialogues. Words and concepts are part of a discourse. A discourse is everything said, written and conveyed about a particular topic within a social network. Although in many cases there is a dominant discourse, there are always alternate discourses, most of which are usually marginalized. The dominant discourse reflects or creates a dominant ideology and is presented as common sense and obvious (hegemonic). Discourses envelop frames and concepts, and they develop around these. They produce words and images that facilitate practices (Tolson 1996).

Context: Modernisation in society and organisation

In discussions of concepts such as the learning organisation and self-managing teams, all sorts of conditions and tendencies are given to explain changing organisational practices, the development of these concepts and the way in which images and concepts can influence organisational practice. Through all these tendencies, developments, and basic conditions of organisational practice, we can distinguish the tendencies of modernisation. These are briefly described below. In Chapter 9 we shall return to them at greater length.

Society and organisational associations in the Western world are characterised by processes of modernisation.[1] Modernisation is a multiple process in which organisations and societies find themselves continually at the intersection of four forces or processes: structure, culture, person and nature (Van der Loo and Van Reijen 1997: 48):

1. differentiation (characteristic of the development of structure: both task differentiation as in the division of labour, and system differentiation where functions turn into separate institutions like childcare, healthcare, etc.)
2. rationalisation (characteristic of the development of culture: ordering and systemising reality with a view to keeping it predictable and controllable)
3. individualisation (characteristic of the development of individuals: individuals attain ever greater freedom of choice and independence) and
4. domestication (characteristic of the development of relations with nature: "making a world in which we are, finally, at home": Ten Bos 2000: 119)[2]

Each of the four aspects mentioned is subject to contradictory developments:

1. The process of differentiation in structure, leads on the one hand to ever-growing specialisation and independence, and on the other to greater mutual dependence of separate parts. Economic activity gets institutionalized in independent enterprises that become dependent on other sectors such as healthcare, infrastructural services, schools. The differentiation of structure is expressed in the development of nation states and political institutions that influence relations between state and citizen (parliamentary democracy, state bureaucracy, welfare state and market economy) (Van Hoof and Ruysseveldt 1996: 24–5).
2. The process of rationalisation, on the one hand supports the ideal of universal communication, consultation and measurability, but also enables individual patterns of choice for actors, and so forms of pluralism. Van Hoof and Ruysseveldt observe the development of a secular culture with a prominent place for science (1996: 25). Through modernisation, organisations have become more rational, but not more manageable or predictable, according to Van der Loo and Van Reijen (1977), Bahlmann and Meesters (1999, the latter with a reference to Boulding, 1956). See also the literature on vicious circles of organisation (for instance Vroom

---

[1] Some authors prefer to speak of the process of postmodernism in a late modern stage (Koot and Verweel 2000, Frissen 1989).

[2] Commodification is also regarded as an element of modernisation: even more aspects of human action are subject to market exchange (Van Hoof and Van Ruysseveldt: 173).

1980, who worked this out for bureaucracy, Crozier 1963, Masuch 1985).

3. The process of individualisation reinforces the search for an identity of oneself, but also leads to a development in which organisations (also by their products or services) develop into providers of identity for actors like managers, employees and customers, and this gets stronger as existing ideological movements or frameworks disappear (such as found in churches, trade unions, politics). Individualisation is sometimes paralleled by the rise of an urbanised social pattern (Van Hoof and Ruysseveldt 1996: 24–5).

4. Domestication leads to the control of the natural environment but also to discussion of the boundary between nature and man, and to transgression of the boundary between man and nature, for instance by genetic manipulation. The independent stance toward nature is based on technology, at the same time dependence on technology has grown strongly, it has become a matter of course to deploy technology for solving problems.[3]

Modernisation was already perceptible in the era of the Enlightenment, when under the influence of rationalisation the transition from a traditional to a modern society took place, and modern forms of organisation developed. The transition was described by a number of scholars in the 19th century. Tönnies introduced the distinction between *Gemeinschaft* and *Gesellschaft*, communities based on affective ties, strong solidarity, and mutual ties, respectively on economic ties, goal and interest-driven action (Van Hoof and van Ruysseveldt 1996: 135). Durkheim used the well-known pair of concepts of mechanical and organic solidarity, the first based on the fact that people resemble each other, the second on a greater division of labour (Van Hoof and van Ruysseveldt 1996: 117–8). These pairs of concepts indicate a transition to social relationships where the functional aspect is primary, and which are businesslike and rationally calculating, goal-oriented, by nature. This rationalisation or increase of goal rationality, comprises according to Max Weber both cognitive control of reality, and a practical control of reality through a better adaptation of means to goals. The increase in goal rationality – also called instrumental or technical rationality – can be distinguished from value rationality where actions are related to values, for instance the honour of an army, from an affective, emotion-driven rationality, and also from traditional action. Morgan (1986: 37) has remarked that through substantial or value rationality an entire situation can be taken into account, a comprehensive view can be given through the values concerned

---

[3] Gephart (1996) links postmodernism to a form of society in which Nature has been replaced with "technology as the 'other' of our society".

(Van Hoof and Ruysseveldt 1996: 127, Kalberg 1980). The process of ratio-nalisation creates tensions between social, relational, human relations and functional or business relations between people, and the tensions are visible in the development of organisations (Mastenbroek 1981, Bahlmann and Meesters 1999, Verweel 1987 and 2000).

Development: Life world and system world

The relationship between the human as an aim in itself and the human as a means in the framework of goal-driven work, for instance in organisations, has also been referred to as the difference between the logic of the life world and that of the system world (Habermas 1981, Verweel 2000, Bailey 1977). We can distinguish the system world from the life world through the following three criteria:

1. Habermas (Van Hoof and Ruysseveldt 1996: 302 ff.) distinguishes communicative action, aimed at arriving at a shared definition of the situation together with others – to be found in the *life world*, from strategic action aimed at achieving goals – to be found in the *system world*. Actors acting communicatively are in search of a shared definition of the situation and seek agreement on three aspects: *what is true?* (truth: reference to a shared objective reality), *what is normatively valid?* (reference to shared agreements and norms) and *what is sincere?* (Sincerity refers to the subjective world of the speaker, the subjective validity of the expressions of the communicator: there is no lying, no foul play, no tactical play. Sincerity is connected to: Who am I? It asks the question: what is the basis of my actions?) Strategic action is based on goal rationality. Communicative action can be goal rational and value rational, and so comprises various rationality aspects.

2. When applied to human action in a work organisation communicative action means (life world): *making meaningful and giving meaning to* the organisation and by and for participants, and so refers to a *jointly built and shared process of giving meaning*. The latter, in its most sophisticated form, may refer to a system that is entirely constructed by the members of the system. Such a system, then, has four aspects:

1. Delimitation of membership (who are the members).
2. Autonomy of task performance, the autonomy to fulfil tasks in accordance with one's own insights.
3. Autonomy of task design and autonomy of the design of the organisation as a system, including the determination of the aims or goals of the organisation.
4. The right to distribute yields or revenues.

These elements can also be found in ideas concerning radical liberalism, anarchism, and organisational democratisation (and they have connections with, for instance, empowerment, modern sociotechnical systems thinking). They extend the concept of 'autonomy of workers' into a fundamentally different view of organising. Of course, there are many ways (and national varieties) to organize the process of creating shared meaning: participation from workplace consultation to codermination of major company decisions, from functional to structural, from shareholder to stakeholder model[4].

3. A life world is characterised by the existence of courage and the power of individuals for expressing moral doubts. Autonomous people are people who have the self-confidence to express their moral doubt on actions, events, situations (Ten Bos 1998, p. III), they have the guts to disagree, to express a minority opinion. The presence of autonomous behaviour and the possibility of minority viewpoints are preconditions for the coming into play of life world elements. This autonomy, or courage is about the expression of something essential to a person or to his or her being there.

In this book we analyse organisation concepts in which the tension between life and system world, strategic (or goal) rationality, and rationality aimed at communicative human relations will be visible: learning organisation, self-managing teams, organisation culture, customer-friendly organisation. We also analyse the 'new images' of manager and employee, and also in these conceptualizations aspects of these tensions can be recognised.

The analyses are made by Dutch researchers from different disciplinary backgrounds (anthropology, management studies, sociology, economics) and offer insights into the reception of these concepts and changing images of actors in this North-western European country. They also give an overview of the discourses to which the concepts are linked in both universitary and practitioners communities.

---

[4] When we want to establish the presence of shared meaning, we should indicate criteria and this can be done in several ways: we present participants with questions and leave matters to their subjective impressions. We can also take into account the degree to which their voice is heard, and to which they are experienced in giving voice, and meaning, and with being heard. That is why we need a well-founded choice of instrument to determine that "degree of communicative action – so the extent of giving meaning – in an organisational context". Without such a reasoned choice there is little we can say about communicative action or about the boundaries and presence of a life world in human action in a labour organisation.

Since individuals define their life world themselves, it is possible that individuals grow strongly attached to authority (for instance Protestant ethics) in an organisation as an aspect of jointly produced and shared meaning, so as part of their life world, when this relates to their images of social order and the basis of authority and community. The distinction between life world and system world that individuals make, is therefore strongly dependent on their norms and values and the vision of the institutions in which they participate.

Summaries of the articles

In Chapter 2 René ten Bos examines the idea of Learning Organisation or LO. First he traces the origins of the concept. He develops the thesis that LO is a term used in a situation of 'hegemonic disorganisation' which points to the right of high ranking members of organisations to withdraw from reality. He develops four statements on LO: the concept implies learning for the few; it emphasizes not the most natural ways of learning; learning is seen as possible only in a fictitious world; its criticism of centralization and hierarchy is not taken to its conclusion.

In Chapter 3 Peter Leisink shows that the new concept of selfmanaging teams finds its roots in ideas about the humanization of work and sociotechnics. Sociotechnics distinguishes the worlds of work or tasksystem and the life or social system and applied these to the concept of selfmanaging teams. However, recent theoretical developments in Dutch sociotechnics are more directed towards efficiency. A study of selfmanaging teams in a buscompany reveals different value attached to financial targets and efficiency between topmanagement and employees and documents the devolution of selfmanagement into top down control.

In Chapter 4 Jan Boessenkool analyses the most popular organisation concept of the last 20 years, organisation culture, by comparing theoretical debates and research in the USA and the Netherlands. The concept turns out to be inadequate. Instrumentalism, stressing integration and control dominates and there is no place for diversity and fragmentation. Culture is a container concept, necessitating an approach which focuses on the creation of meaning and understanding instead of on 'how to do changing'.

In Chapter 5 Carl Rohde and Hans van der Loo analyse customer-friendliness. They decsribe the change from target group approaches via life style segmentation towards vision-based narratives developed by socially responsible firms. There is a change from 'logic of utility' to 'logic of sign'. Customers demand more social relations, enjoyment, gain, comfort and community and customer-friendly organisations face the fragmented customer. Creativity is vital in this encounter. Paradoxically the customer revolution in postmodernism goes hand in hand with increased dependency of customers on organisations for the fullfilment of their social needs.

In Chapter 6 Willem Koot analyses the new manager and starts by reviewing old and new leadership and contingency approaches. The new leadership approach contrast transactional and transformational and links leadership with culture and management of meaning. A study of Dutch managers shows the contrast between reality and the idealized images (being heroes, visonairies, hard and soft) coming from the world of popular management books. Managers are forced to front stage images (everything under control) and a back stage feeling of constant uncertainty. The manager is under continuous and ambiguous pressures.

In Chapter 7 Ton Korver analyses the concept of the New Employee. Labour supply is changing from manufacturing to services, primary processes from things to people and symbols, personnel management from 'personnel' to human resource(s), competencies, employability and from 'management' to mobilisation. Diversity initiatives and female parttime employment give an impression of the suboptimal side of the labour market. The new employee is defined not so much by selfdesign or entrepreneurial spirit, but by choicemaking in career, presentation and the balance between work, family, care. When the necessary social networks are absent, choicemaking increases loneliness.

In Chapter 8 Bert van Hees and Paul Verweel explain the criteria for discerning between life, system and partisan worlds and assess the concepts covered in this book in terms of these. They give an overview of the uses to which these concepts are put and functions and outcomes related to their use. The quality of the concepts is considered and linked to the 'industry' which builds them, discerning between production and use circuits of meaning. In the last part the links between the concepts and modernization processes are considered, laying the ground for the last chapter.

In Chapter 9 Bert van Hees and Paul Verweel analyse management and work organisation in the information age. The network-project paradigm of management offers its personal and social costs of networking and the network society changes the place and meaning of work. There are five major tendencies: subjectivation and soft management, 'mediatisation', diversity, financialisation and the interconnectedness of work and private life. The network-project and network society reshapes system, life and partisan worlds to the extent that instrumental empathy takes its place. Liberation is still in question and the authors offer four visions, four ways to enlarge freedom: the humanizing organisation, the individualizing organisation, the compensating organisation and the imploding organisation. In their conclusions they see incoherent and patchwork freedom spots.

Conclusion

Organisation concepts incorporate social and theoretical developments in different ways. They draw the attention of managers to approaches and objects of analysis, they include the answers to questions and insecurities. At the same time they fulfil a number of other functions, such as that of buzzword, part of management rhetoric, organising scientists and practitioners into knowledge communities, they have political meaning, they position and mobilise people in organisations and offer opportunities for (re)using old and new insights in creative ways for particular, local circumstances.

In the following chapters we shall see how concepts are developed and used, which assumptions determine their form and content, in what force fields they develop, and what the consequences are for theory and practice. We shall also discuss the functions of actual concretisations they have for actors and organisations. In Chapters 2 to 7 the authors have worked out concepts and images in their own ways. This diversity has led to a range of arguments. After Chapter 1, the following chapters contain, consecutively, four images of organisation or organisation aspects and two images of actors: The Learning organisation, Self-managing teams, Organisation culture, Client-friendly organisation, The new images of the manager, The new images of the employee. In Chapter 8 we will draw up the balance of the quality and complexity of the concepts analysed, and in Chapter 9 that of the aspects of modernisation mentioned by the authors. The focus will be on the contrast between the place of life world and system world in the life in organisations, which will yield a number of theoretical questions, also relevant for practice. In conclusion we shall seek to answer the question about ways of achieving emancipation in work, development of the life world in human relations, and communication in the labour organisation.

References

Bahlmann, T. & B. Meesters (1998). *De organisatie die nooit bestond.* (The organization that never existed) Schoonhoven: Academic service.

Bailey, F. (1977). *Morality and expediency – the folklore of academic politics.* Oxford: Basil Blackwell.

Boje, D.M., R.P. Gephart jr. & T.J. Thatchenkery (1996). *Postmodern management and organisation theory.* London: Sage.

Bolman, L.G. & T.E. Deal (1991). *Reframing organizations. The leadership Kaleidoscope.* Jossey-Bass.

Crozier, M. (1963). *Le phénomène bureaucratique.* Paris: Seuil.

Frissen, P. (1989). *Bureaucratische cultuur en informatisering.* (Bureaucratic culture and informatisation) Den Haag: SDA.

Gephart, R.P. (1996). Management, social issues and the postmodern era. In D.M. Boje, R.P. Gephart jr. & T.J. Thatchenkery, *Postmodern management and organisation theory* (21–45). New York: Sage.

Habermas, J. (1981). *Theorie des kommunikativen Handelns.* (Theory of communicative action) Frankfurt am Main: Suhrkamp (2 Baende).

Kalberg, S. (1980). Max Weber's types of rationality. *American Journal of Sociology, 85,* 1145–1179.

Economy and Society Volume 29, Number 1, February 2000. Issue on Shareholder value.

Mastenbroek, W.F.G. (1982). *Conflicthantering en organisatieontwikkeling.* (Coping with conflict and organisation development)Alphen aan de Rijn: Samson.

Masuch, M. (1985). Vicious circles. *Administrative Science Quarterly, 30,* 14–33.

Morgan, G. (1986). *Images of organization.* Sage.

Opp, K.D. (2002). *Methodologie der Sozialwissenschaften.* (Methodology of social sciences) Westdeutscher Verlag.

Ten Bos, R. (2000). *Fashion and utopia in management thinking.* Amsterdam & Philadelphia: John Benjamins.

Tolson, A. (1996). *Mediations: Text and discourse in media studies.* Arnold Publishing Co.

Van Hoof, J. and Van Ruysseveldt, J. (1996). Sociologie en de moderne samenleving (Sociology and modern society), Boom.

Van Veen, K. (2000). Meningen over managementmodes. (Opinions on management fashions) *Management and Organisation 5 (6).*

Van der Loo and Van Rijen (1997). *Paradoxen van modernisering.* Muiderberg: Coutinho. (Paradox of modernisation).

Verweel, P. (1987). *Universiteit: Verandering en planning.* Utrecht: ICAU. (University: Changes and planning).

Verweel, P. (2000). *Betekenisgeving in organisaties: de rationalisering van het sociale.* Oratie. Utrecht: CERES. (Meaning in organisations: the rationalisation of the social aspect.)

Vroom, C.W. (1980). *Bureaucratie, het veelzijdig instrument van de macht.* (Bureaucracy, the multi-faceted instrument of power) Alphen aan de Rijn: Samson.

Chapter 2

The nurseries of the learning organisation

René ten Bos (Schouten & Nelissen)

Introduction: where does the idea of learning organisations originate from?

The general complaint about the learning organisation, even from people who claim to be supporters of this concept, is that it is so badly defined (Garvin, 1995). This is the reason why various authors writing on this subject (Swieringa and Wierdsma, 1990) claim that the journey to the promised land of the learning organisation is more important than one's presence in it. This is logical; there is little to learn in promised lands. Everything necessary for a fruitful and happy life would already appear to have been learnt in such places. On the other hand, others (Pedler, Burgoyne and Boydell, 1991) have claimed that glimpses of the promised land can be seen, and they therefore hope that those that have had them will write and tell them as much as possible about their own glimpses, so that others will also be able to gain an idea of what the promised land looks like.

But where do ideas about this promised land come from? It is unclear where it exactly originated from in general literature. Some authors claim that the ideas relating to learning in organisations date back at least as far as Mozes, even if they are not, unfortunately, clear about their reasons for supposing this (Pedler, Burgoyne and Boydell, 1991: 2). Others claim the honor for themselves, and maintain that they were already experimenting with such ideas more than half a century ago. I am not thinking here of Peter Drucker, someone who is known to claim that he was the originator of almost all management ideas. I am thinking, however, of Reg Revans, an almost forgotten name in management literature. I would like to introduce him as the person that coined the term 'learning organisation', although I am not entirely sure that this is the case.

When the elderly Reg Revans (1984) reflects upon his academic career, he cannot resist explaining in detail how, shortly after the Second World War, he was working on what would become known, many years later, as *action learning*, *quality circles*, and *organisational development*. At the same time, he also claims that it was he, and his colleagues, who initiated the concept of the *'learning community'*. This concept was introduced in 1959, during a lecture (entitled: *'The hospital as an organism'*) at a congress that had been organized by *The Institute of Management Sciences* in Paris. Research conducted in the academic hospital in Manchester had revealed that patients being cared for by nurses who found it easy to learn, and were able to obtain information quickly, were discharged earlier than patients whose nurses evidently did not possess such characteristics. Such results were important news in a time of rapidly increasing healthcare costs. If a new idea is not only interesting but also useful, then you're on to something. Revans immediately recognized the relevance of the discovery. In essence, it meant that ...

> ... we had left behind the idea of a small group as a learning microcosm, and that we had stumbled upon the idea of an entire institute as a learning community; for example, a hospital in which more than two thousand people work ... (Revans, 1984: 10–11)

Thus, if we are to believe Revans, it was at this congress that an already slumbering interest in *learning in organisations* first became a reflection upon a *'learning community'*, and, once such a progression has occurred, the idea of a *'learning organisation'* is not far behind. Revans also adds, for that matter, that such revolutionary ideas were ridiculed in 1959, particularly where the idea crucial to the learning organisation was concerned, that is that organisations have a collective will that transcends the will of individuals. If we are to believe Revans, the time was not yet ripe for these kinds of ideas. It would be some years, under the colors of such terms as *organisational development,* before the ideas generated by Revans and his colleagues would gain more acceptance. Revans himself admits that he only published these ideas in 1971, in his book *Designing Effective Managers*.

Revans is probably exaggerating his intellectual solitude. There were, undoubtedly, kindred spirits. Such contemporaries as Michel Polyani (1957) and Cyert and March (1963) have been at least as influential as Revans, if not more so. Polyani, a former chemist, developed the still very popular notion of *'tacit* knowledge', described by him as a type of individual knowledge that is generated by the active creation and organisation of experiences. The ongoing creation of new experiences would later occupy a prominent place in the literature about learning in organisations. Cyert and March, both pupils of Herbert Simon, were pioneers in the field of decision-making theory, and, in a recent article by Silvia Gherardi (1999: 105), are referred to as the actual inventors of the term *'organisational learning'*, something that they chiefly understand to mean a continual organisational adjustment process. Other names that one continually encounters in general literature are Simon, (1947), Lindblom (1959), Holt (1964), Weick (1969), Bateson (1972), Duke (1974), and Argyris and Schon (1974), all of whom, with their ideas on such subjects as 'limited rationality', 'incrementalism', 'constructing realities', 'loosely coupled systems', 'gaming', 'learning to learn' or 'deutero-learning', in their own way were to become important sources of inspiration for the literature about learning organisations. Far less numerous are references to the work of pragmatic philosophers such as John Dewey, who, in the nineteen-thirties, wrote a number of books about the educational or edifying character of organisations, or Richard Rorty (1980) who, many years later, would adopt the same theme, even though he was not so much concerned with organisation, but with philosophy (Kolb, 1984; Czarniawska, 1997; Weaver, 1997). In the last section in particular, I will return in detail to the subject of pragmatism as the almost-forgotten source of inspiration in literature about learning in organisations and learning organisations. For the time being, it is sufficient to conclude that a characteristic common to all literature must be sought in a thorough rejection of the rationalistic portrayal of mankind, and the trust in rational planning, based on this, that is typical of much traditional literature about management and organisation.

Nowhere was this rejection of strict, rational planning more clearly expressed than in Michael's book *Learning to Plan and Planning to Learn* that was published in 1973, and has recently been reprinted (1996). Subjects were described in this book that much later would become essential to such people as De Geus (1988) and Senge (1990): error tolerance, feedback, holism, long-term orientation, environmental awareness, etc. However, whereas the work of De Geus and Senge is characterized by an unconcealed optimism about the ability of organisations to learn, Michael is far more sceptical. Although he does not consider it impossible that companies will one day contribute to social learning processes ('*civil learning*'), in his preface to the 1996 edition, he warns against too much optimism in this respect (1996: 28–30). It would mean, for example, that companies would have to relinquish their one-sided orientation on shareholders' interests, or that their knowledge and skills would constantly have to be used for the benefit of society as a whole. And this is now by no means the situation. Therefore, almost quarter of a century after writing his book, Michael concludes that it still refers to a possibly still very distant future, which we can only hope will one day materialize.

It is not surprising, then, that Michael's work does not focus on organisations as such. Rather, Michael discusses learning processes that occur in society as such (1997: 325). His book particularly concerns the psychological resistance that could thwart such processes. Besides this, no mention is made to learning organisations; while such people as De Geus and Senge assume that learning organisations do exist somewhere in reality, and can and must be studied if we are ever to be able to facilitate perfect learning processes. This is often the way with management concepts: what once

26

appeared to be a quite innocent heuristic concept ('civil learning' or 'learning in organisations'), used by social scientists in order to be able to construct certain social realities, is converted by consultants and gurus into a term that effortlessly refers to actual organisations, and then sets a standard for more or less anxious followers. In the process, a certain alienation in respect of the original ideas always occurs. The focus is no longer on government policymakers, or social scientists that are interested in the question of how our society should progress from here, just as Michael is, but rather, on managers who have to achieve a profit, but who also want to retain a clear conscience.

Senge (1990: 15) himself makes it quite clear that he was initially not very interested in business management. He agreed with such people as Michael that solutions for the 'Big Issues' should be a particular responsibility of government and the scientific community. At the time, he was particularly inspired by Jay Forrester, a computer scientist who supervised Senge, when he was writing his dissertation about system dynamics, amongst other things. He learned from Forrester that many policymakers did not have a very holistic view of reality, as a result of which they proposed solutions within certain domains that caused all kinds of more serious problems elsewhere. He must somewhere have been disappointed in the possibilities open to public sector policymakers to start thinking differently, because, around 1975, thus approximately three years after Michael's publication, he increasingly places all his hope in those "business leaders" that he meets as a computer scientist at MIT. He describes these people as "thoughtful people, deeply aware of the inadequacies of prevailing ways of managing". They work for such companies as Apple, Hanover Insurance, Polaroid and, of course, also for Shell, where Arie de Geus, a later ally, worked, and where extensive experiments were carried out with scenario planning. Gradually, he realizes that the potential for revolutionary changes should not be sought in the public but in the business sector:

> Gradually, I came to realize why business is the locus of innovation in an open society. Despite whatever hold past thinking may have on the business mind, business has a freedom to experiment missing in the public sector and, often, in nonprofit organisations. It also has a clear "bottom line", so that experiments can be evaluated, at least in principle, by objective criteria (1990: 15).

Such ideas as these are also often held by other gurus. Mintzberg (1994), for whom learning capacity is just as crucial as it is for Senge, claims that business managers are pre-eminently able to relieve us of our technological and rationalistic straitjacket. The hope of a better world must not be sought from government or science, but from business, nowhere else. Of course such messages as these are very much welcomed by the business community. They contribute to the image of dynamics and flexibility that they like to radiate. Nobody, then, is surprised any more by such professors as Shosana Zuboff, from Harvard, who unblushingly claims that learning is "the new type of labour ... the heart of each production activity" (quoted in: Wooldridge and Micklethwait, 1997: 138–139). This ties in very nicely with the self-marketing that has become so important for companies in the information age. Literature about the learning organisation is perfect for companies wishing to manifest themselves as attractive organisations. They adopt the ideals of those that share Michael's lack of hope in business.

In other words, idealism is no longer the privilege of groups from the political or religious margins. Idealism has become orthodox in management literature. Senge is the most striking example of this. To begin with (1990: 6), he directs his book towards managers wanting to understand the art of building learning organisations, but then also towards parents wishing to learn something from their children (because children have, as we will see later in the chapter, much to teach parents about learning) and to citizens. As we have seen, quarter of a century ago, Michael was still directing himself towards society as a whole. Such shifts in orientation indicate that the context in which ideas about the learning organisation were able to blossom have now disappeared or changed.

Bill Cooke recently showed (1999) that many popular ideas about organisational changes originate from radical-left circles. Edgar Schein, one of the gurus on the subject of culture management, something that he perceives as a collective learning process, derived his views on the possibility of change and innovation from research that he conducted into the Chinese communist party in the nineteen-fifties. Schein observed that this party had been pre-eminently successful in the realization of behavioral and mental changes. In 1962, Schein wrote frankly that the Chinese methods possibly no longer appear so "mysterious, different or awful when we forget their gruesome communist ideology and just concentrate on their methods" (Quoted in: Cooke, 1999: 95). Cooke (1999: 97) then concludes that the left-wing origin of many ideas is concealed in modern management literature. Where Schein was still aware of the cruelty that accompanied this method, whether or not intentionally, this is concealed in current management literature. I suspect that Cooke's observations also apply to Senge, even if further historiographical research is necessary. But if this suspicion is correct, Senge must, somewhere in the whole process that led him to write for managers, have hit upon the idea of tempering the left-wing, idealistic and quasi-religious enthusiasm, in order to make it as accessible as possible for business. How better than to portray managers themselves as idealistic innovators?

What is more, his contacts with people from the business community gave him the opportunity to reinforce his belief that learning organisations do exist. He finds, from these personal contacts, that the type of idealistic leaders and managers that he dreams of do exist, but in places where he had not previously expected them. People like De Geus (Shell) or William O'Brien (Hanover Insurance) convince him that learning in learning organisations can become reality. Now, discussions about learning in organisations have long been plagued by (pragmatic) doubt about the realistic ontology behind such statements as "Hanover Insurance is a learning organisation" or "The Royal Infirmary in Manchester is a learning community". In other words, there has always been doubt in the more academic literature about the so-called discovery made by Revans in 1959; doubt that is completely ignored by Senge and De Geus. The ontological status of a learning insurance company or a learning hospital is however, to voice this carefully, uncertain. Only the most persistent idealist or post-structuralist will dare to deny that learning and unlearning occurs in hospitals; the claim that learning hospitals exist will, by contrast, encounter far more doubt. The best evidence for the problem outlined here is supplied by the texts written by De Geus and Senge themselves: they appear to be more about learning processes in people, whether or not employed by certain organisations, than about learning organisations (Jacques, 1996: 9). In the words of Rorty (1980: 359), they are more concerned with *Bildung* (understood here as the training, education, and self-transformation of people) than with *knowledge* (understood to mean the establishment of a certain number of indisputable descriptions in respect of a certain type of reality), even if they do not always appear to realize this themselves.

Thus, it often appears as if indisputable knowledge is concerned, as if the promised land has already been charted. This sells better too: in general, calling upon people to change and to become idealistic is doomed to failure if you do not have some strong knowledge to back you up. This is the reason why we encounter many different definitions of the term learning organisation (Garrett, 1990: 77; De Geus, 1997: 35). The most well-known originates from Senge himself. He speaks of ...

> ... organisations where people continually expand their capacity to create the results they truly desire, where new and expansive patterns of thinking are nurtured, where collective aspiration is set free, and where people are continually learning how to learn together (Senge, 1990: 3).

Of course, this is a definition that requires further definitions to be given. What, for example, is understood by 'expansive', 'learning capacity' and 'creativity'? Such conceptual problems have often resulted in objections to learning organisations, particularly from a practical point of view. Garvin (1995) claims, for example, that you must be able to construct learning organisations if they are to be of any practical value. Thus, criticism of this concept comes from two sides: some academics claim that conceptual clarity is ontological deceit; consultants claim that conceptual clarity is the least that may be expected, if it is to be of interest to managers. Thus, supporters of the learning organisation are caught between two fires.

Criticism is, however, often expressed from a sort of underlying sympathy for the ideas which underlie the concept. However unclear, both academics and people in the field are evidently mesmerized by the idea of learning in organisations and learning organisations. After all, who could be against expansive thinking, learning processes or creativity? Who, in other words, would not dare to endorse such idealism, certainly if we consider that it can easily be combined with financial gain? No-one, right? Yet, I do want to dismiss this sympathy, and rummage subversively in the promised land, a place which I fear and believe not to be at all so beautiful or heavenly. I want to chart the cruelty that such people as Cooke believe is concealed. I will do this by extending a number of extreme images central to the literature about learning organisations. I will discuss nurseries, gardens and many other microcosmic spaces encountered in and around the learning organisation. I will myself also add the necessary images. Men like Odysseus, apes or ape men, but also the dying on the graveyards, from Homer up to the First World War, will be reviewed. All to criticize the courtesy with which the subject is usually approached. Why? Because I occasionally meet managers who are fanatical about these ideas, and approach their subordinates armed with feelings of urgency, and full of love, hardly realizing what damage they are causing with their emphasis on an eternal willingness to change. But also because the optimism that characterizes the literature that I will discuss here can make me feel very miserable.

Firstly, I take offence at the idea that learning appears to represent a type of value which requires no further discussion, as if people are always preoccupied with self-transformation, that is realized on a magnificent quest, in search of the unknown and the mysterious. Rorty (1980: 360) has pointed out that such forms of education and transformation are not permanent, and will, sooner or later, be reduced to normal learning processes, the only aim of which is the refinement of what is already known. The idea that people in organisations are flexible, always and everywhere, expansive, involved and creative is nothing less than ghastly, just as a utopia is in many respects ghastly (Achterhuis, 1998: 12). Secondly, it is an illusion to believe that learning organisations are free of suppression and power. In this respect too, a parallel can be drawn with a utopia (Achterhuis, 1998: 66). My criticism here particularly relates to what I will refer to as *hegemonic disorganisation*. In short, I understand this to mean the right of high-ranking members of the organisation in particular to withdraw, in all kinds of ways, from the reality of the organisation in question, where the reality itself just remains what it is, right down to its very smallest details. It is true that all these people are advocating a form of institutionalized change, but I want to show that we should regard this instead as a type of organized other-worldliness. As I interpret it, the literature offers sufficient points of departure for it to be possible to substantiate this statement. It is supported by four sub statements about the learning organisation that I will discuss in the following section. They throw a threatening shadow over the promised land.

Hegemonic disorganisation

The four sub statements that I will discuss are:

1. In literature about the learning organisation, relevant learning is reserved for only a few people.
2. The learning methods which are emphasized – breaking through boundaries, learning other things, etc. – are not the most natural ways of learning, not for children and certainly not for adults.
3. Only in a fictitious world, often referred to as a "microcosmos", which consists of a number of mental models, is learning and experimentation possible; the most important step towards hegemonic disorganisation is taken here.
4. Nowhere does the criticism of centralization and hierarchy result in the full support of democratization initiatives.

Who learns and who does not?

I have always been surprised about the idea that organisations could learn, not only because learning, as authors have quite rightly commented (see, for example, Weick and Westley, 1996), appears to be reserved for people not organisations, but particularly also because I have always noticed during the various activities that I have carried out for numerous organisations during my life, just how much learning must, indeed, be excluded from the organisational process. If any learning did occur, then this was not intended for anyone holding the position of warehouseman, a position I have often occupied when employed by an employment agency. I remember a supervisor once telling me that I was far too intelligent to last long as a conveyor-belt employee, however hard I tried to beguile him with my work. Don't think, talk about nothing, and listen to Radio 3: these were the ingredients for an efficient contribution. I felt like one of Odysseus' rowers: lots of wax in your ears, so that you remain deaf to the signals around you, and besides this, rowing as quickly as you possibly can (see also: Horkheimer and Adorno, 1987). Then five o'clock will come around in almost no time at all. Of course my colleagues and I were also to blame for the apparent absence of learning, and the resulting monomania. As soon as experimentation or improvisation was required, because someone was ill, or because a consultant had visited the company, the consequence of which was that one of us had to work in a different department, Odysseus would notice a silent but persistent dissatisfaction amongst his men. Mindless work is one thing, the rowers thought, but you'll never be able to take away our sense of belonging to a group. Good riddance to enriching work.

Now, you could of course say that I was not working in learning organisations, but the manager in these organisations did, in any event, possess the vocabulary that would later become so characteristic of such authors as Senge. They talked about job enrichment, learning processes, quality impulses, culture changes and other such things. A certain affinity with the 'learning in organisations' theme was thus certainly present. But more important than this is Odysseus' lesson that learning in organisations is evidently not intended for everyone, unless we are referring to the learning process by means of which one can very quickly subordinate oneself to the prevailing course of events. In that case, learning is a question of survival, not a question of variation, change or disorganisation, as intended by supporters of the learning organisation, for without variation, change or disorganisation, you will not be able to cope with turbulent situations. In other words, there are *relevant* learning processes and *irrelevant* learning processes in organisations. The former result in innovation and change; the latter result in more of the same.

In a text that has acquired classic status, at least in this field, and in a quite unmistakable manner, De Geus (1988), with Senge one of the more important thinkers in the field of the learning organisation, has given a clear explanation of the difference between relevant and irrelevant learning processes: "The only relevant learning process in a company", he writes, "is the learning process experienced by those people that have the power to act" (1988: 67).

The true aim of the planning process, regarded by De Geus as a learning process, is " ... not the making of plans, but the changing of the microcosmos, that is to say, of the mental models envisaged by the people in charge".

Relevant learning is, thus, a privilege reserved for Odysseus and others in a position of authority. The rest have to row. Row fast.

Natural learning: 'habituation' and imitation

Now, Adam Smith in particular was of the opinion that we should not be overly condescending about what has just been referred to as irrelevant learning processes. To him, work was nothing more and nothing less than a necessary evil, and if workers could be induced to do this work as efficiently as possible, then it would be possible to temper this evil as far as possible, certainly if it were also met with a fair reward (Grint, 1998). This attitude towards labor is incredibly pessimistic, although this will not have been experienced as such by everyone in Smith's time. In any event, Smith's splendid vision of the blessings of the division of labor had the side effect that the work of task specialists did not become any more humane because of it. Smith was very well aware of the fact that it was only bearable for 'stupid' people.

Here too a type of learning process is involved, albeit in the opposite direction. In ethology, it later became known by the name of 'habituation'. This is a type of learning that we could encounter "along the entire phylogenetic scale (...), from single-celled organisms to human beings" (Estes, 1978: 245–246, *quoted in*: Murphy, 1993: 65). The idea behind this is simple: if we just repeat a certain stimulus as often as possible, then the organism will, sooner or later, cease to respond. In other words: sooner or later, habituation to a certain environment results in an absence of response. Smith had a fundamental understanding of the fact that *learning not to react* is the simplest and most natural way of learning. Habituation makes it possible for us to cope with and accept all kinds of damaging influences, such as the monomaniacal work of the task specialist. A very concrete consequence of habituation is that "our social and natural environment become indiscernable to us" (Murphy, 1993: 66). We always need strangers if we are to understand who we are, Murphy wisely adds.

Of course, this has important consequences for our reflection about Odysseus' rowers. Supporters of the learning organisation always claim that nothing is more natural than learning, but, according to biologists at least, the most natural way of learning is just not to respond, not something that the rower is supposed to do in the learning organisation. Invariably, learning organisations are described in terms of conscious behavioral change and almost unlimited developmental scope, something that becomes apparent in Senge's discussion of 'personal mastery', for example. Here, the point is not to submit to depressing reality. If you have to hold on to something, hold on to extreme ambition, the dream that far exceeds reality. Such personal mastery facilitates a creative tension, which exceeds the emotional tension of realism (Senge, 1990: 150–153). In such *new age* atmospheres, such concepts as habituation are not very useful. No, while ignoring biological insights into the process, you will even start to say that adjusting to reality is unnatural.

Neither is any attention paid to imitation as a learning process; another natural learning process. A short quote from Aristotle's *Poetics*:

> From childhood onwards, imitation is natural for humans, and one of the advantages that they have over the lower species is the fact that they are the creatures that imitate most in the world, and learn the fastest by imitation (Poetics, 1448b).

Of course, we do not necessarily have to accept Aristotle as an authority, but even today there seems to be a considerable degree of consensus that the best imitators are to be found at the top of the above-mentioned phylogenetic ladder (see De Waal, 1996: 88, for example). There is also evidence that most people from the business community obtain their best ideas by emulation or copying (Bhide, 1994).

Nevertheless, in the literature about learning organisations, attention to the learning effects of imitation is quite scant. Authors prefer to emphasize the unique, creative ability of the human being, as well as his ability to transform himself and develop again and again in an experimental learning process (see also: De Geus, 1997: 76). According to Senge, a good description of the conceptualization of mankind that underlies the learning organisation is the one provided by the Japanese businessman Kazuo Inamori:

> Whether it is research and development, company management, or any other aspect of business, the active force is "people". And people have their own will, their own mind, and their own way of thinking. If the employees themselves are not sufficiently motivated to challenge the goals of growth and technological development, (...) there will simply be no growth ... and no technological development (Quoted in: Senge, 1990: 139–140).

Thus, according to Inamori, to be able to utilize people's potential, we must obtain a new understanding of their unconscious mind, willpower and *'action of the heart'*. If we regard people in this way, we do not generally regard them as imitators, but as creators, artists, visionaries.

And so a second crucial way of learning is simply pushed under the carpet. What is more, imitation has obtained an extraordinarily negative connotation, not only in the literature about learning organisations, but also in the business world itself. The famous, but not unambiguous, appeal by Hamel and Prahalad (1994) for companies to embrace the so-called core competency approach, was successful particularly because this involves *non-imitable* skills and advantages before anything else, something for which Japanese companies in particular appeared to have had the patent for many years. This is particularly ironic when one considers that it was these Japanese businessmen who were frequently called imitating apes by Anglo-Saxon and other confrères, or, as an old Victorian tradition has it: 'Japanzees' (pronounce: *'djappenzees'*). In 1913, the year that the physiologist Charles Ritchet was awarded the Nobel Prize, he was still claiming that the Japanese were chimpanzees, that is to say, "babbling imitation people somewhere between ape and man" (*Quoted in*: Schwartz, 1996: 368).

Imitation of the world in the nursery

In the literature about learning organisations, attention is paid to imitation, but never in the sense of copying, while almost all biological research indicates that, besides habituation, copying is the most important way of learning, particularly for those apes that we call people (Murphy, 1993: 70; De Waal, 1996: 88). Adult specimens set the example, and children imitate them. Somehow this notion is not compatible with the learning organisation's conceptualization of mankind. Although Senge (190: 314) is interested in how children learn, he never discusses imitation as a form of copying. On the contrary, in the nursery's own small "microcosmos", where children are able to play safely, they are engrossed, in solitary saintliness, by blocks, and by doing so learning, "*by teaching themselves*", the basic principles of spatial geometry and mechanics (ibid.; *my italics*).

De Geus (1988: 67) also finds the idea of education a little difficult. He points to scientific research that has demonstrated that education is a form of knowledge transfer where generally no more than 25 % of what is taught is retained. What is more, education supposes authority, something that those that should teach managers and board members, namely the planning specialists, per definition do not have. As soon as this specialist enters the boardroom, he loses his authority and is unable to teach. Fathers and mothers are *non grata* in the nursery. Therefore, the imitation that occurs there is imitation of the outside world, not copying.

The same laws of learning apply to both the nursery and the boardroom. If there is no education here, all that remains is the creative use of the "mental models that people in authority envisage." Now, De Geus refers to these mental models as '*microcosmos*', a term that is also used by Senge. A microcosmos is a room where children and directors are by themselves. A sophisticated solipsistic circle, because in this room they are exposed to nothing but their own models and images:

> The discipline of working with mental models starts with turning the mirror inward; learning to unearth our internal pictures of the world, to bring them to the surface and hold them rigorously to scrutiny (Senge, 1990: 8).

Here too the comparison with Odysseus' journey past the Sirens is appropriate, as these strange creatures, a mixture of bird and nymph, did not sing their own song, but a song that had already, for a long time, been familiar to Odysseus and all of the others, who, incidentally, did not survive. According to Sloterdijk (1998: 496–497), the irresistibility of the Sirens did not lie in the seductiveness of their voices, that were more ugly than beautiful, or in the beauty of the melody, but in the fact that they sang what the sea heroes that passed by most wanted to hear, as if "sung from the position of the listener himself". They would have sung songs about Achilles (or whoever else) and his heroic deeds, were it not that this hero coincidentally never sailed past the high meadow "strewn with the blanching bones of their victims". Odysseus did sail past, and he too would have finished up in this graveyard if he had not been warned about it by Circe. Thus, the Sirens sang songs that he alone could understand, not only because they were about him, but particularly because they sang it in such a manner that it seemed as if the hero himself were singing them, or, even better, was hearing them from within himself:

> Come here Odysseus, who is famous throughout the world; you who are the pride of the Greek knights! Let your ship drift ashore, because you must first hear our voices! No-one has ever sailed past here on their dark ships without hearing our voices, which are as sweet as honey. And there is no-one who has not returned home wiser and happier. We know about everything that happened on the broad plains before Troy ... and we always know what will happen on earth, that brings forth so much (Homer, 1959: 590; with some occasional changes by myself).

Brilliant psychotechnics, according to Sloterdijk (1998: 499, 500), which enables the hero to believe himself deaf to the 'noises of the world', and, by doing so, only have ears for his own song, his own desire. Sirens market *avant la lettre*, because they know better than the consuming heroes themselves what they desire. Full of auto-erotic and solipsistic excitement, the hero then sinks away into a sonospherical microcosmos. There are no stories more beautiful than those that you want to tell and hear told about yourself.

The literature on learning organisations also contains clever psychotechnics. I am thinking here, for example, of Senge's attempts, discussed above, to depict those managers who have to read his books, as idealistic pioneers. But I am particularly thinking of his opinion about the functioning of the human mind. This is described as a mirror that exposes images of the world, which images can be studied. Philosophers like Rorty (1980) and Dennett (1993: 32–33) have branded such opinions as superstition. Nevertheless, the claim that you are alone with, and in charge of your images, even if these do reflect something that is apparently outside of yourself, is something so 'natural' that its rhetorical effect is enormous. Who would not allow himself to be carried away by the idea that you can be the master of your own thoughts and actions, that everything will work out, and that you will, sometime, be home again? It is only this that makes it credible to managers that some adjustment of mental models is sufficient to be able to cope with the complexity of the outside world. In other words, you can become your own hero. Senge is to managers what Sirens were to Odysseus. De Geus (1997: 65) sings along with the Sirens when he discusses scenario planning:

> The mythological elements of the hero's journey, such as those described by Campbell [in his book *The Hero with a Thousand Faces*], do indeed appear to draw a quite good response from most business people. The departure, the belly of the wale, the initiation to the road of tribulations, and, finally, the homecoming (after having earned the freedom to live); all have their parallels in scenario stories. In my experience, several scenarios, that were the best

understood and remembered the longest at Shell, contained elements of Joseph Campbell's description of the timeless 'adventure'.

What Sirens are to a hero like Odysseus, are "the accelerators of an economic recession" or "the threat of low oil prices" for the "(company) hero" that De Geus talks about.

Such things as 'developing creative tension', 'leverage' and other such fabrications that adorn books written by Senge (1990) or Hamel and Prahalad (1994) must also be regarded as psychotechnics. Such ideas gain their rhetorical power because they fit in so well with the naive beliefs about the workings of the human mind. A lever according to my own image of reality is, of course, completely different to a lever according to certain aspects of reality itself. And then I have not even yet posed the question of to what extent we ourselves are the master of our own constructions. To what extent are these not influenced by the outside world? To what extent do we really understand the manner in which constructions, models, paradigms get us in our grasp? Despite all his emphasis on dynamic complexity, Senge's views on the human mind are, mildly speaking, oversimplified, and he wrongly makes it seem as if we already know all this (for criticism of a similar nature, see: Griffin, Shaw and Stacey, 1998).

Such simplifications are encountered frequently. De Geus (1997: 79–83) talks about games, where reality is imitated, something that he believes is to be recommended, because 'play' is the best way to learn, at least in the world of business. De Geus is therefore surprised that in most companies games are not regarded as instructional devices. Instead, learning occurs via experience, and "reality itself is experimented with", something that he is evidently surprised about. According to De Geus, we should be able to experiment in the business world without being afraid of the consequences that reality has in store for us. Here too, a comparison which at first sight appears obvious plays an important role:

> For example, a girl places part of her reality into a doll. In her imagination, the doll is her little brother or her boyfriend. She experiments (plays) with it. Because the doll is only a toy, she can do this without being afraid of any consequences. She can mutilate it, and discover that certain acts do indeed lead to mutilation. She can throw it up into the air, or let it fall to the ground, in a way that her mother would never allow her to do with her small, living, brother (1997: 81).

This passage elicits a personal outpouring from me. I have two small children at home. Just as we, their parents, never allow them to stick a pen into each other's eyes, neither may they stick one into a doll's eyes. Not even in the nursery. The image of children autonomously experimenting in their own small microcosmos is entirely illusory.

But the illusion is effortlessly extrapolated to organisational contexts. De Geus claims that "toys" – a word that he himself uses – are also used at Shell (1997: 81). However, these are not called dolls, but computer models. And, as we know, the modern-day army also has its toys: entire computer simulations, referred to by De Geus (ibid.) as "war games" occur before any concrete action is taken. The predecessors to these computerized war games were of course the small model soldiers, with which officers could enact their own 'Kriegspiel'. These little tin soldiers were once positioned in a two-by-four meter landscape of painted rivers and minute matchstick bridges.

Don't get me wrong; I can quite understand De Geus' dislike of recklessness or, as he calls it, "Rambo-management" (1987: 82). But the question is whether the nursery, any more than reality, creates Rambos or, in the case of the little girl that sticks things into her doll's eyes, Rambas. Let us consider some generals from the start of this century, who, in their own small microcosmos in the headquarters, are standing, cigars in hands, around a table on which tin soldiers, motionless and riveted silently to their bayonets, are spread over a paper-maché landscape. Will these people act as De Geus expects the little girl in the nursery to act? Will they realize that the murder of tin soldiers, carefully pushed over with the little finger of the left hand, is simulating a horrible reality? Or will they, rather, be under the illusion that they know what it would have been like to be a soldier, living or dying, on the battlefields of Verdun or Ieperen? Will they not instead just become insensitive to that reality? Schwartz (1996: 260) points out that this is always the problem with simulation. "Does simulation represent insight or flight, imagination or denial?", he wonders in a probing manner. And the answer that he gives is not one that supporters of the learning organisation will be able to appreciate.

Imagine how it could be in the nurseries of the generals and their officers. During the "Kriegspiel" (Schwartz, 1996: 265) there was often a warm and intimate atmosphere among the befriended generals, who, just as in a game of Stratego – far removed from the darkness of the battlefield, and enjoying a glass of cognac – tried to outdo each other. Imagine also that, as we have seen, De Geus professed to be speaking about the only learning processes relevant to organisations, and that he explicitly reserved for "those in charge". The right of senior executives to learn and play in the microcosmos of the nursery – the only ideal alternative for the boardroom – has everything to do with hegemony. It is Odysseus' right, chained to the mast, to experiment with the sensual temptations of the Sirens only intended for him. In reality, outside this microcosmos, people row, plod on, fight and die. Schwartz tells us about a famous major, an experienced strategist in paper-maché countries, who burst into tears when finally confronted with a real battlefield. He could not understand how his plans and maneuvers could have such devastating consequences.

Anyway, the major mentioned above was, in any event, presented with reality as a sort of ethical gift. The technical refinement of the simulation and the whole amusement esthetics that often go with it, entail that reality itself will, sooner or later, conform to the simulation. Nuclear war games can be won on a computer screen, and if you win this type of game often enough, the temptation will be great to believe that nuclear wars can also be won (Schwartz, 1996: 266). Eventually, war itself becomes a game, played from computer screens, with the aid of IFF (Identify Friend or Foe) software. Gary Klein (1998), an American decision theoretician, observes that it is exactly those people who continually withdraw from reality by continuing to rely on planning and other alienation techniques that make increasingly less adequate decisions. Of course, this behavior results in a *self-fulfilling prophecy*, because the longer you delay your visit to reality, the more you have to rely on the procedures and scenarios that have been devised for you. Klein, who presents various empirical data to support his claims, opposes the idea that people are in fact helpless creatures who may only be brought together in the planning room if a good decision is to be possible. In every-day reality, people rarely make optimal decisions, but equally seldom do they make catastrophic decisions. This might not be a score to get enthusi-astic about, but we needn't become too enthusiastic about the score for plan-ning and simulation games either (Klein, 1998: 106; Mintzberg, 1994). Normally, people make reasonably good decisions, even in tense situations, or under time pressure; this is certainly the case if they possess the necessary experience. And these decisions only become worse, certainly when made by experienced people, the greater the reliance on the above-mentioned alien-ation techniques.

In other words: experienced people do not belong in the nursery, at least on the condition that they do not continually strive for optimal decisions. Klein therefore claims that people do not do this. He re-introduces the term coined by Herbert Simon (1960) 'satisficing decisions' to indicate how people arrive at decisions outside the nursery. People may be rationally-lim-ited creatures, but this does not mean that we should lock them up in a nurs-ery as potential Rambos and Rambas. Which is to say, that I have my doubts about the whole notion of a microcosmos, in which decisive learning moments are constructed by important people. I find this an other-worldly idea, in the literal sense of the word. It distances these people from reality and, whether this be willingly or unwillingly, they will have to learn from this reality. And this is not possible by simulating reality and searching for border experiences within the simulacrum, as Weick and Westley (1996: 453) have suggested, but by imitating people from said reality, or by just not reacting and quietly adapting. Not that there are no other ways of learning in said reality, but imitation and adjustment are more frequent and more natural. Neither do such learning processes correspond to the definition of the learning organisation, even if they do appear to offer a perfect description of learning processes in nearly all actual organisations. If during my time as a warehouseman, I had to learn something, then it was the way in which an experienced colleague stacked or carried sacks or boxes. Watching and copying exactly what I had seen, that was the motto. And what other motto should I have had?

Of course I understand that errors made by people with far-reaching powers of decision can often have major consequences, and that these can, if only for this reason, be improved during a simulation. But the price that we have to pay for this is enormous. Due to various types of planning techniques and strategic simulations, an organisation's leaders are increasingly distanced from what is happening within and around the organisation. In general, they do not possess the 'soft' information that is necessary for the really important decisions to be made; information that is often possessed by their subordinates. This other-worldliness is not restricted to bank managers who do not know what an avocado is – this is something that is relatively innocent – but extends to bosses like Gerlach Cerfontaine, Director of Schiphol, who say that they would prefer to deal only with the prime minister. The two of them together in the prime minister's little tower, the curtains well-drawn, they can cope with the turbulent world outside. This is pervaded by the same sort of homesickness as that which the major must have experienced when he found himself in the middle of the smoking graveyard of the First World War, and thought back to his tin soldiers.

You could say that the above-mentioned simulation also gives rise to a remarkable type of error tolerance; something that I have discussed in detail elsewhere (1998). The idea is simple. You learn from your mistakes. Great. But these do have their price. This is why it is better if they are not made (in reality), even if this is sometimes unavoidable. Depending on the consequences resulting from the error, reality can mercilessly punish the person that made the error. This is not good, because it leads to fear in people who make errors, and this, in its turn, again undermines the ability of the people in charge to learn. In the end, because the relevant learning capacity is reserved for them, they are the only ones who are allowed to make mistakes. The learning organisation must, therefore, advocate a moment of hegemonic disorganisation. This disorganisation is exactly the microcosmos referred to by Senge and De Geus, and enables senior executives to withdraw from reality. It is the team training in the sticks, the computer simulation, the table of tin soldiers, but also, as already said, the boardroom that has deteriorated into a nursery, to which those in charge have an exclusive right, and where they can giggle about the stupid mistakes that they made earlier in the game. Only in the nursery can one really learn = play = experiment.

I have my doubts about the notion that people learn from the mistakes that they make, certainly if these are made in the nursery, and certainly if they can only be reprimanded by other inhabitants of the microsphere of which they form a part. The emphasis placed on error tolerance is yet more proof of the contempt that is felt for such more everyday learning processes as imitation. In everyday reality, the exemplary behavior of a certain leader or colleague probably results in a substantially greater learning effect than can be achieved by making a mistake. To say the least, such aspects are not taken into consideration. People who must continually break through their own intellectual, instinctive and behavioral boundaries in order to continually be able to do new things, cannot suffice with the imitation of good behavior. This would only amount to the standardization and institutionalization of success, and if anything is to be institutionalized in the learning organisation, then it is change. Once again, learning in the learning organisation is shifting boundaries, and boundaries are shifted more easily in a simulated world than in the real world. This is why imitation does not relate to the exemplary behavior of actual leaders, but to reality as a simulation.

Democracy and roses

Of course, Odysseus did not advocate it, neither did the soldiers around the table with their little tin soldiers. Yet, democracy does exercise the minds around the learning organisation. Because learning entails the overturning of hierarchy, some hope, even the critical theorists amongst them (for example: Clegg c.s., 1996), that the learning organisation will be able to start something like a democratic revolt. Well then, what are we to make of such expectations? Are they groundless or realistic?

One thing first: democracy is not something desired by everyone, certainly not in organisations. It generates fear and uncertainty if performance is required. Fulop and Rifkin (1997: 57) allude to the creation of a learning space in which managers do not have any privileged access to the truth, and in which the hierarchy can be turned upside down. However, both authors refer to the unavoidable feelings of fear by which such a learning space is accompanied, because it must be possible to question anything here, including someone's own knowledge and position. It is, thus, important that this learning space is not confused with the nursery, which is intended to somewhat reduce feelings of fear. They quite rightly reproach Senge for paying no attention to such negative emotions, but this, of course, has its own small strategic objectives (Fulop and Rifkin, 1997: 61; Ten Bos, 1998: 12).

Senge (1990) does not in any way remove hierarchy. Yet, he does often refer to its fundamental flaws. However, the word 'democracy' does not form part of his vocabulary. He is more concerned with a meritocracy, in which people dare to speak their minds, face-to-face (ibid.: 182). This is referred to as 'openness' and is one of the values that can be used to destroy the hierarchical culture that exists in many organisations. Nevertheless, I cannot help associating this notion with the nursery, to which few have

41

access. Of course, in the nature of things, such a meritocracy remains hierarchical, but rank is not determined on the basis of someone's length of service or position, but on the basis of performance.

There is something else which can have quite clear anti-democratic consequences: Senge's dislike of politics and all other things negative, such as the feelings of fear and uncertainty already referred to. In his opinion (ibid.: 60), political decision-making is "counterproductive" because this concerns a process in which factors are considered that do not bear any relation "to the intrinsic merits of alternative courses of action" – for example, building one's own power base, "looking good", or "pleasing the boss". Here too we see the tendency to optimize and idealize the decision-making process; something that must be realized by banning the political and the emotional, insofar as the latter is not 'positive'. What is more, such language, just as the language in which a sovereign 'I' is assumed, which is the boss in his own room, appeals to managers and employers who often detest politics and other fear and anxiety- generating phenomena anyway. Thus, some clever psychotechnics are again the case here. To the great satisfaction of employers, the political and (an important part of the) emotional reality in organisations is simply pushed aside as unproductive. A common vision (1990: 273–274) replaces the democratic decision-making process. In the nursery, serious discussion is only possible within the framework of this vision.

Hamel and Prahalad (1994: 140) have also put up a good show in the discussion, and argue for a democratization of strategy, in the sense that strategy becomes the business of each employee employed by the organisation. However, whether people really have something to contribute may be called into question. In an interview with Gibson (1997: 91), Hamel said that this is a democracy according to a Greek model, not "one vote per person", but a democracy based on what people can contribute intellectually. Thus, once again, a meritocracy, and probably not even according to a Greek model. The responsibility for strategy development is distributed throughout the organisation, something that we would barely dare to claim from the old Greek city-state. For that matter, this distribution of strategic responsibility must, just as is the case with Senge, result in "one single vision that has the entire organisation in its grasp" (ibid.). This, dear reader, is the comment that concludes Hamel's defense of strategic democracy. Nowhere in this literature do we see an appeal for pluralism or the corresponding democratic discussion. If democracy is about anything, it is about discussion. However, too much discussion is a risky business.

De Geus (1997: 208) is slightly clearer about the role of the democracy in the learning organisation. He quotes Popper, who apparently once said that the essential idea of democracy is that we can rid ourselves of a leader without the need for a crisis. According to Popper, this possibility is more important than the right to vote. We have just seen that the latter also appeals, in any event, to many supporters of the learning organisation. De Geus is matter-of-fact and, reflecting on his comprehensive work experience, states that in "companies where employees were not able to rid themselves of their managers, we did not concern ourselves about any claim to democracy" (ibid.).

In practice, there appeared to be one minimal variant at the most: if you were not satisfied, you could always use your democratic right to leave the company. Such observations are at least honest and straight-to-the-point, and, as such, food for thought. Yet De Geus is also ambiguous. He argues for shared-power ethics; something which he takes significantly further than his conceptual allies do. This idea is linked to his opinion that the entire organisation can never learn if a small group appears to be predestined to learn (1997: 214). In itself, this idea is sympathetic, if you at least feel warm sympathy for democracy, but, in the light of earlier remarks about relevant and irrelevant learning processes and those who should benefit from the fruits of these, I am unable to place this myself. Is this really about non-hegemonic disorganisation?

Earlier in his text, De Geus discusses tolerance. Here too he uses a lovely image. If you want the largest and most beautiful roses in the area, you have to prune aggressively (1997: 162). More than three branches per plant are then absolutely forbidden. You cannot tolerate anything, and everything must be kept under strict control. The trouble is that the plant as such could suffer irrecoverable damage as a result, for example if frost occurs in the spring. The plant could cope far better with such "unpredictable" events if it were not pruned. In the long term, tolerance is probably better for the plant than vigorous control. The metaphor of the garden is often criticized in literature (see, for example, Ten Bos and Willmott, 2001), but this was partly due to the fact that it resulted in an image of the weeding and pruning gardener who aggressively destroyed anything that was a weed. De Geus knows more about gardening, and says that this determination is often unfortunate. The image of the gardener controlling everything within his domain does remain intact, a little like the officers with their tin soldiers, although he does sometimes allow some good and tightly organized disorganisation. This disorganisation can be interpreted as tolerance. How far does it extend?

It is, and continues to be, the tolerance of hegemony, because to what extent you permit overgrowth is entirely in the hands of the gardeners in their enclosed garden at the top of the organisation. It is all very well to say that nobody may have too much power in organisations (1997: 213), but the distributive code lies with the gardeners themselves. Managers should not any longer wish to control everything themselves. They must create a context. They must say the following to their subordinates: "Go ahead (...).

You are free to make mistakes within the framework of the learning that we have undergone together. I will observe" (1990: 215).

Elsewhere (1990: 173) De Geus writes that what is involved is the creation of space in which to experiment and to take risks, but, at the same time, people must not expect to be able to "do what they want to do at the expense of the common aim of the organisation". Organisations need people who want independence, but who also wish to be effectively controlled.

I was of the opinion that this leaves the dream of a democracy in tatters. Possibly it only concerns an idea that belongs in the virtual microcosmos of the nursery, to which only the bosses have access. Possibly, upon further consideration, it was only a fascinating toy that belongs in the realms of hegemonic disorganisation, but that, just as all other toys, is cast aside when it has served its often ephemeral purpose.

Concluding remarks: a question of mood?

Ideas about learning in organisations and learning organisations are heading for a golden future, for example because they reflect the increasing interest that organisations have for flexibility and turbulence. For example, Volberda's (1998) recent development of the *'flexible firm'* concept is heavily indebted to such ideas. For the rest, it still remains to be seen whether organisations that have become entirely flexible will continue to invest in learning processes. In times where permanent positions are under pressure, it is almost inevitable that investment in employee development will decrease, at least from an organisational perspective. If knowledge is lacking, this will simply be hired in. Temporary contracts, often a pre-eminent characteristic of flexible organisations, could, thus, sometimes work out unfavorably for the learning capacity of *organisations*. Or, in other words: flexibilization causes the responsibility for learning to shift from the organisation to the individual him/herself, if, at least, he or she wishes to remain an attractive party in the labor market (Tregaskis, 1997: 540). Of course, this links up to my contention that the literature about learning organisations is directed more towards the individual person than towards organisations.

Also, the ideas discussed are suffused with an atmosphere of optimism that is welcomed in a time described by many in terms of chaos and turbulence. There is a way out of the choking reality. I have sought to temper this optimism with a sort of pessimism that can also be found in the work of Michel Foucault (1975). You can never escape power, not even in learning organisations. There will always be violence, restraint, exclusion and abuse. If Foucault (1976) has made anything clear then it is the fact that the replacement of physical violence by more subtle, more 'psychotechnical' forms of violence only implies a change in the type of violence used, not its disappearance. Not that Foucault thinks that organisations are bad, not at all, but he believes that organisations, just as everything else in the world, are *dangerous*. It is this sense of danger that I have particularly wished to stimulate in this article. The other-worldliness and the escapism of senior executives is dangerous, certainly if we are not aware of it. Thus, something always remains to be done. I share Foucault's ideas about "pessimistic hyperactivism" (*quoted in*: Weaver, 1997: 43).

At the same time I am not blind to the attractive aspects of the ideas that I have put in a pessimistic light. The desire to learn differently, to change oneself by learning, to see larger relationships through learning, is understandable. Long ago, John Holt, one of De Geus' sources of inspiration, wrote about learning processes, that he quite rightly condemned:

> At school, children learn that the wrong answers, insecurity and confusion are crimes. Schools want Right Answers, and childen are taught various strategies to help them to worm these answers out of the teacher, which help them to make her believe that she thinks that they know what they do not know. They learn how to avoid, bluff, simulate and deceive ... What children actually learn is that they must never get into trouble, that this is something for other children, that they are embroiled in a vicious competitive struggle with other children, that, in other words, each human is the natural enemy of man (*quoted in*: Michael, 1996: 152).

In the introduction I have pointed to the idealistic inspiration on which the work about the learning organisation is based. We need not necessarily share Senge's optimism about business managers, but he is not alone. In 1930, the pragmatic philosopher John Dewey placed subjects on the agenda that would only much later be given a place in the thoughts about learning in organisations and learning organisations. At that time, he already believed that companies and organisations could contribute to a very different type of education of people than the way in which Holt's children were being educated (Weaver, 1997: 38–41; see also Rorty, 1980: 369 et seq). He was of the opinion that the old individualism of the Enlightenment, to which the autonomous individual was central, would make way for a "collectively constructed individual", that, on the one hand, is free, but, on the other hand, realizes that his fate is connected to the community of which he forms a part. Companies play a decisive role here. According to Dewey, the large company could remove one of humanity's oldest problems, namely the problem of loneliness. A sense of belonging and community is promoted by organisations, certainly if the profit imperative is put into some perspective. Organisations can be places where people can pre-eminently be formed into good citizens, where there will always be room for what seems unacceptable, where truths can be imbedded into contexts, and never be made absolute, where the aim is not material self-enrichment but the education and transformation of people (see also: Rorty, 1980: 359, 360, 379).

The difference between Dewey and Foucault therefore appears to result in a choice between romantic optimism and realistic pessimism. However, Weaver (1997: 44) correctly remarks that Foucault and Dewey agree on many points. They are both convinced that organisations can change people. In other words, people are not rigid, autonomous and lonely rocks that cannot be influenced by changing contexts and larger wholes. This is exactly the reason why, despite all of the rhetoric about autonomous and individual employees, the learning organisation is also anchored in the pragmatic tradition. After further consideration, this rhetoric appears to be no more than a marketing instrument designed to entice and mislead individual consumers. To be able to change people, supporters of the learning organisation must believe that employees are susceptible to what is happening within their organisations.

This susceptibility forms a source of hope to Dewey, because organisations can help to bring forward a 'new' type of person, one that is more directed towards a sense of community; for Foucault, but also for someone like Saul (1997), this susceptibility is rather a source of despair, which ensures that a person disappears in a surge of violence, however subtle the forms of this violence might be. With the exception of someone like Donald Michael, who, as we have seen, shares Foucault's pessimism about companies, and focuses more on society as a whole, most supporters of the learning organisations share Dewey's optimism about the ability of organisations to realize happiness. Weaver may be right when he states that all of these differences have less to do with theoretical disagreement than with different moods.

Nietzsche may have been right when he said that all of the differences in opinion can eventually be traced back to our moods.

References

Achterhuis, H. (1998). *De erfenis van de utopie.* (The heritage of the utopia) Amsterdam: Ambo.

Argyris, C. and D. Schon (1974). *Theory in Practice.* San Francisco (Ca.): Jossey-Bass.

Bateson, G. (1972). *Steps to an Ecology of Mind.* New York: Ballantine Books.

Bhide, A. (1994). How entrepreneurs craft strategies that work. *Harvard Business Review,* 72 (2), 15–161.

Bos, R. ten (1998). Lerende organisaties en foutentolerantie. (Learning organisations and tolerance of mistakes). *M&O,* 52 (2), 7–20.

Bos, R. ten, H. Willmott (2001). Towards a post-dualistic business ethics: interweaving reason and emotion in working life. *Journal of Management Studies* (in press).

Clegg, S., M. Barrett, T. Clarke, L. Dwyer, J. Gray, S. Kemp and J. Marceau (1996). Management knowledge for the future: Innovation, Embryos and New Paradigms. In S. Cleg and G. Palmer (Eds.) *The Politics of Management Knowledge* (190–236). London: Sage.

Cooke, B. (1999). Writing the left out of management theory: the historiography of the management of change. *Organisation*, 6 (1), 81–105.

Cyert, R., J. Marsh (1963). *A Behavioral Theory of the Firm*. Englewood Cliffs (NJ): Prentice Hall.

Czarniawska, B. (1997). Learning organisation in a changing institutional order: Examples from city management in Warsaw. *Management Learning*, 28 (4), 475–495.

Dennett, D. (1993, 1991). *Consciousness Explained*. Harmondsworth: Penguin.

Duke, R. (1974). *Gaming. The Future's Language*. Beverly Hills (Ca.): Sage.

Estes, W. (Ed.) (1978). *Handbook of Learning and Cognitive Processes. Vol. 6*. New York (NY): John Wiley.

Foucault, M. (1975). *Surveillir et Punir: Naissance the la Prison*. Paris: Gallimard.

Fulop, L., W. Rifkin (1997). Representing fear in learning in organizations. *Management Learning*, 28 (1), 45–63.

Garratt, B. (1990). *Creating a Learning Organisation, a Guide to Leadership, Learning, and Development*. Cambridge: Simon & Schuster.

Garvin, D. (1995, 1993). Building a learning organisation. In P. Frost, V. Mitchell and W. Nord (Eds.), *Managerial Reality. Balancing Technique, Practice, and Values. Second Edition* (386–400). New York (NY): HarperCollins. (Originally in: *Harvard Business Review*, 71 (4)).

Geus, A. de (1988). Planning als leerproces. *Holland Management Review, Autumn*, 16, 65–70.

Geus, A. de (1997). *De levende onderneming. Over leven en leren in een turbulente omgeving*. (The living firm) Schiedam: Scriptum.

Gherardi, S. (1999). Learning as problem-driven or learning in the face of mystery. *Organisation Studies*, 20 (1), 101–124.

Gibson, R. (1997). *Rethinking the future. Visies op leiderschap, organisaties, markten en de wereld*. Zaltbommel: Thema.

Griffin, D., P. Shaw and R. Stacey (1998). Speaking of complexity in management theory and practice. *Organisation*, 5 (3), 315–339.

Hamel, G. and C. K. Prahalad (1994). *De strijd om de toekomst. Baanbrekende strategieën voor marktleiderschap en het creëren van nieuwe markten*. Schiedam: Scriptum. (The struggle for the future.)

Holt, J. (1964). *How Children Fail, and How Children Learn*. New York: Pitman.

Homeros (1959). *Ilias & Odyssea*. Kemppische Bookhandel-Retie.

Horkheimer, M. and T. Adorno (1987, 1947). *Dialectiek van de verlichting*. (Dialectics of the enlightenment) *Filosofische fragmenten*. Nijmegen: SUN.

E. Jacques (1996). *Requisite organization: a total system for effective managerial organization and managerial leadership for the 21st century*. Arlington: Cason Hall.

Kieser, A. (1997). Rhetoric and myth in management fashion. *Organisation*, 4 (1), 49–74.

Klein, G. (1998). *Sources of Power. How People Make Decisions*. Cambridge (Ma.): MIT Press.

Kolb, D. (1984). *Experiential Learning: Experience as the Source of Learning and Development*. Englewood Cliffs (NJ): Prentice Hall.

Lindblom, C. (1959). The science of muddling through. *Public Administration Review, 19,* 78–88.

Michael, D. (1996, 1973). *Learning to Plan and Planning to Learn*. Alexandria (Vi.): Miles Rivers Press.

Micklethwait, J. and A. Wooldridge (1996). *The Witch Doctors. What the Management Gurus Are Saying, Why It Matters and How to Make Sense of It*. London: Heinemann.

Mintzberg, H. (1994). *The Rise and Fall of Strategic Planning*. Englewood Cliffs (NJ): Prentice-Hall.

Murphy, J. (1993). *The Moral Economy of Labor: Aristotelian Themes in Economic Theory*. New Haven/London: Yale University Press.

Pedler, M., J. Burgoyne and T. Boydell (1991). *The Learning Company. A Strategy for Sustainable Development*. New York (NY) McGraw-Hill.

Polanyi, M. (1957). *Personal Knowledge*. London: Routledge.

Revans, R. (1984). Action learning: half a life time spent. In R. Revans: *The Sequence of Managerial Achievement* (7–28). Bradford: MCB University Press.

Rorty, R. (1986, 1980). *Philosophy and the Mirror of Nature*. Oxford: Blackwell.

Saul, J. (1997). *The Unconscious Civilization*. New York: Penguin.

Schwartz, H. (1996). *The Culture of the Copy. Striking Likenesses, Unreasonable Facsimiles*. New York: Zone Books.

Senge, P. (1990). *The Fifth Discipline*. New York (NY): Doubleday.

Simon, H. (1947). *Administrative Behavior*. New York: MacMillan.

Simon, H. (1960). *The New Science of Management Decision*. New York (NY): Harper & Row.

Sloterdijk, P. (1998). *Sphären I: Blasen*. Frankfurt am Main: Suhrkamp.

Swieringa, J. and A. Wierdsma (1990). *Op weg naar een lerende organisatie*. (On the way to a learning organisation). Groningen: Wolters-Noordhoff.

Tregaskis, O. (1997). The 'non-permanent' reality! *Employee Relations, 19* (6), 535–554.

Volberda, H. (1998). *Building the Flexible Firm*. Oxford: Oxford University Press.

Waal, F. de (1997). (Good natured: the origins of right and wrong in humans and other animals). *Van nature goed. Over de oorsprong van goed en kwaad in mensen en andere dieren*. Amsterdam: Contact.

Weaver, W. (1997). Dewey or Foucault?: Organisation and administration as edification and as violence. *Organisation, 4* (1), 31–48.

Weick, K. (1979, 1969). *The Social Psychology of Organisation*. Reading (Ma.): Addison-Wesley.

Weick, K. and F. Westley (1996). Organisational learning: Affirming an oxymoron. In S. Clegg, C. Hardy and W. Nord (Eds.), *Handbook of Organisation Studies* (440–458). London: Sage.

Chapter 3

Self managing teams: practice and rhetoric of organisational performance and bonding

Peter Leisink

Introduction

The concept of self-managing teams is increasingly popular in management and organisation publications and it is a fitting item in the constant flow of rising and disappearing management concepts (cf. Grint, 1997; Karsten, Van Veen, 1998). Working in groups nowadays even bears 'a halo of good, correct and modern entrepreneurship' (Van der Zee, 1998: 8). The term 'self-managing team' refers to a fixed group of employees who are collectively responsible for (a circumscribed task in) the total process of manufacturing and delivering products or services to a customer, where the team plans and monitors the process of production and, relatively independently, solves minor problems of execution, and works on the improvement of processes and methods without appealing to management or services departments (cf. van Amelsvoort, Scholtes, 1994: 11; Van Ewijk-Hoevenaars, Den Hertog, Van Jaarsveld, 1995: 61). The concept of 'self-management' is used to denote the basic principles of the management structure of an organisation, which means that the team has the organisational capacity to manage the process, and management and staff services are available for creating the right conditions (Kuipers, van Amelsvoort, 1990: 121; van Amelsvoort, Scholtes, 1994: 11).

The ideas subsumed under the concept of self-management look familiar, at first glance. During the 1970s they were known by the concept of (semi) autonomous groups, which had a large following in the human relations movement (cf. Van Assen, Den Hertog, 1980). The term 'autonomous groups' and several other terms were used for a long time before the term 'self-managing teams' became popular. Whether the image of self-managing teams is really a sign of a new perspective, or rather a rhetorical innovation, will become clear when the theoretical roots of the concept, its contents and implied practice have been subjected to analysis.

During the 1970s the human relations movement was the influential perspective of research and practice of organisational change. At present, movements like human resource management and modern sociotechnical systems theory are dominant. Although the theoretical perspectives may be subject to change, a constant factor is the way in which the organization is conceptualized. Is the organisation primarily viewed as the domain of production where the rationality of the primary process and objective-driven management dominates, or is the organisation primarily regarded as a community in which social relations are central, making these relations and the quality of human life an aim in themselves? The fact that these different views can be combined into a dual perspective on organisations, makes them suitable for the analytical aims of this chapter, they are the ideal typical extremes of a continuum: organisation as the domain of production versus organisation as a community.

With this analytical differentiation the image or concept of self-management in different theoretical perspectives can be analysed and compared. Three perspectives will be discussed: modern sociotechnical systems theory, human resources management, and constructivism. The analysis of meanings attributed to the image of self-management, will not be limited to theoretical discourse. A practical case of self-managing teams will illustrate how conceptual ambiguity in organisational practice results in stressed relationships between different objectives with changing consequences. Finally, the balance will be drawn up of the meaning which theory and practice attributed to self-management, and the prediction is made that in all probability a new concept will be proposed for putting the same themes on the agenda.

Self-managing teams

It may be typical for popular images in general, but once they have become popular it is extremely difficult to trace the term back to their origins. The concept is employed by everyone, its use taken for granted, as if it has no specific theoretical roots. This is certainly true of self-managing teams. Thus, Yeatts and Hyten (1998) regard the human resource perspective (starting with Miles, but going back on McGregor and Maslow) and the participative-management perspective (Lawler, among others) – which are both regarded as resulting from the human relations approach – as the relevant theoretical movements for self-management. There is no denying that these perspectives are useful for recognising the importance of elements which are relevant for self-managing teams. Thus, for instance, the importance of social relations has been demonstrated by the human relations approach. The disadvantage of this historical approach is, however, that the combination of elements into a new concept is hard to retrace. Nevertheless, the concept of self-managing teams is regarded by many (among whom Yeatts and Hyten, 1998: 17) as the direct result of modern sociotechnical systems theory.

Self-managing teams and modern sociotechnical systems theory

In the Netherlands, modern sociotechnical systems theory is currently the most influential approach to integral organisation innovation based on the principle of self-management. In the world of organisation consultants and science sociotechnical systems theory is prominently present. Publications (for instance De Sitter, 1981; Kuipers, Van Amersfoort, 1990) respectfully refer to the London-based Tavistock Institute of Human Relations, which researched and implemented a classic example of sociotechnical organisation development (Trist, Higgin, Murray, Pollock, 1963). This concerned the replacement of the shift system of fixed specialised tasks in a predetermined stage in the cycle of coal mining, by a system of shifts where the members of shifts could perform all the tasks in the cycle and could thus regulate their own work and timetable, and shifts could relieve each other in a flexible way. In comparison to the old method of production, not only did the quality of work rise but so did productivity. 'Modern' sociotechnical systems theory, when compared to 'old' sociotechnical systems theory, is not exclusively focused on the micro level of the working group (with task rotation, task extension, and task enhancement), but on the integral refurbishment of the organisation as a whole with its production, management, support and information systems (Kuipers, Van Amelsvoort, 1990: 9). In addition, according to Kuipers and Van Amelsvoort (1990: 9) modern sociotechnical systems theory 'is not only aimed at the quality of work as an isolated functional requirement of the organisation', but the combination of functional requirements in the field of flexibility, order flow control, product quality, potential for innovation, and the quality of work is of importance.

In Dutch modern sociotechnical systems theory the central figure has been De Sitter, who laid the scientific foundations and made an important contribution to the success of organisation consultancy based on these principles. The argumentation and points of departure for the ideas which we now indicate with the concept of self-management, were systematically worked out by De Sitter in 'Op weg naar nieuwe fabrieken en kantoren' [The road to new factories and offices], a study commissioned by the Scientific Council for Government Policy [WRR] (De Sitter, 1980). For the organisational concretisation of these ideas the unwieldy term 'self-sufficient product groups' was coined, and the casual way in which it was introduced (De Sitter, 1981:

239) illustrates that sociotechnical systems theory is not the most 'fashionable tool of management', as De Sitter himself remarked (1981: 164).

De Sitter's central thesis is that there is a close and complementary connection between the quality of the organisation, work and labour relations. The Taylorist organisation based on the principle of division between executive, monitoring and regulatory tasks, and the division of each of these tasks, has negative consequences in the field of efficiency and effectiveness (prone to failures, inflexibility), in that of the quality of work (finding expression in alienation and increasing discrepancy between rising levels of education of workers and falling levels of functions) and in that of labour relations (segmentation). De Sitter posits the need for an integrated policy for tackling the interconnected problems of work, organisation and labour relations. The key role for implementing change is in the structure of the production organisation. The interventions in the division of labour and the addition of managing tasks to operational tasks not only diminishes the complexity of the labour organisation and enhances the flexibility of the potential for innovation, but at the same time it can improve the quality of work and labour relations. De Sitter (1981: 15) explicitly claims that his work 'is a plea for relinquishing the thesis of the opposition between so-called social and economic requirements, and to seriously implement policies that stimulate the development of organisational structures, in which rising quality of work, improving labour relations and work motivation, setting the trend of improving efficiency and effectiveness, become complementary and mutually reinforcing over time.' International organisational practice and scientific analysis are at the basis of De Sitter's plea for integrated organisation development.

De Sitter regards regulatory capacity as the central feature of quality of work (De Sitter, 1980: 58); increased regulatory capacity at work means, for instance, that work offers more learning opportunities and leads to frequent communication and consultation between management and workers. It is remarkable how he distances himself from 'ideologically coloured justification' in terms of 'humanisation' and 'democratisation' (De Sitter, 1981: 241) and how he argues for the objective necessity of redesign based on numerous research outcomes in the field of organisation of production (production of efficiency losses, increased productivity) and the organisation as a living community (better quality of work, less alienation).

De Sitter's work is at the basis of a growing practice in organisation consultancy during the '80s and '90s, which in several publications reported on the experiences gained in the application of sociotechnical theories in the practice of organisational innovation.

The development of modern sociotechnical systems theory entered *a new phase* with the publication of 'the first introduction to sociotechnical systems theory as an integral system of organisation design' (Kuipers, van

Amelsvoort, 1990). This handbook furnished a systematic treatment of modern sociotechnical systems theory, including exemplary cases that such a paradigm calls for.

The independent production unit, according to Kuipers and Van Amelsvoort (1990: 121), is the basic unit of the production organisation because at that level there is room for manoeuvre for redesigning the organisation to comply with modern requirements. A number of terms are used for the independent production unit: production cell, (semi)autonomous group, production cluster, self organising group, production island, or complete task group. Unequivocal, however, is the endeavour to use available leeway in and around the group 'to enhance the involvement of the members in the work and in the group in order to increase the regulatory capacity of the group, so that the group can independently solve problems that arise at the local level and within the task domain' (Kuipers, van Amelsvoort, 1990: 121). This formulation, as pars pro toto, calls for two remarks relating to the interpretation of the theoretical perspective in terms of the organisation as a production unit and/or to the organisation as a living community.

Firstly, the involvement that is referred to, together with the motivation of members of the group plays a central role in generating the human qualities which are of importance for the functioning of autonomous groups (Kuipers, van Amelsvoort, 1990: 137). According to Kuipers and Van Amelsvoort the integrated structure of the production organisation, which offers the possibility of actively influencing the whole, leads to involvement and motivation, whereas a non-cohesive structure with widely implemented division of labour leads to alienation. The central sociotechnical point of departure, therefore, is to design group tasks in such a fashion that alienation is replaced by 'structural room for manoeuvre and necessity to exert influence', 'to co-operate on useful products or services', 'to solve problems that arise in relation to other people on the basis of mutual agreement', 'to go on learning, so that a person can go on functioning in changing circumstances and can continue to be a fully functioning member of the group whose contribution to the group increases over the years' (Kuipers, van Amelsvoort, 1990: 140). The underlying assumption in the structural approach is that 'the structural necessity' as worked out above, will indeed lead to the need for influence and participation, to interest in the whole, to activation of social needs and ongoing personal development. Beside the structure of the work organisation, goalsetting and reward structuring can also contribute to this.

The reasons for this structural approach can be found in the criticism on experience approaches as found in Maslow and Herzberg, but also in the distance sociotechnicians wish to keep from ideologically determined standards. Thus, Kuipers and Van Amelsvoort (1990: 20) emphasise that the autonomous group should not be regarded as an 'ideologically determined sociotechnical standard prescription', but as a result of the 'logic of the sociotechnical structural construction'. This objectivist approach does, however, raise the question whether it is correct to interpret these sociotechnical statements about 'improvement of the quality of work' and 'reduction of alienation' as references to the organisation as a living community. Presuming that the adequacy of an interpretation demands that the interpretation be based on the commonsense meaning attributed by the actors to whose reality the statement refers (cf. Giddens, 1976), we should like to know whether the members of the group who have observed 'objective' improvements in their situation, subjectively also interpret their reality in terms of (more) community.

Secondly, in the above quotation, involvement is instrumentalised i.e. linked to improvement of organisational performance. There are other instances of statements that point to the instrumentalisation of the quality of work for organisational performance. The results of a consistent application of this sociotechnical concept are only formulated in terms of improved performance: reduction of overhead costs, reduction in the variable production costs, enhanced productivity, reduction of processing times, stock reductions, reduction of absenteeism and staff turnover, increased flexibility and potential for innovation, and improvement of product quality (Kuipers, van Amelsvoort, 1990: 10). Whereas for De Sitter (1980, 1981) the idea is feasible that the objectives of integral organisation development are of equal importance, Kuipers and Van Amelsvoort tend towards a subordination of quality of work to other organisational function demands. This instrumentalisation implies that meanings attached to the concept of self-management are restricted to the domain of the organisation as production. Indeed, the idea of the organisation as a community is based on the idea of community as an aim in itself, with human interaction as intrinsic value in the organisation and not as functionality for the improvement of performance.

Beside the consecutive editions of the handbook for sociotechnical design there are other publications based on organisation consultancy, as remarked before. 'Self-managing Teams' (van Amelsvoort, Scholtes, 1994) first published in 1993 and reprinted several times aims to be 'a guide' for organisations implementing self-managing teams. As the title of the book makes clear, the term self-managing teams is explicitly used here, and a Dutch equivalent [self steering teams] is introduced for 'self-directed teams' (Wellins, Byham, Wilson, 1991) or 'self-managing teams' (Manz, Sims, 1987). The guide for organisations implementing self-managing teams, mentions beside 'essential improvement of performance' a second reason for working in teams, the possibility for enhancing people's involvement and to give them (back) a meaningful task (van Amelsvoort, Scholtes, 1994: 18–19). The authors seem to give objectives in the domain of the organisation as production and the organisation as living community equal standing, but the former domain is emphasized: "... people are the most important resource in the organisation and self-managing teams ... a powerful means of fostering and deploying this asset" (van Amelsvoort, Scholtes, 1994: 19). The quotation makes clear that in this context self-management is a 'means' of 'deploying' human capital, that is to say: deploying assets in the domain of the production.

Self-managing teams and human resource management

Human resource management has several variants which take a different approach to the relation between company strategy and personnel strategy, and between the objectives of developing human capacities and production-driven deployment of human resources (e.g. Kluytmans, Vander Meeren, 1992; De Nijs, 1992; Storey, 1992). De Nijs (1992) differentiates between the Michigan model aiming at high performance, and the Harvard model aiming at high commitment. The first bases itself on integration of personnel management into the strategic policy of the company to such an extent that the content of personnel policy comes to depend on company strategy; the second aims at integration of personnel management into an integral strategy on organisation development based on new concepts of production (with functional flexibility, participation etc) in which the focus is on commitment of employees and development of capacities. This second variant, in the opinion of sociotechnical organisation consultants (see van Ewijk-Hoevenaars, den Hertog, van Jaarsveld, 1995: 32), by aiming at integral organisation development offers room for modern sociotechnical systems theory. Since the previous section has already paid extensive attention to sociotechnical systems theory, this second variant of HRM will not receive separate treatment here.

The relevance of the existence of differing variants for determining the meaning of the concept of self-management is easily indicated: the variants of HRM which focus on the company strategy will probably give meaning to the concept of self-management by means of a primary link to the organisation as production, whereas variants which focus on commitment and personnel development will leave room for determining the meaning of self-management in the direction of organisation as community.

One of the central ideas of HRM is that human talents contribute to the organisation and that organisations must learn how to employ the capacities of their personnel better and more fully. Instrumental in this process are teamwork and performance management with the aid of, for instance, the high-performance cycle of Locke and Latham, which is discussed by

Kluytmans and Vander Meeren (1992), as well as by Yeatts and Hyten (1998). The high-performance cycle not only seeks to enhance performance of the organisation, but gives job satisfaction a place in the model. Satisfaction arises as a result of being able to perform at a high level. The interpretation of this job satisfaction in terms of Maslow's theory of human need for self-respect and self actualisation refers to subjective meanings which are linked to the organisation as a community. The double meaning of this satisfaction, however, appears from the fact that this satisfaction has a direct effect on performance because of the enhanced involvement and willingness to accept new challenges that it generates in the employee. The high-performance cycle makes this meaning instrumental for the rationality of production. Another illustration in this connection is that Yeatts and Hyten (1998: 48), in their initial theoretical framework, measure the performance of teams both by customer satisfaction and by worker satisfaction, thus expressing the double objective of HRM. In doing so, they follow a large number of theoretical models – those of McGrath, Gladstein, Pearce and Ravlin, Hackman, Sunderstrom et al, Campion, Cohen – all of whom, when discussing criteria for effectivity of teams, include worker satisfaction. In their theoretical models it is difficult to determine whether worker satisfaction has been instrumentally restricted to functionality for (even) higher performance. It is significant, however that Yeatts and Hyten (1998: 53), in their final model of criteria for measuring performance restrict themselves to customer satisfaction and economic viability.

On closer analysis, Yeatts and Hyten's model turns out to link the meaning of self-managing teams to the domain of production, in accordance with the Michigan model of HRM which gives priority to company strategy. In view of the variety of human resource management strands, this conclusion cannot be generalised to HRM in its widest meaning. What this analysis does show, is that the double objective of HRM goes together with an ambiguous determination of the meaning of self-managing teams, so that different interested parties can all be convinced that the concept has something to offer them. No doubt, this is the reason that has most contributed to the popularity of both HRM and to that of the concept of self-managing teams.

Self-managing teams and constructivism

Constructivism is especially known as a cognitive theoretical approach differing from positivism in that it regards discourse about the world not as a direct reflection of that world but as a product of human interaction (e.g. Gergen, 1985, 1999). This assumption about the central role of signification or sense-making is taken by De Moor (1995) as a point of departure for working out a constructivist perspective on teamwork and participative management. From this perspective social reality, including the organisation as social reality, does not exist as an objective, substantive reality. 'There is an inter-subjective reality which is formed as the ongoing interaction between people. This reality does not exist outside human interaction. The organisation-as-social-reality is created and maintained in interaction' (De Moor, 1995:7). It is because of their capacity to communicate that people are able to construct and maintain social realities. In his analysis of the concept of 'communication', De Moor differentiates between 'exchange of information' among people and the element of 'making common' which arises because people interact in a certain context and arrive at mutual understandings or commonsense making. The mutual understanding which arises is the binding factor by which people form a community. An organisation can only come into being where people communicate or interact (de Moor, 1995:8–9). In this context De Moor refers to Weick (1979).

Constructivism in a general sense, then, takes the organisation as community as its point of departure, because it regards the organisation as social reality, which is the result of connections which people make in their interactions so that they arrive at mutual understandings by which they are linked. According to De Moor (1995: 12) it is especially true of teams that they are a social construct. There are teams in all sorts and sizes, says De Moor, but he agrees with Grayson as 'one of the better attempts at defining a team, in this case the self-managing working group: (...) a form of labour organisation which attributes responsibility to workers for the regulation, organisation and control of their work and the conditions directly related to it. This includes the definition of specific group responsibilities and autonomy as undertaking tasks in a way which is determined by the group itself. Within limits the group is free to take decisions on its daily activities' (de Moor, 1995: 34–35). Characteristics of a well-functioning team include (de Moor, 1995: 17–19):

- a team derives its reason for existence from the realisation of a mission which is clear to all members, on which they all agree and of which there are fully aware
- members of the team realise that the achievement of the objectives is determined by participative cooperation in which the different team roles (including that of team leader) are mutually geared to form a cooperative structure
- within the team there is an atmosphere of mutual trust and an open attitude to the participative input by others
- the team transcends the performance that individual members can produce, with customer satisfaction as the most important criterion
- the team leader monitors essential conditions, coaches the functioning of the team as a whole, and stimulates the motivation of all members

De Moor does not subordinate community characteristics of a team to its production performance. In the constructivist perspective the signification of self-managing teams remains linked to both the production-domain and the community-domain.

The meaning of self-managing teams in the theoretical perspectives

The three theoretical perspectives can be compared with reference to the meaning they give to self-managing teams within the organisation as domain of production or to the organisation as community. See Table 3.1.

Table 3.1. The labelling of goals of self-managing teams by different theoretical perspectives.

Perspectives	Domain of production	Subsumption of social goals in func-tion of production	Domain of community
De Sitter *Sociotechnics*	– higher productivity and efficiency – greater innovative potential – more flexibility		– better quality of work/less alienation – better labour relations/less segmentation
Kuipers & Van Amelsvoort *Sociotechnics (new phase)*	– higher productivity and efficiency – greater innovative potential – more flexibility	– better quality of work – better labour relations	
Yeatts & Hyten *HRM*	– customer satisfaction – economic viability	– worker satis-faction	
De Moor *Constructivism*	– excellence of per-formance		– making common sense – developing mutualties

None of the perspectives analysed reduces the meaning of self-management exclusively to the view of the organisation as a domain of production, but there are clear differences.

Modern sociotechnical systems theory is a movement with a large follow-ing in the Netherlands. It would appear that with the development of this theoretical perspective the variation in the signification of the concept of self-management has been limited. De Sitter attributed equal importance to self-managing teams in the field of higher productivity and efficiency, more innovative potential and flexibility on the one hand, and in the field of bet-ter quality of work (less alienation) and labour conditions (less segmentation) on the other hand. His objective scientific approach to quality of work and labour relations regards the meaning of this as system-theoretical consequences and does not connect these to subjective or ideological signification of 'community'. However, with the more recent systematisation of the sociotechnical systems theory the emphasis in meaning shifts towards improvement of performance and efficiency and increased flexibility and potential for innovation. The improvement of the quality of work and working conditions is regarded as functional for increased involvement as a condition for enhancing regulatory capacity and problem solving potential in aid of better production performance. The meaning of self-management for the organisation community as an aim in itself appears to be absent, although mention is made of advantages of self-managing teams in meeting human needs for discussion and social contacts, and offering possibilities for adaptation of work to individual capabilities and ambitions.

The high-performance variant of HRM worked out by Yeatts and Hyten gives meaning to self-managing teams in the domain of production through customer satisfaction and economic viability, and in the domain of community it attributes secondary meaning to worker satisfaction as the results of self-management. Yeatts and Hyten appear not to attach any meaning to self-management as a form of inter-human relations.

De Moor's constructivist perspective gives meaning to self-management by postulating excellence of performance in the domain of production, and by emphasising common sense making and group bonding in the domain of community as aims in themselves. These two meanings are of equal importance and this distinguishes De Moor's constructivism from the other theoretical perspectives, but not from De Sitter's.

The dominance of modern sociotechnical systems theory and human resource management perspectives in organisation and management publications implies that the meaning of self-management lies overwhelmingly in the instrumental function of self-managing teams for the improvement of organisational performance. In the Dutch field of organisation and management publications the constructivist perspective forms a modest undercurrent, which may well be drawing more attention at conferences and seminars as a spiritual and philosophical variant (cf. Cornelis, 1997). In summary, the conclusion is that the theoretical perspectives analysed give significance to self-management by referring to the view of the organisation as a domain of production. There has been a shift in signification in comparison to the theoretical perspective of the humanisation of labour, dominant in the 1970s, which linked the meaning of the semi-autonomous groups to human values of humanisation and democratisation.

Analysis of a case of self-managing teams in a bus company may serve to show existence and operation of the counterforces aimed at the organisation as domain of community.

Organisational practice of self-managing teams

The interest in new forms of labour organisation, such as self-managing teams, is an international phenomenon. When we wish to establish to what extent new forms of organisational practice have in fact been developed, a real problem is a large variation of terms, and the at least as large variation of practice referred to by these terms. In the first part it has already become clear that the term 'teams' in modern sociotechnical systems theory has gained a specific meaning that differs from the term 'teams' in everyday organisational practice, ranging from management-team and project team to multidisciplinary team, which may sometimes indicate a fixed group with group responsibility for the execution and regulation of the entire task, and in other cases may merely indicate a discussion platform for autonomous professionals. Against this background statements like that in the World Labour Report 1997–98 to the effect that there 'has been rapid expansion of teamwork during the last decade' (ILO, 1997: 94), as well as figures that indicate that in the United States about 2 % and in Germany 7 % of workers are now working in self-managing teams (quoted in de Leede and Stoker, 1996: 311), should be put into proper perspective. A European comparative study into group work, which points to the methodological problem of definition and operationalisation, comes to the conclusion that about 4 % of labour organisations in 10 European countries make use of self-managing teams (European Foundation for the improvement of living and working conditions, 1999). After Sweden, the Netherlands have the highest percentage of companies in which groups of workers have extensive rights and responsibilities to perform their work without constant reporting to superiors (Huijgen and Benders, 1998). The interest in self-management is not limited to the manufacturing industry; at least as much interest has been shown by service organisations, including the public sector (see Benders, van Amelsvoort, 2000; Teske, Schneider, 1994), although some critical remarks have been made on the application of the sociotechnical team concept in the professional service industry (see Kapteyn, 1999).

International research indicates that economic objectives dominate the introduction of self-managing teams. The World Labour Report 1997–98 signifies that during the 1970s the objective was to improve the quality of work, to humanise work content and to increase productivity, but that nowadays the primary objective is to raise productivity and improve positions in competition (ILO, 1997: 94). The study into group work in Europe also indicates that economic objectives such as reduction of costs, reduction of turnover cycle, reduction of absenteeism, and quality improvement form the primary motive for introduction, and in connection with this, although less often, the quality of work is mentioned. The same picture emerges from a study concerning eleven industrial companies in the Netherlands, where economic aims (efficiency, improvement of competitive position, improved flexibility, reduction of turnover cycle and cost reduction) are the most important motive for introduction of task groups and only five out of eleven companies have improvement of the quality of work as an equivalent objective (de Leede, Stoker, 1996: 312). In organisational practice the importance of self-managing teams appears to lie in the domain of production. In the light of the earlier link between autonomous groups and humanisation of work, the current situation raises the question whether there are counterforces in the organisation that try to mitigate the one-sided focus on economic objectives. Insight into the tensions between the different aims and the concomitant organisational dynamics can be gained in a study of the long term development of self-managing teams in a bus company. The case covers a period of three years.

Ambiguity of aims and organisational dynamics: self-managing teams in a bus company

Over the past decade public transport has undergone great changes, and privatisation and market conformity are the dominant forces in this process. Public road transport in the mid-1980s was carried out by bus companies which were part of Holding VSN, which was 100 % publicly owned. At the moment, Connexxion, legal successor to VSN, operates about 70 % of the market for bus transport, and companies owned by British and French multinationals operate regional and city transport in large parts of the Netherlands. This chapter discusses the organisation of the exploitation of bus transport.

By way of experiment, the government decided in 1995 to entrust regional transport in the province of Zuid Limburg to Vancom (part of an American privately owned transport company, that later sold its Dutch assets to the British Arriva). Vancom claimed it would be able to realise an extension of the bus services for the same amount of government subsidy, and the key to this improvement was the exploitation of bus transport by self-managing teams (see Leemans, 1996). Firstly, improvement of services would have to yield an increase in the number of passengers and the level of revenue. In addition, savings could be achieved by reduction of overhead costs and supporting functions of which the former bus company had many, since it was a machine bureaucracy, and at the same time management functions were to be entrusted to drivers. Vancom claimed that only 10 per cent of its staff worked in indirect functions, against 25 per cent in other bus companies. The self-managing teams, beside running the actual bus service on a certain route, were made responsible for planning (of rosters, services, detours etc.), technical matters (cleaning, minor repairs, etc.), administration, regional marketing and personnel matters. Within each team a group of four or five drivers was responsible for the tasks in one of these five fields, and the idea was for the groups to learn to do it in all these fields in due course. In view of the required capacities needed to fulfil these tasks, drivers were selected by means of assessments and then trained. After some time it turned out that the drivers were positive about the new way of working, were better satisfied and more involved in the organisation (Leemans, 1996). Travellers were more divided, being positive about customer friendliness of the drivers, comfort and cleanliness of the buses, but negative about the total service (routes, number of stops, connections, punctuality) (Consumentengids, 1996).

Vancom certainly challenged Dutch bus transport, and the government was firmly decided in favour of ongoing privatisation in public transport. As early as May 1996, VSN published the policy paper 'Transformer', in which the introduction of self-managing teams was advocated from the point of view of exploitation efficiency, but internal disagreement precluded a decision to enforce introduction. In the meantime several bus companies had already started small-scale introduction of self-managing teams, for instance the bus company concerned in this case study.

VSN was one of the largest in the Netherlands and had a structure of business units responsible for transport in certain regions, and each region was subdivided into districts. In the early 1990s District A had already introduced self-managing teams as a solution for drivers who could no longer take the stress of city traffic for medical reasons, but who were willing and able to run school bus services and to shuttle tourists to and from a local recreation area. The objective behind self-managing teams was to offer fitting employment to this specific category of drivers, in combination with high-quality custom transport.

The experience gained by these teams formed the basis for a wider introduction of self-managing teams in district A in 1995. On a voluntary basis drivers could sign up for teams which were responsible for transport on a certain route. A reason for making participation voluntary was connected to the fact that so-called route-bound exploitation (drivers have the same route every day) was associated with monotony by the drivers, as this would lead to a loss of the variation in work in comparison to the traditional system where drivers were deployed on all routes in a certain district. Although the loss of this type of variation is compensated by variation that arises out of managing tasks to be carried out by the teams (as in the earlier example of Vancom, but on a more modest scale), the idea of route-bound exploitation aroused so much subjective resistance in drivers, that district management decided to leave them the choice. Eventually, out of 180 drivers in district A, 140 signed up for self-managing teams. The 10 teams together with district management entered upon a process of change which had been initiated by management based upon a bottom-up process in which drivers would be given every opportunity to take initiatives and to make proposals, since that would be the best basis for involvement and participation.

After a one year experience and increasing interest from other districts but also reservations and criticism by the works council, central management decided that the initiative which had been taken at the de-central level, should have the status of 'experiment' and that there was to be an evaluation (review) to arrive at a motivated decision about working with self-managing teams. Here only those elements will be discussed that throw light on the diverse sense-making of the concept of self-managing teams by the various parties involved.

In the question formulated by management as a guideline for the evaluation (review), self-managing teams were not presented as an objective, but as a means that was to contribute to 'improvement of business results in the field of quality, efficiency (costs), flexibility, and motivation and involvement'. It is interesting to note the variety in the objectives mentioned: the quality as well as the costs of service, and in addition operational flexibility as well as motivation and involvement of drivers. There was no indication which of these should take priority.

Earlier research had already shown that driver motivation was primarily dependent on the actual driving of the bus (driving skill) and the contacts with passengers, followed by interaction with colleagues, appreciation and esteem from supervisors, and being entrusted with certain responsibilities (Van der Giessen, 1994). The motives drivers gave nearly without exception refer to the domain of the organisation as community.

In the light of the objectives which companies wished to achieve by the introduction of self-managing teams and which turn out to be mainly of a business nature, it is interesting to find out how the relations between the various objectives are assessed by the management of the bus company under discussion (Hienkens, 1997). As a rule, district management in the bus company is in constant contact with the drivers, and this was certainly true for district A. A national strike over flexible working hours in the bus industry had, however, troubled relations on the shop floor and earlier activities undertaken to stimulate involvement of drivers in the organisation were negatively affected. In this context the most important reason for the management of district A to take the initiative for introducing self-managing teams was the conviction that this would increase motivation and involvement of drivers. In addition, self-management would contribute to improvement of customer services and the quality of the service as a whole. In time, the district management was persuaded that efficiency would also improve. The district management, however, found out that there was a clear field of tension between the objectives of quality and efficiency improvements; priority of the one is at the cost of the other, and vice versa. In the sense-making by district management, then, there is equal ranking of motivation/ involvement, referring to the domain of community, and quality of service, referring to the domain of production.

In the period 1996–1998 external pressure on the bus industry increased. Politicians decided to reduce government subsidies and ongoing preparations for market conformity and competition urged Holding VSN to raise the efficiency of the bus companies. This external pressure was palpable in the relative importance given to objectives of self-managing teams by the management, especially by strategic management. Interviews with members of central management showed the following emphasis: 'in the end it is a relationship between quality and price that is important, and we will come out on top on the basis of price and quality, not on the basis of motivated drivers' (Hienkens, 1997:16). In assessing the price-quality relationship a division was becoming manifest. Some members of central management thought: 'competition is about price only, that has been proved, not so much about quality. Efficiency must improve, that is an objective and a hard and fast target.' Other managers were of the opinion that: 'in the end quality is most important' (Hienkens, 1997:17). It is interesting that the various people and groups within the organisation were not aware of these differences in sense making that turned out to exist at the level of central management.

The strong emphasis which was gradually placed on the criterion of the price-quality relationship in public transport was also manifest in the assessment of the results of an employee satisfaction survey held across the organisation. In the study, the drivers in the self-managing teams in district A turned out to have the most positive judgments of being client-centered (e.g. being able to give passengers information, being able to react to passenger wishes). In addition, not only drivers had this opinion; passengers were also more positive about the service rendered by the drivers in the self-managing teams than about that of the others working in the traditional fashion. The employee satisfaction survey, furthermore, showed that the drivers in self-managing teams were most positive about the degree of independence in their work. Most drivers thought that self-management affects first of all the quality of service positively, as it does driver motivation, followed in importance by flexibility of service and, finally, efficiency and cost control.

In the autumn of 1997, when central management drew up the balance of the year's experimentation with self-managing teams the positive assessment of the quality of service and about motivation/involvement of drivers was duly noted. On this basis management decided to continue working with self-managing teams in district A, but not to introduce self-managing teams in the entire organisation. The financial effects were not convincing according to management. They concluded: 'should the continued deployment of self-managing teams lead to sufficiently sound economic results, management is of the opinion that the team-approach could be a fitting organisational approach to tackle the future.' This makes clear that good economic results had become the first criterion.

This assessment by management confirmed the sceptical attitude that the works council had evinced from the beginning, to the effect that introduction of self-managing teams was only based on arguments about efficiency. The works council expected the introduction of self-management to lead to loss of jobs, to agreements on working times that ran contrary to collective agreements, to dismissal of seniors and people with a medical indication who would not be up to the increased work pressures, and to the loss of mutual solidarity. Although the research results explicitly contradicted some of the fears of the works council – drivers working traditionally, for instance, made the most negative assessment of their work pressures and drivers in self-managing teams were most positive in this respect – the works council kept up its opposition to working in self-managing teams. Basing themselves on collective agreements and the legal responsibilities of the works council, and with the justification that 'people need protection against themselves', the works council blocked several proposals made by self-managing teams about the running of the bus service for which they were responsible.

In this context it was extremely difficult for district management to keep up their credibility for the drivers and to create desirable conditions for the ongoing development of working in self-managing teams. The basic requirements for district management for a bottom-up process of change with a maximum of room for initiatives and proposals by the teams threatened to become incredible because drivers saw that their proposals were not accepted, but had no insight into considerations underlying such decisions. In addition, the duality of the roles played by district management, i.e. that of coach of the teams and in-line responsibility for the execution of central management decisions, led to confusion in the teams. The analysis of these developments made district management decide that an extra investment in internal communication was essential in order to keep up the confidence between management and drivers, and that it was desirable that operational coaching of the teams should take place by service managers.

District management had more difficulty in coping with the lack of co-operation of internal offices (see Sips, Hovelynck, 1998), especially supporting services which felt threatened because of delegation of certain tasks to self-managing teams. The 'experimental' status of self-management in district A and the conditions which the central management made for the introduction of self-managing teams in the entire organisation, led to a situation where the conditions for an integrated sociotechnical redesign were lacking, and where district management, when amalgamating executive and management tasks, came to depend on the co-operation of supporting services

65

on a voluntary and personal basis. A discussion about structural review of place and tasks of supporting services did not take place because central management, in 1998, because of a planned reorganisation, decided to freeze the situation in district A and not to extend the introduction of self-managing teams to the rest of the bus company.

Conclusion

The context and frames of meaning into which a new concept like self-management teams is introduced initially affects the reception of the new concept. In the case of self-managing teams: this meant that apparent continuity with earlier concepts of semi-autonomous groups and humanisation made for expectations of sensemaking tending towards the organisation as community. The concept of self-managing teams, however, is formulated in another language game, in which sociotechnical jargon reformulates 'humanisation' as 'quality of work' and 'regulatory capacity', complemented with other meanings like 'improved performance'. In the first instance, in De Sitter's elaborations there is a sensemaking in which there is a balanced reference to the domain of production and community. In later sociotechnical elaborations a certain ambiguity remains, but compared to the earlier humanisation movement there is an unmistakable instrumentalisation of the quality of work to production objectives.

It is interesting that in the theoretical discourse there is some room for ambiguity, which in the practice of organisation is regarded as misleading. In the bus company, but also in other organisations such as a national chain of supermarkets, it was decided after a time to discard the term 'self-management' because it raised the wrong expectations with employees. For it was never really the intention that employees should actually manage themselves, management would go on providing frameworks. The rhetorical power of the term 'self-management' became apparent, however, in the supermarket company where the alternative introduced was called 'process management', but after a year it had still not filtered down to the shop floor. Employees went on thinking in terms of self-management, but had not really expected to become entirely self-managing without frameworks provided by management. This incident illustrates on the one hand that employees had developed a substantial degree of scepticism during their working lives, and on the other hand that sensitivity about the frontiers of control in management had hardly changed.

From the point of view of organisational practice, the theoretical approach of self-management can be criticized because of the lack of problematisation of the tensions that arise between diverging goals. Giving equal weight to objectives like improvement of productivity, efficiency, flexibility and potential for innovation on one hand, and better quality of work and working conditions (sociotechnical), or mutuality/solidarity (de Moor) on the other is idealistic because the forcefield of parties and interests in organisational practice is ignored. The meaning of self-management, to an important extent is created by the dynamics in this forcefield, but this is not recognised in theoretical discussions on self-management. There is implicit agreement with dominant regimes of truth and the organisation is regarded from the point of view of management (Van der Zee, 1998: 12).

In addition, the lack of problematisation of the tensions that arise between the diverging goals of self-management makes the plea for coaching or participatory management that accompanies the theoretical perspectives on self-management implausible. When, in organisational practice, self-management works in the direction of improvement of productivity and efficiency, the shop floor will regard coaching as a subtly packaged strategy of control by management, and regard it as empty rhetoric.

When the expectations which the theoretical concept of self management evokes diverge from reality to the extent assumed here, the rhetorical function of the concept (cf. Karsten, van Veen, 1998: 8), which is to activate people and motivate them, will also be affected. Current knowledge about self-management in organisational practice points in the direction of the dominant meaning given to production objectives to the detriment of community objectives also proposed. It is not overstretching the imagination to predict that the rhetorical function of the concept of self-management will be exhausted and the need will be felt for a new concept to fulfil this function. Perhaps the significance which in public debate is given to the balance between working and living will figure in this. A concept that succeeds self-management will need a more credible appeal to images which give meaning to the organization as community.

References

Amelsvoort, P. van, G. Scholtes (1994). *Zelfsturende teams. Ontwerpen, invoeren en begeleiden*. Vlijmen: ST-Groep.

Assen, A. van, J. den Hertog (1980). Werkbeleving en werkstructurering. In C. de Galan, M. van Gils, P. van Strien (eds), *Humanisering van de Arbeid* (49–77). Assen: Van Gorcum.

Benders, J., P. Van Amelsvoort (eds) (2000). *Zelfsturende teams in de dienstverlening*. Utrecht: Lemma.

Bolwijn, P., T. Kumpe (1998). *Marktgericht ondernemen; management van continuïteit en verandering*. Assen: van Gorcum.

Consumentengids (1996). Sommige busverbindingen beter door concurrentie. In *Consumentengids*, April 1996, 260–261.

Cornelis, A. (1997). *Logica van het gevoel*. Amsterdam/Brussel/Middelburg: Stichting Essence.

European Foundation for the improvement of living and working conditions (1999). *Useful but unused – Group work in Europe*. Dublin: European Foundation for the improvement of living and working conditions.

Ewijk-Hoevenaars, A. van, J. den Hertog, J. van Jaarsveld (1995). *Naar eenvoud in organisatie. Werken met zelfsturende eenheden*. Deventer: Kluwer Bedrijfswetenschappen.

Gergen, K. (1985). The social constructionist movement in modern psychology. In *American Psychologist, 40* (3), 266–275.

Gergen, K. (1999). *An invitation to social construction*. London, Thousand Oaks, New Delhi: Sage.

Giddens, A. (1976). *New rules of sociological method*. London: Hutchinson.

Giessen, J. van de (1994). *Motivatie als voorwaarde in het veranderingsproces*. Onderzoeksverslag, Universiteit Utrecht.

Grint, K. (1997). *Fuzzy Management; Contemporary Ideas and Practices at Work*. Oxford: Oxford University Press.

Groep Sociotechniek (1987). *Het flexibele bedrijf*. Deventer: Kluwer.

Hienkens, M. (1997). *Rapportage van onderzoek naar verzelfstandiging en exploitatieteams; De invalshoek van management en ondersteunende diensten*. Onderzoeksverslag, Universiteit Utrecht.

Huijgen, F., J. Benders (1998). Het vallende kwartje; directe participatie in Nederland en Europa. In *Tijdschrift voor Arbeidsvraagstukken, 14*, (2), 113–127.

International Labour Office (1997). *World Labour Report 1997–98: Industrial relations, democracy and social stability*. Geneva: International Labour Office.

Kapteyn, L. (1999). Zelfsturing in de non-profit-sector: geen recept voor koekjesmanagement'. In *Gids voor personeelsmanagement, 78* (4), 25–29.

Karsten, L., K. van Veen (1998). *Managementconcepten in beweging: tussen feit en vluchtigheid*. Assen: Van Gorcum.

Kluytmans, F., W. Van der Meeren (red.) (1992). *Management van human resources*. Deventer: Kluwer Bedrijfswetenschappen, Heerlen: Open Universiteit.

Kuipers, H., P. van Amelsvoort (1990). *Slagvaardig organiseren. Inleiding in de sociotechniek als integrale ontwerpleer*. Deventer: Kluwer Bedrijfsinformatie.

Leede, J. de, J. Stoker (1996). 'Taakgroepen in de Nederlandse industrie: één concept met vele toepassingen'. In *Tijdschrift voor Arbeidsvraagstukken, 12* (4), 310–319.

Leemans, A. (1996). Het team doet het, tenzij ... In *Gids voor Personeelsmanagement, 75* (4), 50–53.

Manz, C., H. Sims (1987). Leading workers to lead themselves: the external leadership of self-managing work teams. In *Administrative Science Quarterly, 32*, 106–128.

Moor, W. de (1995). *Teamwerk en participatief management*. Houten/Diegem: Bohn Stafleu Van Loghum.

Nijs, W. de (1992). De personele component. In J. Doorewaard, W. de Nijs (eds), *Integraal Management* (85–106). Leiden/Antwerpen: Stenfert Kroese.

POST-groep (1991). *Onderweg naar nieuwe fabrieken en kantoren*. Deventer: Kluwer Bedrijfswetenschappen.

Sips, K., J. Hovelynck (1998). De rol van externe contacten in het ontwikkelen van zelfsturing. In: *Opleiding en ontwikkeling*, 1998–9, 19–24.

Sitter, L.U. de (1980). Kenmerken en functies van de kwaliteit van de arbeid. In J.J.J., van Dijck, J.A.P. van Hoof, A.L.Mok, W.F. de Nijs (eds), *Kwaliteit van de Arbeid* (43–80). Leiden/Antwerpen: Stenfert Kroese.

Sitter, L.U. de (1981). *Op weg naar nieuwe fabrieken en kantoren*. Deventer: Kluwer.

Storey, J. (1992). *Developments in the management of human resources*. Oxford: Blackwell.

Teske, P., M. Schneider (1994). The bureaucratic entrepreneur: the case of city managers. In *Public Administration Review*, *54* (4), 331–340.

Trist, E., G. Higgin, H. Murray, A. Pollock (1963). *Organizational choice*. London: Tavistock Publications.

Weick, K. (1979). *The social psychology of organizing*. Reading MA: Addison Wesley.

Wellins, R., W. Byham, J. Wilson (1991). *Empowered teams, creating self-directed workgroups that improve quality, productivity, and participation*. San Francisco: Jossey-Bass Publishers.

Yeatts, D.E., C. Hyten (1998). *High-performing self-managed work teams. A comparison of theory and practice*. Thousand Oaks, London, New Delhi: Sage.

Zee, H. van der, (1998). Het heilige geloof in zelfsturing. In *Opleiding en ontwikkeling*, 1998–9, 7–13.

Chapter 4

Organisational culture: a concept's strengths and weaknesses

Jan Boessenkool

Introduction

Has the culture concept had its day, in the context of how organizations think and act, or is its popularity still to peak? Undoubtedly, time will tell; all the same, at the beginning of this new century, it would not do any harm to weigh up its pros and cons. In this contribution, I would like to do this – in a broad sense – by describing the images that were and are current, and also by comparing these with the development of my own thoughts on the culture concept over the last ten years.

Many organizations, or, rather, those in charge within such organizations, are in a state of confusion, and searching for (new) answers. This search commences back in the early eighties, when economic stagnation meant that many companies' results were unsatisfactory. Japan's experiences put the West on the track of culture and cultural differences. The fact that the interpretation of these experiences is rather one-sided and distorted does not detract from the popularity of the Japanese success stories. Western managers are finding support in the consensus and harmony that (supposedly) exists in the Japanese business world (Ten Bos, 2000). In hindsight, it has become clear that so-called lifetime employment must be taken with a pinch of salt (Bax, 1991). Nevertheless, the culture concept would appear to offer relief to many: culture in the sense of 'shared values': how do we achieve a situation in which everyone is pulling in the same direction? This perspective has continued to dominate discussions to this day, at first chiefly in the business world, but later, in the nineties, in the not-for-profit sector as well. Everyone started to look for shared core values with which to redetermine and share their deadlocked identities. Managers and executives are continually impeded by differentiation and fragmentation, which ought, preferably, to be banished. Various management courses come up with the instruments and models with which to achieve this, both to identify conflict, via a quick scan, and to change this into a more desirable situation.

The extent to which cultural processes can be influenced always proves disappointing, which does not alter the fact that many stubbornly persist. Many (failed) mergers bear witness to this: it seems as if people either learn nothing, or refuse to learn anything from negative experiences. The odd exception is prepared to reflect more, and sign up for university courses that focus on organizational culture and related concepts. He or she then learns from the academic gurus that cultural differences and diversity are, in general (in our time), not only normal and a matter of course, but can also be valuable and productive, provided they are analyzed and used correctly. But what can managers then actually do with these splendid academic *tours de force* in their real-life situations? Why should these managers suddenly cease to value scarcity of differences and peace in their organizations? After all, difference still sows the seed of misunderstanding and conflict, something that no executive wants. Does the latter not then automatically mean that there is, and always will be, a need for uniformity? Is not the search for core values and a common identity *the* expression of this?

In everyday life, we understand the culture concept to relate to such things as 'values' and 'norms', or 'the way we do things here'. This sounds straightforward. Upon further analysis, however, values and norms prove to be very tricky concepts, just as 'just the way we do things here' is usually far from clear. In organizational reality, far too isolated and instrumental use is generally made of academic insights; this is the reproach quite frequently voiced by academics. Probably because the organizational culture concept refers to too many processes, and processes that are too complex. This indicates both the strength and the weakness of the concept. The wealth offered by the concept is undervalued; at the same time the theory is evidently unable to optimally fit in with organizational practice.

Enthusiastic pioneers

For a clear historical account, I am following the account given by Martin Parker in his recently published book 'Organizational Culture and Identity' (2000). Parker asks himself why *organizational culturalism* has become so popular, and what is wrong with much of the "management guru and textbook writing on this topic" (p. 2). He uses the term 'culturalism' to identify the interest that managers have in cultural manipulation as opposed to the more academic approach, which has not as its primary focus (paid) intervention. Barley et al. (1988) mention this difference at an early stage: the *practitioners' perspective* versus the *academic perspective*. I will return to this distinction at a later point in this chapter. I have already hinted at the difference by pointing to the instrumental use of the culture concept.

Parker thoroughly analyses several works from the early eighties that have

71

set a clear trend in the instrumental and functionalistic perspective, namely Peters and Waterman's *In Search of Excellence* (1982), Ouchi's *Theory Z* (1981) and Deal and Kennedy's *Corporate Cultures* (1982). This trend would appear to be extremely innovative, with regard to writing on organizations, and organizational culture in particular. However, cultural and social aspects had already captured the attention of organizational researchers early in the twentieth century. Although, – see the Hawthorne experiments – , this was particularly aimed towards increasing production, and humans were particularly regarded as production factors.

This does not alter the fact that the early eighties represent a breakthrough for the interest in the concept of organizational culture. The start of this breakthrough is twofold. In 1979, the first conference on organizational culture is held (Barley et al., 1988: 24; Pondy et al, 1983; Parker, 2000: 9). In the same year, Andrew Pettigrew publishes an article in Administrative Science Quarterly, which is known as a forum for "highly quantitative and conservative management theory" (Parker, 2000: 9).

However, the publications mentioned above ensure an overwhelming interest in the concept from that point on. Incidentally, almost all of these publications can be placed within the practitioners' perspective. Interest amongst managers for the great quantity of 'How To' books that follow is due, to a great extent, to a combination of the poor economic situation and prospects in the Western world at the beginning of the eighties, on the one hand, and the Japanese success story, and the threat posed by this, on the other hand.

Parker places the evaluation of the books written by Peters and Waterman, Ouchi and Deal and Kennedy in context, and concludes that "the most relevant element of that context is that which frames the culturalist movement as an attempt to intervene in the identity of the employee just as all organizational control strategies from (at least) Taylor onwards have done" (2000: 25). He quite rightly warns that this should not be taken too seriously, as the claims made are, to a great extent, normative, and are far less about what actually happens in organizations: "most of this work is hence an amalgam of mythologizing and mystification couched in marketable quasi-anthropological language" (idem). It raises the question of whether the current (renewed) interest in diversity, identifications, commitment, loyalty and binding also contains a great degree of normativity, and wishes to provide managers with instruments with which to increase efficiency and productivity, and increase manageability. Are they concerned with ideal situations, or do they seek to express what the actual situation is?

Success and failure are being linked to the leader's vision, to the unity and collectivity on the workfloor, and to the degree to which organizations are able to adapt to changing circumstances. Related to this, culture may be weak or strong, as indicated by Deal and Kennedy. For non-functionalistic anthropologists this is blasphemy, as, after all, for them culture (cultural analysis) is by definition a neutral affair. It is this normative claim in respect of the culture concept that repeatedly surfaces in the practitioners' perspective. The weakness of the concept lies in its instrumental use (prescription) in all of the (new) insights that it generates. Its strength is the fact that it is always able to raise new questions about the state of affairs in modern organizations, and always from a different perspective. In Parker's words (2000: 26): "It is potentially an attempt to understand something quite significant about the constitution of organization and organizing. The tensions, or dualisms, between individualism and collectivism, agency and structure, local and social are all played out in culturalist texts."

In the period between 1985 and 1990, people such as Frissen (1990), Sanders and Neuijen (1988), Tennekes (1990) and Koot (1990) placed the culture concept firmly on the Dutch agenda, prompted, it is true, by mainly American initiatives. Verweel (1987), in his study of organizational practices in universities, touches upon issues relating to the culture concept (1987). Verweel does not focus on organizational culture, but takes the ideology concept and preoccupation with power as his starting point. By doing so, he marks a period of transition within anthropology, from a more Marxistic tradition to a rather humanistic perspective.

Many anthropological colleagues for a long time regarded the growing interest in organizational processes with great suspicion and mistrust (and continue to do so even now). Traditionally, anthropologists are 'supposed to' take the side of the *underdog* in the battle of the classes in society, even if there have been many exeptions to this position over the years. Anthropological research conducted in companies cannot mean anything other than betrayal: studies focusing on workfloor processes, from which management could profit. The innovators are repeatedly associated with ties and *Samsonites*. Koot and others, including myself, have become embroiled in a long struggle to achieve recognition for the new discipline of 'organizational anthropology', a struggle that has not yet been settled today.

Given the popularity enjoyed by academic courses focusing on the '(organizational) culture' concept, there is not any danger of its premature disappearance. What, then, is its content?

Meaning of the organizational culture concept

The content of the concept in respect of organizational culture is closely linked to the meaning given to the concept of culture itself. Various attempts have been made to distinguish between, classify and reduce the meanings to the underlying meta-theoretical and even paradigmatic principles. The concept of culture has an enormous wealth of meanings and derived functions.

It was initially hoped that by discussing and recording these, uniformity would be achieved within the academic discussion, and, possibly, as a result, also within organizational practice. Let us consider some of the contents of the culture concept, on the basis of a number of important and decisive texts, the first American in origin, and the second from The Netherlands.

Administrative Science Quarterly

In the first introductory article of the ASQ special issue, published in 1983, Jelinek et al. identify nine different variants of the culture concept, as used in the other articles. Particular attention is paid to the "potential power of culture as a root metaphor for organization studies. Because the concept of culture in the study of organization is not well developed, a range of approaches seems not only desirable but required" (p. 331). The (guest) editor was able to print nine of the sixty papers that had been submitted. Thus, at that time much was not published.

An important contribution, which later proved to be an influential contribution for The Netherlands, was the one submitted by Linda Smircich. She restricts herself to "the roots of the concept of culture in anthropology" and arrives at five different conceptual relations in organization studies (Smircich, 1983). The first (research) theme is that of Cross-Cultural or Comparative Management, in which both organizations and culture can be regarded as instruments by means of which tasks can be performed, and biological and psychological needs fulfilled (the classic management theory and Malinowski's functionalism). The second theme, Corporate Culture, is based on Radcliffe-Browne's structural-functionalism. Organizations are adaptive organisms, existing by a process of exchange with the environment; e.g. contingency theory.

Smircich's third theme is called Organizational Cognition: organizations as systems of knowledge, and culture as a system of shared cognitions (Goodenough's ethnoscience). Fourthly, she identifies Organizational Symbolism, emphasizing patterns of symbolic discourse, such as language: culture as a system of shared symbols and meanings (e.g. Geertz's symbolic anthropology). The fifth and final theme identified by Smircich is Unconscious Processes and Organization, based on transformational organization theory (organizations as manifestations of unconscious process) on the one hand, and Levi-Strauss' structuralism: Culture is a projection of mind's universal unconscious infrastructure, on the other hand.

What is striking is that the above-mentioned themes always regard culture as either a variable in organizational processes, or, otherwise, a metaphor for organizational life. "Smircich argues that the power and limitations of the culture concept for organizational analysis can only be assessed with reference to the particular purpose the researcher is pursuing" (Jelinek et al., 1983: 332).

For instance, in her contribution, Gregory focuses pre-eminently on the insider's perspective: understanding the (different) meanings that (all) members of an organization themselves give to their behavior and the organizational processes of which they form a part. She also defines culture as "a system of meanings that accompany the myriad of behaviors and practices recognized as a distinct way of life" (Gregory, 1983: 364).

Smith and Simmons (1983) endorse Gregory's "native" views approach, although they particularly have in mind the collective symbolization of earlier experiences in organizations, experiences that are unconsciously, extremely powerful. In his contribution, Barley investigates the signs and semantic codes of a funeral home. These appear to be so manipulable that they are able to influence people and steer people's interpretation of reality. As such, culture can be interpreted "as an enabling mechanism for organized action" (p. 333). Patricia Riley describes the symbols used to create the political image of an organization's culture. Structure and symbols are seen as both the medium of communication and the outcome of interaction. In Riley's contribution, Jelinek et al. see two important relations between power and culture. "First, power is an important aspect of culture, where culture is interpreted as the product-and-process of organization members' sense making through their ongoing interactions" (...) "Second, the *process* by which the power structure is created – the process of structuration – is closely parallel to the process of culturation." As such, structure is nothing more or less than the crystallized meaning of earlier (power) relations and sense making. Riley has a structurationist view of culture here, based on Giddens (1979, 1984), a subject I will return to in the concluding paragraph.

The authors of the following contribution point out the paradox of the unicity claimed by organizations on the basis of cultural manifestations that may also be found in other organizations. Martin et al. do this by comparing stories about seven different organizations, and by identifying the similarities between them. For instance, one always finds equality versus inequality, safety versus a lack of safety, and control versus lack of control. Jones believes that "culture develops as the outcome of negotiation over property rights and the resulting expectations that are created" (p. 334). Culture then translates into the values and norms (or obligations) encountered by members of an organization. Wilkens and Ouchi take the position that culture is not something that all organizations develop. Organizations where bureaucratic norms and rules form the basis for organized actions, such as in bureaucratic and market settings in particular, are not organizations that they consider to have a 'culture'. To them, culture is more about informal consensus in respect of accepted and desirable behavior. In an article, contributed by Broms and Gahmberg, "culture is seen as group values embedded in shared value-laden images or myths". They emphasize the belief that exists in what an organization does and stands for.

With the exception of Wilkens and Ouchi, and Jones, the ASQ authors share the process-oriented character of (organizational) culture and the continual and intersubjective (re)creation of shared meanings, as a result of interaction between the members of an organization. Culture is always cause and effect, at one and the same time a source for and a product of human actions. Giddens' 'duality of structure', the notion central to his structuration theory, fits in with this perfectly.

Besides this, there is a shared emphasis on sense making: how people in organizations try to make sense of their organizational world. This goes beyond the search for formal or (superficial) behavior, but tries to discover the 'why' (the meaning) behind this behavior. The authors suppose an underlying structure of meaning, grounded in field data and abstracted from it, a structure of meaning that would speak to members' understandings (p. 337). However, the underlying structures emphasized differ: myths, unconscious organizational dynamics, or even economic transaction agreements. The process, however, is common.

All contributions are particularly internal in orientation. Barely any attention is paid to the organizational context, or, rather: to the relationship between the inside and the outside. However, the advantage gained lies particularly in the use of culture as a metaphor for organizations and, as such, permanent attention for process and dynamics: from organization to organizing!

On the one hand, the impact of the ASQ special issue was large, namely where it concerns the academic discussion of the concept of organizational culture. However, this discussion was largely restricted to the social-scientific world, and, within it, to the anthropological discipline in particular. On the other hand, its impact was minimal. It is true that the ideas presented have been used and abused from all sides, but this has occurred mainly in an instrumental sense. The insights referred to by the authors have barely influenced the reality of everyday organizational processes and management ideas. This is not surprising, as it is only possible for real insiders to understand the material presented above. This shows the complexity of the culture concept and related perspectives from which organizational processes may be viewed, but at the same time it is clear that it will never be possible to achieve uniformity in this complexity. Should it be? Maybe not, but this does make it difficult to allow others (course participants, managers) to share the insights, to such an extent that they can also actually do something with them. In many management courses on organizational culture, the ASQ insights are not mentioned, or only very briefly. Course participants with many years of management experience are flabbergasted when they are confronted with the quantity and complexity of the concept of organizational culture. Although the concept has not stood still since 1983, we should not overestimate the insights that followed. It would seem that most of what can be said, or, in any case, what is most important to say, was already said then. I will now discuss several interesting Dutch publications.

Dutch publications

In 1990, two publications focusing explicitly on organizational culture are published in The Netherlands. The first was written by the public administration expert Paul Frisser (1986, 1990). Frissen particularly builds on Smircich's work (mentioned above), and he almost integrally adopts the categorization used by Smircich in the ASQ special issue (see Frissen and Van Westerlaak, 1990: 33–40):

- Culture as a contingency factor: the organizational environment is at the forefront, with social culture on the one hand (such as national or regional culture) and the cultural background of the organizational members on the other hand.
- Culture as a subsystem: in this vision, culture forms a separate part of organizations, just as structure and technology are, for example.
- Culture as an aspect system: here, culture is (just as control is) a quality that exists throughout the organization, "a dimension of all structures and processes" (p. 35).
- The organization as a cultural phenomenon: "Organizations are important cultural artifacts themselves" (Morey and Luthans, 1985: 221); Frissen and Van Westerlaak also quote Smircich, saying that culture is a 'root metaphor' for organizations: culture as "the central characteristic" of social processes in general, and, therefore, also of organizations (pp. 35–36).

The third variant is easier to mention than to understand; what does 'a dimension of' mean? Does everything that we encounter in organizations consist, in some small way, of culture? And which part then, exactly? How do we find out?

The last variant also raises questions. If culture is a metaphor for organizations, then this is not consistent with the definition of organizations as cultural phenomena. After all, the latter regards organizations as cultures, not merely as a (central) characteristic of organizations. And, in turn, the latter is barely distinct from culture as an aspect system. The metaphor variant supposes that organizations are not really cultures, but are similar to them (they *look alike!*). As such, nothing is being said about what they actually *are*.

What is essential is the difference between *having culture* and *being cul-*

ture, a difference that has far-reaching consequences for any research, and change projects based on this. The first strongly encourages instrumental use, while there can be no question of this in the second.

The other reaction to the relationship between culture and organizations, comes from an anthropologist. With so much interest for a concept as pre-eminently anthropological as culture, anthropologists could not stand on the sidelines. Koot was disturbed about the abuse being made of the culture concept by all kinds of organizational experts, as is evident from his early publications. He (together with others) exposes a number of "Myths about Corporate Culture" (Koot, 1988; Koot, Staarman and Verbeek, 1989; Koot, 1989).

Twelve case studies based on actual empirical and qualitative research into the 'fiction and reality of organizational culture' (Koot and Hogema, 1990), demonstrate that (organizational) culture cannot be isolated from the rest of the organization, as many publications would have it. Organizational culture from an anthropological perspective means taking into account the difference between fiction and reality, between the formal and the informal organization, the strategic use of culture, informal networks, subcultures and the interweaving of organization and environment. All themes that emerged in the early ASQ work, and that have proved relevant to date, and have gained the necessary depth in numerous studies since then. However, it must also be mentioned that this anthropological perspective has never progressed much further than the courses provided by the University of Utrecht (Organizational Anthropology) and the Free University (Culture, Organization and Management). The dominant image, certainly in The Netherlands, is, in fact, on balance, that culture is particularly about shared values and norms, and the more model-based and quantitative approach of the concept, with strong influences from psychology and sociology. The mainstream continues to be: culture as a phenomenon that can be isolated and manipulated. Or, in the words of Van Frissen (and Smircich): culture as a subsystem, in addition to the structure and strategy subsystems.

Of course, a number of other authors have preoccupied themselves with organizational culture in The Netherlands, but their work has barely gained publicity outside their own circle (Olila, 1989, for example). No attempts have been made to link the organizational concept from various disciplines, in order to arrive at a meta-theory. The attributed visions and probably also (and particularly) the methodological approaches on which these are based, are evidently so far apart that any advances would be wrong, rather than desirable[1].

---

[1] At the Center for Policy and Management, where various disciplines have been brought together, some progress has been made amongst a group of anthropologists, several sociologists and linguists. As yet, there is more multi-disciplinarity than interdisciplinarity.

The search for a meta theory: Martin

In the early nineties, the overwhelming number of publications focusing more or less explicitly on organizational culture caused several American authors to compare the many approaches, whether or not with the aim of arriving at a synthesis.

In 1985, the first textbook is published (Schein, 1985), as are several review articles (by Ouchi and Wilkins 1985, amongst others). In the same year, a critical reflection is published by Frost et al. (1985). Criticism focuses particularly on the (alleged) functionalistic character of these approaches. This is followed by a phase in which the theory is defined in more detail, and a certain degree of disciplining and the formation of author networks occurs.

The books by Martin (1992) and Trice and Beyer (1993) have a "state of the art" character. The authors explicitly state the necessity they felt to establish order in the very pluriform approaches of (organizational) culture (Martin) and the pluriform description of reality (Trice and Beyer). To this end, Trice and Beyer have included as many as 1200, and Martin some 300 publications in their bibliographies. Trice and Beyer have used research material from various disciplines, and attempt (in line with their implicit desire for unity): "the first synthesis of the growing literature in this developing field". An important motivator is the neglected central role played by culture in human behavior in organization studies.

Martin introduces three perspectives on culture, which she distills from the theoretical state of affairs current at the time. The "unity" approach regards culture as "the social glue that binds". Organizational practice portrays itself as a heaven of harmony and homogeneity. Martin is of the opinion that this is the (concept of) culture that managers want. As many other writers have done before them, they claim that a culture based on transparency, consistency and consensus results in a more effective organization, in which any form of ambiguity is considered deviant or even detrimental.

Apparently, competing subcultures exist in the differentiation approach. Theoretical and empirical attention is focused on the numerous contradictions that exist between groups and departments. There are (major) differences between informal behavior and the proclaimed culture of unity. This approach logically also pays attention to power processes.

In the fragmentation approach, ambiguity forms the essence of cultural description. It emerges from this perspective that culture is interpreted very differently by the organizational members. Unexpected similarities and differences exist right across all groups and departments (subcultures). Attention is paid to personal sense making. In this perspective, ambiguity and dissensus form the core of culture.

Although Martin is herself allied to the fragmentation perspective, she rejects the claim that it is possible to choose between the three perspectives, this for empirical and theoretical reasons. Although, empirically, one of the perspectives may dominate for a while, this does not alter the fact that elements of the other two perspectives are present at the same time. From a theoretical point of view, none of the three perspectives is able to cover the complexity of organizational culture. Martin is of the opinion that most researchers have their own dominant perspective; the other two help the researcher to correct the dominant perspective's weaknesses.

Particularly by her addition of the fragmentation perspective, which up to that point had been underexposed, Martin makes an interesting move, in order to avoid the simplification of complex cultural processes. Frost et al. found Martin's (and Meyerson's, 1988) three perspectives so interesting and innovative that, in 1991, they dedicated a whole book to them: "Reframing Organizational Culture". However, they place perspectives next to each other, thus creating the impression that the corresponding cultural elements occur separately in the organization. It would be more obvious to study the corresponding cultural forms and concepts in conjunction with each other. The pursuit of unity may, for example, actually cause unwanted conflicts to occur, while attention paid to differentiation may result in harmony.

The search for synthesis: Trice and Beyer

The title of the first chapter of Trice and Beyer's (1993) book – How and Why Organizations are Cultures – is an important indicator of where they belong within the various approaches in respect of culture. To them, organizations *are* cultures (compare with Smircich, 1983, and Frissen, 1990, amongst others). Culture consists of content ("the substance of organizational cultures") and the various forms in which these are communicated (symbols, language, practices, etc.). From their point of view, culture is the collective answer to the uncertainties and chaos inevitable in human experience, and in organizations. The authors refer to the content, or components, of these answers to uncertainties, fears and ambiguities as ideologies ("shared, emotionally charged belief systems").

Although reality is far too complex to include everything, the cultural approach is far more comprehensive than rational theories. Cultures are collective, emotional, historical, symbolic, dynamic, fuzzy, etc. According to Trice and Beyer, it is precisely as a result of this that cultures, besides rational considerations, determine human behavior in general, and organizational behavior in particular. Although they take the position that organizations are cultures, for them the essence of culture is consensus (for Martin dissensus): "to avoid endless confusion, it seems sensible to reserve the term culture for situations in which there is some core of consensus" (1993: 15).

This causes some surprise when compared with their definition of culture, in which "ambiguity and fuzziness" are essential components. Trice and Beyer intended their extensive work to form a bridge between theory and practice, a theoretical synthesis that can also be applied in organizational practice. The disadvantage of their more functionalistic and application-oriented approach is the insufficient amount of attention paid to the concept's orientation towards process. As such, their work belongs largely to the tradition of the "practitioners' perspective" (Barley et al., 1988). This perspective pays particular attention to the question of what culture is in practice, and how it can be used as a manager's tool. Trice and Beyer also pay a relatively great deal of attention to rational processes, and tend to look for simplification in the complex cultural issue, possibly to provide managers with instruments after all. As such, they overestimate, to my thinking, the rationality of organizational actions.

An overview

Trice and Beyer present a large number of approaches and show the enormous versatility of the culture concept. At the same time, this is a weakness, because there is barely any problematization, leaving you with the question of 'where to begin?'. The book by Martin is more appealing, particularly due to her eye opener that these phenomena may be regarded from different perspectives, thus facilitating different insights. What is more, her approach touches far more directly on organizational members' interests and positions, and, as such, the closely related power and identity processes.

Although he may be placed in the same academic tradition as Martin, Alvesson (1993) quickly voices his criticism of the "emphasis on ambiguity as a 'central feature of organizational culture'" (p. 110). He continues: "This interest in ambiguity can perhaps be seen as a reflection of the Zeitgeist" (idem). Alvesson recognizes that ambiguity is a central aspect of organizations, but is more inclined to regard it as a "modification of the 'differentiation view' ..." (p. 117). He does not wish to regard Martin's (and Meyerson's) three perspectives as competing and conflicting approaches, but places them next to each other: "The perspective I am proposing can be called a *multiple cultural configuration view*. (...) Organizational cultures are then understandable not as unitary wholes or as stable sets of subcultures but as mixtures of cultural manifestations of different levels and kinds" (p. 118). Alvesson takes ambiguity seriously, without making it the center of his analysis. By doing so, he opens "the possibility of 'explaining' much uncertainty, confusion and contradiction" (p. 118).

The approach of Parker (2000) is related to Alvesson's. "From the early 1980s onward there was an explosion of enthusiasm for writing about and managing something called 'organizational culture'. The central assumption behind this rise of interest seemed to be that a hard 'scientific' management of institutions could and should be augmented with, or even displaced by, an approach that stressed a softer, more humane understanding of human values and culture." The time study engineer was to be replaced by the organizational anthropologist: "… there are important insights to be gained from applying the term 'culture' to organizations, but … much of the writing … has been most unreflexive about its core assumptions".

It would appear that Parker is trying to breath new life back into the academic and more reflexive approach to organizational culture. To this end, he first presents "the history of ideas about culture in organizations" and the reasons for the concept's popularity, to subsequently arrive at a "rather different way of thinking about organizations and culture. To put it simply, organizational cultures should be seen as 'fragmented unities' in which members identify themselves as collective at some times and divided at others", thus Parker (2000: 1). Parker also argues for the elimination of the time-honored opposition between structures and actors, – "in sum, organizational culture both as a constraint and as an everyday accomplishment". Following on from this, he also regards organizations and identities (of employees) as two sides of the same coin, entirely in line with Giddens' duality concept (1984): "If organizations shape the identities of their members, should managers seek to influence these identities in order to manage more effectively?" An important basic assumption for Parker is "the idea of culture as an 'us' and 'them' claim, an identification" (p. 3), which he links to the relationship between 'structuralist and social constructionist accounts': "In terms, of the structure/agency dualism I suggest that both culture and organization can be regarded as mediating terms between the determination of generalities and the agency of individuals" (p. 4). After analyzing several early bestsellers (Peters and Waterman, 1982; Deal and Kennedy, 1982, and Ouchi, 1981), Parker states that we should not take 'managerial culturalist literature' too seriously, because these are less about "what organizations are like than about what they should be like. It is prescriptive rather than descriptive" (Parker, 2000: 25). The problem of the functionalistic theory-based organizational literature is that it fixes rigidly on consensus by means of shared values, and barely leaves room for the differences in meaning that always exist and, as such, different interpretations, conflicts, fuzziness and ambiguity. In fact, (organizational) culture is usually reduced to shared values and norms. As such, Deal and Kennedy are able to speak of strong and weak cultures, which conflicts with the assumption that, as ongoing social constructions, organizations do not have any cultures, but are cultures (Smircich, 1983, 1985).

For Parker too, this assumption results in three general principles: "Firstly, that terms like 'organization' and 'culture' should be understood as processes that, in some way, draw together history and everyday practice, or what sociologists call structure and agency. Secondly, that these processes continually involve making shifting and temporary stabilizations of meaning with a wide variety of human and non-human resources. Finally, that these meanings are contested because there are always competing understandings of what people and organizations are and should be doing" (Parker, 2000: 81). The social construction process of meanings is continually concerned with unity and diversity, that which we have in common, and that in which we differ, or in Martin's terms, that which integrates, differentiates and fragments (Martin, 1992). This is about the continuing drawing of (cultural) boundaries, both in and between organizations. In other words, the core is formed by inclusion and exclusion mechanisms (according to De Ruijter, 1996). Everyday practice teaches us that, diametrically opposed to this core, the dominant approach is that of 'everyone pulling in the same direction'. Rational steering is supplemented by a normative mission-driven approach. Steering very rarely occurs on the basis of an analysis of current content, but far more often on the basis of desired content.

Functions: from means of competition to increased reflexivity

The attention paid in the past to organizational culture was particularly inspired by the wish to influence human behavior in such a manner that production would increase. Essentially, the mainstream has never deviated from this. Until the nineteen-sixties and seventies, as a production factor, the individual plays a subordinate role. For many years, market developments and technological improvements barely gave any cause to demand attention for the so-called soft side of life in organizations. Around 1980, this changes drastically, due to intensified competition between Japan and the United States, amongst other countries. Given technical possibilities (in the market) that are more or less equal, it has been found that the individual and culture can be decisive. Almost self-evidently, cultural aspects are isolated from their context and from the wider culture concept (see the success factors described by Peters and Waterman, for example). You would have to be crazy not to use these, and first take time to calmly reflect upon whether the approach is scientifically sound. Parker speaks of "a practitioner-consultant model that regards culture as a normative glue that can be managed to ensure that organizations are more efficient" (2000: 220).

> People prefer to leave the latter to the academics, a great many of whom, as we have seen, started to concern themselves with the organizational culture issue from the start of the nineteen-eighties. Broadly speaking, these academics may be categorized into two groups. Firstly, those who particularly wish to support managers, by further increasing the practicability of the difficult

'culture' concept, resulting in all sorts of useful and less useful handbooks. The second groups consists of academics who (strongly) resist the instrumental character and the supposed flexibility of isolated aspects of culture. Parker refers to the first group of academics as "academic but functionalist", and the second group as anti-functionalist, with the starting point that organizations are cultures (2000: 221).

Whatever the case may be, the culture concept has preoccupied many in the last twenty years, offering direct support for management and debate with colleagues at business schools and universities. However, the urge for controllability, flexibility and increased production continues to be just as prominent. It is striking that, particularly in courses intended for management, real depth is (still) lacking in respect of the culture concept, and that these are always intended to increase the efficiency of production processes (including service). The instrumentality level of such courses has hardly decreased. Evidently, they still meet a need, and participants believe that they will be able to optimize their own performance by 'learning tricks'. In practice, they would appear to be disappointed in this, as numerous conversations with course participants reveal. Sooner or later, they encounter something unanticipated by the tricks, something that requires unforeseen action to be taken.

More academic (reflection-focused) courses are intended to bring relief. But do they? On the surface of it, the answer is 'yes'. The richness of the culture concept provides so many new insights and perspectives that participants continually indicate that they have learnt a lot, on the basis of which new initiatives start within their organizations. It is an interesting question, whether these new insights are directly related to the culture concept, or whether the latter is 'only' a (very handy) means of better understanding organizational processes, in this case the actions of organizational members.

All in all, twenty years of organizational culture have proved very fruitful. It has particularly demonstrated that organizational processes may be viewed from many different perspectives. It makes it possible to ask numerous questions about organizational processes. The pitfall always is that people are far too quickly inclined to believe that they have understood these processes, and suggest solutions that do not then appear to work.

Is this satisfactory? Has the concept given us what we had hoped or expected? For many, probably not. The danger is that we will throw it onto the great pile of all those management and organizational concepts that regularly come and go. And, as such, all of the enriching insights that the culture concept has produced in respect of organizational processes may hang in the balance. It is precisely these insights that must be maintained. Possibly, we will have to increase the functionality of these insights for those who should be able to profit from them on a day-to-day basis. The fact that this causes the culture concept itself to disappear into the background is a shame, but no more than that. It is probably the destiny of all concepts: their magic is always just temporary. This will also be the destiny shared by the successors of the culture concept. In the last paragraph, we saw that these have already presented themselves.

Future

People act on the basis of interpretation and sense making. Sense and meaning are not fixed, but are always realized during social construction processes. What is more, they are the subject of ongoing discussion and negotiation. To be able to understand meanings, we must gain insights into their creation, thus in the processes which precede them. Meanings and actions result from these processes. Organizations may be regarded as ongoing social and sense making construction processes. If we wish to be able to influence these processes effectively in any way, then we have to analyze them thoroughly.

We talk of management or meaning. Is meaning not just another term for culture? On the one hand it is; after all, for many, culture is particularly a system and process of patterns of sense making. On the other hand, it is a far more neutral term, which will not allow the questions of 'whose meaning is at issue?' and 'how has this meaning been created?' to be ignored. Meaning offers the manager possibilities for control, provided he has sufficiently informed himself about the sense making of those concerned, and the 'why' behind it.

Within the framework of management or meaning, Verweel (2000) calls upon the reader to focus on the issue of (renewed) binding, now that time-honored forms of identification have ceased to be of use for many. This search ought not to be accompanied by a one-sided integration approach. As such, he opposes the instrumentalization and mechanization of the social and the cultural. The concept of binding touches upon another important part of the culture concept, namely that of identity (compare, for example, Parker and Alvesson). Verweel wishes to approach the 'binding' concept analytically, but it poses the risk, just as the culture concept does, that people will start to search for "the social glue that binds", the shared values and norms. This would, then, fit perfectly into the instrumental integrative perspective favored by managers, something that Verweel wishes to resist, given his emphasis on organizations as communities.

A second approach is De Ruijter's (2000) who points to the stratification of society and organizations, and uses the metaphor of the arena. De Ruijter demands attention for management or diversity, in the sense of multiculturalism. Multiculturalism is more than ethnic diversity. The concept wishes to indicate the diversity of meanings. De Ruijter argues for the co-ordination of differences (in meanings). By doing so, he is suggesting that harmony

85

becomes possible due to a better understanding of (each other's) differences, and, as such, conflicts can be avoided. This is at odds with the arena model, which states that sense making (and thus also any reconciliation) concerns positions and interests, and is, thus, highly power related: how great is the chance that those with less power in the co-ordination process could play a significant role?

Would it not, in any event from an academic perspective, be more accurate and more correct to concentrate on the analysis of current organizational processes without continually wishing to indicate how they could be different or better? Do we not fall back in the pitfall of functionalism and normativity by doing the latter? Is it not also our academic task to help those, who want our help, to increase their reflexive ability, by teaching them to ask the right questions in their own organizational practice? Daily practice requires rapid decisions and changes. There is no time for reflection, or time is very rarely taken for this, in any event (also compare Koot and Sabelis, 2000). It is this divide between academic thinking and practical use that is evidently so difficult to span, or which translates itself into almost ridiculous solutions. Management at a large hospital decides that it should, indeed, take more time for reflection; and then decides to reserve ten minutes for reflection during its meetings ... Reflection is also a question of nerve, after all reflection often results in greater uncertainty (compare Alvesson and Wilmots, 1996).

In the analysis of organizational processes, there should be a focus on the process of sense making (meaning), as this is the basis for (collective organizational) actions. The analysis of organizational processes will thus (always) have to concentrate on retrieving the origin of these meanings. Meanings are formed by earlier experiences, and are continually (re)produced in interactions. At the same time, this is a process of negotiation. Thus, what is concerned is the analysis of these interactions, from the realization that it is a 'struggle' in which participants participate from different positions and interests. Many dislike the conflict and arena metaphors. I prefer them, because they express the fact that a struggle is involved, and they do not create the illusion that organizational practice is focused on consensus and harmony. The basic principle is differences, not about resolving differences, but about the extent to which the struggle can be fought openly, and the extent to which the other is taken seriously[2]. The issue of identity is connected to this. The culture concept's promise has not been lost, but gains a deserved place in a context of organizations as political and cultural phenomena (Czarniawska-Joerges, 1992).

---

[2] Elsewhere, the arena model is elaborated on in more detail (see, for example, Anthonissen and Boessenkool, 1998.

References

Alvesson, M. (1993). *Cultural Perspectives on Organizations*. Cambridge: Cambridge University Press.

Alvesson, M. and H. Wilmott (1996). *Making Sense of Management. A Critical Introduction*. London: Sage.

Anthonissen A. and J. Boessenkool (1998). *Betekenissen van Besturen: Variaties in bestuurlijk handelen*. Utrecht: ISOR.

ASQ, Administrative Science Quarterly (1983). Special issue on Organizational Culture, 28 (3), 331–502.

Barley, S., G. Meyer and D. Gash (1988). Cultures of Culture: Academics, Practitioners and the Pragmatics of Normative Control. *Administrative Science Quarterly, 33*, 24–60.

Bax, E.H. (1991). *Organisatiecultuur, technologie en management in een veranderende samenleving*. Utrecht: Het Spectrum.

Bos, R. ten (2000). *Fashion and utopia in management thinking*.

Broms, H. and H. Gahmberg (1983). Communication to Self in Organizations and Cultures. *Administrative Science Quarterly, 28*, 482–495.

Czarniawska-Joerges, B. (1992). *Exploring Complex Organizations: A Cultural Perspective*. Newbury Park, CA: Sage.

Deal T. and A. Kennedy (1982). *Corporate Cultures*. Reading, MA: Addison-Wesley.

Eriksen, T.H. (1995). *Small Places, Large Issues: An Introduction to Social and Cultural Anthropology*. London: Pluto Press.

Frissen, P. (1989). *Bureaucratische cultuur en informatisering*. Den Haag: SDA.

Frissen, P. and J. van Westerlaak (1990). *Organisatiecultuur*. Schoonhoven: Academic Service.

Frost, P., L. Moore, M. Louis, C. Lundberg and J. Martin (Eds.) (1985). *Organizational Culture*. Beverly Hills, CA: Sage.

Frost, P., L. Moore, M. Louis, C. Lundberg and J. Martin (Eds.) (1991). Reframing *Organizational Culture*. Newbury Park, CA: Sage.

Giddens, A. (1979). *Central Problems in Social Theory*. London: MacMillan Press.

Giddens, A. (1984). *The Constitution of Society*. Cambridge: Polity Press.

Gregory, K. (1983). Native View Paradigms: Multiple Cultures and Culture Conflicts in Organizations. *Administrative Science Quarterly, 28*, 359–376.

Jelinek M., L. Smircich and Paul Hirsch (1983). lntroduction: A Code of Many Colors, *Administrative Science Quarterly, 28*, 331–338.

Jones, G. (1983). Transaction Costs, Property Rights and Organizational Culture. *Administrative Science Quarery, 28*, 454–467.

Koot, W. and I. Hogema (1990). *Organisatiecultuur: Fictie en Werkelijkheid*. Muiderberg: Coutinho.

Koot, W., M. Staarman and J. Verbeek (1989). *Mythen over Corporate Culture*. Utrecht: ISOR.

Martin, J. (1992). *Cultures in Organizations: Three Perspectives*. New York: Oxford University Press.

Martin, J. and D. Meyerson (1988). Organizational Cultures and the Denial, Channeling and Acknowledgrnent of Ambiguity. In L. Pondy, R. Boland and H. Thomas *Managing Ambiguity and* Change (93–125). Chichester: JohnWiley.

Martin, J., M. Feldman, M. Hatch and S. Sitkin (1983). The Uniqueness Paradox in Organizational Stories. *Administrative Science Quarterly, 28*, 438–453.

Ouchi, W.G. (1981). *Theory Z*. Reading, MA: Addison-Wesley.

Parker, M. (2000). *Organizational Culture and Identity*. London: Sage.

Peters, T. and M. Watennan (1982). *In Search of Excellence*. New York: Harper and Row.

Pondy L., P. Frost, G. Morgan and T. Dandridge (Eds.) (1983). *Organizational Symbolism*. Greenwich, CT: JAI Press.

Riley, P. (1983). A Structurationist Account of Political Culture. *Administrative Science Quarterly, 28*, 414–437.

Ruijter, A. de (1996). Betekenisconstructie en sturing in een complexe wereld. In M. Gastelaars and G. Hagelstein (Eds.), *Management of meaning: Besturen en organiseren als processen van betekenisgeving* (9–24). Utrecht: ISOR/CBM.

Ruijter, A. de (2000). Oratie KUB.

Sanders, G. and B. Neuijen (1988). *Bedrijfscultuur: diagnose en beïnvloeding*. Assen/Maastricht: Van Gorcum.

Schein, E. (1985). *Organizational Culture and Leadership*. San Francisco: Jossey Bass.

Smircich, L. (1983). Concepts of Culture and Organizational Analysis. *Administrative Science Quarterly, 28*, 339–359.

Smith K. and v. Simmons (1983). A Rumplestilskin Organization: Metaphors on Metaphors in Field Research. *Administrative Science Quarterly, 28*, 377–392.

Tennekes, J. (1990). *De onbekende dimensie*. Leuven/Apeldoorn: Garant.

Trice H. and J. Beyer (1993). *The Cultures of Work Organizations*. Englewood Cliffs, NJ: Prentice Hall.

Verweel, P. (1987). *Universiteit: verandering en planning*. Utrecht: ICAU.

Verweel, P. (2000). *Betekenisgeving in organisatiestudies: De mechanisering van het sociale*. Utrecht: ISOR.

Wilkins A. and W. Ouchi (1983). Efficient Cultures. *Administrative Science Quarterly, 28*, 468–481.

Chapter 5

The customer-friendly organisation

Carl Rohde and Hans van der Loo

Introduction

The term 'customer-friendly organization' is actually a strange one. After all, all organizations want to sell. And everyone knows that it is easier to sell using honey than using vinegar. Customer-friendliness appears as the most basic and most self-evident form of 'honey' production. The description 'customer-friendly' for an organization should therefore be too self-evident for words – after all, this is a basic requirement.

Despite this, the description 'customer-friendly' is anything but simple and obvious. Otherwise it could never have attracted so much attention, particularly in recent decades. The image of the customer-friendly organization has even grown to become an insistent symbol of our society; a society that, in all its districts and regions, is penetrated by the Marketing Idea.

It is this prevailing marketing idea that not merely convinces everyone and everything of the necessity of client-friendly operation. It is the same marketing idea that suggests, or even insists, that more and more systematic attention must be paid to everything that customer-friendliness may involve, both actually and ideally, and how we can then refine customer-friendliness and realize it still more effectively. Because after all, this is the core concept, customer-friendliness, of the core idea of our society, marketing.

The quest for what customer-friendliness involves, including the competitive desire to realize customer-friendliness more and more effectively, has demonstrated how much the concept of and the striving for customer-friendliness proceeds in phases of constant further refinement. Customer-friendliness is largely a historical construct. And it is precisely its historical variability that means that there has to be constant work on the image of the customer-friendly organization. It means that customer-friendliness immediately loses the all-too-convenient 'self-evident' label that we ascribed to it just a few lines above.

Under the surface, as its deep motivation, the customer-friendly organization's imperative scarcely changes. But on the surface, customer-friendliness is constantly adopting new forms. On the surface, though, they meant something different at the start of this century than they did in the thirties, fifties and eighties and will do in the new millennium.

Development of the concept

The major sources for the image of the customer-friendly organization all show that customer-friendliness is a concept in motion – from the past through the present to its further perfection in future. Inasmuch as we can describe the image of the customer-friendly organization as a cliché – what could be more basic and self-evident? – it is nevertheless a cliché that is constantly, from occurrence to occurrence, charged with new meanings.

The beginning: selling and sales

Terms such as consumer and consumption first arose in the last century. More specifically, they arose in the period when the first large-scale industrial manufacturers were looking for and finding a market to sell their goods.[1] This was the period of the scarcity economy. As yet, there were no sophisticated consumers, except in the upper stratum of society. The mass consumer still had to be 'nurtured', so to speak. At that stage, there was still very little to that nurturing; in a scarcity economy, the mass simply consumes what it can get and use. Sophisticated marketing techniques are unnecessary. Sales territories are there for the taking, so to speak. So all the attention and energy have to be focused on manufacturing and distribution – purchasers will buy anyway.

In this context, marketing, in the sense of building up a sophisticated knowledge of the consumer, is not needed at all. Quite simply, selling is the imperative. The purchasers are no more and no less than the end users of the products provided[2], and not yet full-grown consumers. It will be clear that the concept of customer-friendliness will not be developed under these circumstances. In the scarcity economy, organizations and companies remain essentially 'production oriented'. And can be so without any problems.

Fables of abundance: from selling to marketing

The exclusive focus on manufacturing and distributing disappears as soon as the scarcity economy is transformed into the affluent society. This is a gradual process. One that actually had already commenced in America in

---

[1] "*Consumer* as a predominant term was the creation of large-scale industrial manufacturers and their agents. It implies … the using up of what is going to be produced." Williams, R. (1983) *Keywords: A Vocabulary of Culture and Society*. Fontana, London. Pg 78–79.

[2] "To say *user* rather than consumer is still to express a relevant distinction." Williams, R. (1983) *Keywords: A Vocabulary of Culture and Society*. Fontana, London. Pg 78–79.

the last century, that reached a high point in the fifties and sixties of this century (when North America achieved a hitherto unknown level of prosperity and the contours of the welfare state were developing in Western Europe[3]), but that has continued right up to the present date.

As far as thinking and action on customer-friendliness is concerned, that long period really consists of one basic movement: constant expansion and refinement. Increasingly, products are encountering competing products on the market. Hardly any product still sells itself simply on its own terms. As a first response to this situation, historically speaking, manufacturers start to embellish their products by linking them with images, symbols and myths that appeal to a wide public. We can call these 'fables of abundance'. They are the archetypes that the advertising industry is still using to this day.

For instance, even in the nineteenth century we can see that the narrative of a fresh, pure rural society is used to make products more attractive – the vine-covered country cottage, the rosy-cheeked babies on baskets full of corn and fruits, the young farm labourers radiating health and vitality etc.[4]

Together, they nourish the so attractive back-to-the-simple-life and back-to-nature motif. The impressive narrative of constant technological progress is also exploited commercially – the doctor who perfects nutrition and (somewhat later) prescribes cigarettes because of their relaxing effect. In the first decades of this century, Gillette is already praising its razor blades with the slogan 'From Boston to Bombay', making use of yet another advertising narrative – cosmopolitanism and world-wide product recognition.[5]

As soon as prosperity increases and products have to start competing for consumers' favour, we see their manufacturers joining with the advertising industry to construct a second, symbolic layer around their products. A symbolic layer that always symbolizes a version of the good life – the natural life, the rich life, the life of social standing, the technologically advanced life. Their object is always to increase the product's attractiveness in its consumers' eyes.

It is no longer enough to offer products to consumers. From then on, the products also have to be provided with an attractive ambience. Selling alone no longer works; consumers are becoming more selective. The marketing matters. In a modern society that is less and less characterized by scarcity, it becomes important to focus on the collective emotions that motivate potential consumers.

---

[3] Swaan, A. de (1989) *Zorg en de staat.* Bert Bakker, Amsterdam.

[4] "The late-nineteenth-century ideal of gemeinschaft – the self-sufficient, organic community – achieved its embodiment in commercial imagery long before it was codified in sociological texts." Lears, J. (1994) *Fables of abundance. A cultural history of advertising in America.* Basic Books, New York. Pg 103.

[5] Lears, J. (1994) *Fables of abundance. A cultural history of advertising in America.* Basic Books, New York. Pg 163.

As the competition for consumers' favour grows fiercer – that is, the further we advance into the 20th century – we find that marketing and marketing communications become more and more emotive. "Soup can produce emotions. You can write as emotionally about ham as about Christianity", stated the J. Walter Thomson advertising bureau back in 1923.[6] And since then the idea has spread. Naturally, the emotions in question are always those that appeal to consumers. Manufacturers are invited by the advertising industry, and simultaneously forced by consumers who have moved beyond the scarcity economy, to focus more on these consumers. In one way or another, we can describe this as a customer-friendly orientation.

The intensification of customer-friendliness

The affluent society crystallized for the first time in North America in the 1950s and 1960s. And that is where full awareness blossoms of how important it is to serve the consumer as appropriately as possible – to implement customer-friendliness as fully as possible.

Drucker puts it as follows in 1954:

> The customer is the foundation of a business and keeps it in existence. He alone gives employment. And it is to supply the customer that society entrusts wealth-producing resources to the business enterprise ... Because it is its purpose to create a consumer, any business has two – and only these two – basic functions: marketing and innovation. ... Marketing is ... much broader than selling. ... It is the whole business seen from the point of view of its final result, that is, the consumer's point of view.[7]

This definitively puts aside selling for marketing. The paradigm of the product-driven organization has been abandoned, at least on paper. From the early sixties, we see the image of the customer-friendly organization gaining in advertising allure. It is subject to constant further development and refinement. The target-group approach (1960s) and the lifestyle approach (1970s) become part of it, as do customer loyalty, customer satisfaction and customer delight programmes (1980s), which analyse, develop and implement the finest details of the process of achieving maximum customer-friendliness. EPOS (electronic point of sale) takes off in the 1990s. Even if it primarily represents a very effective (because computerized) form of distribution, EPOS is also an instrument to serve customers more quickly and more efficiently,[8] and therefore belongs in this summary of the ongoing attention paid

---

[6] Lears, J. (1994) *Fables of abundance. A cultural history of advertising in America.* Basic Books, New York. Pg 227.

[7] Quoted in Brown, S. (1995) *Postmodern marketing.* Routledge, London, New York. Pg 31.

[8] Gay, P. du (ed) (1997) *Productions of Culture/Cultures of Productions.* Sage, London. Pg 169–175.

to customer-friendliness. Call-centres and information helplines are spreading in the 1990s.

Apart from this expansion and refinement of thinking and action on customer-friendliness, the image of the customer-friendly organization also becomes established in more and more areas of modern society. It operates as a paradigm not only in the commercial provision of goods and services, but also in the government and administrative area, and even in the elevated sphere of museums, the arts and the theatre. Nowadays, a company can provide its business relations and customers with a dinner under Rembrandt's 'The Night Watch', while just 15 years ago this would have been rejected out of hand as an unheard-of concession to commerce. Now theatres no longer provide just a play any more; they sell packages that include at least a cup of coffee and guaranteed parking. And all this is done in the name of customer-friendliness.

Classical approaches

What takes place in society is summarized and reflected in the specialist academic literature, and so there have been numerous treatments of the growing power of the consumer since the late fifties.[9] Here, I propose to deal with two classic sources for the image of the customer-friendly organization, Levitt and Kotler.

While marketing is certainly not merely a post-Second World War phenomenon, marketing ideas only crystallize completely in the late 1950s and early 1960s. This is illustrated not only by Drucker, as shown by the quotation in 2.3; Levitt and Kotler do the same. Levitt, who gained such fame in the 1960s with his 'economies of scale' globalization theory, had already written a much-talked-of article in the *Harvard Business Review* in 1960 not only warning of the risks run by a company if it does not serve its customer according to his or her whim, but also warning of the risks if the company does not develop a keen eye for the customer's potential future wishes, and of course if it does not then act appropriately.[10] Levitt's article is a pressing invitation to develop more extensive forms of service and customer-friendliness. For example, not to think of consumer leisure in competitive terms such as either television or radio or an evening out, but to see all these as forms of entertainment and then analyse how consumers can be served most

---

[9] "The shift in power from production to consumption." Miller, D. (ed) (1995) *Acknowledging consumption*. Routledge, London. Pg 7.

[10] Levitt, T. (1960) *Marketing Myopia*. Harvard Business Review 38. "Marketing myopia: companies' failure to respond to the changing requirements of consumers; their preoccupation with the products they produce rather than the markets they serve; a tendency to define their purpose and customer needs too narrowly (railroads rather than transportation, movies as opposed to entertainment etc.)...". Summery in Brown, S. (1995) *Postmodern marketing*. Routledge, London, New York. Pg 32.

effectively. It is this switch to deeper and more innovative forms of customer-friendliness that has made Disney the market leader in the entertainment industry.

In broad outline, Kotler applies the same ideas as Levitt, but he has elaborated them increasingly in a growing series of articles and textbooks. In his *Principle of Marketing*, constantly revised since the 1960s, he describes the various phases that marketing has gone through with considerable consistency.[11] In Kotler's view, the focus of attention in marketing shifts from (1) the manufacturing process itself to (2) the product and its qualities, to (3) selling, to (4) marketing as a much wider and at the same time more intensified form of selling, to (5) a 'societal marketing concept' – a form of marketing that also takes accounts of the wishes consumers cherish for such things as a pleasant environment ('green' products), a humane world (no child labour), 'caring' business (fair-price policies towards the Third World, good personnel policies at home). Translating this to our theme of customer-friendliness, this represents a development which, as with Levitt, invites an increasingly broad and far-reaching response to consumers' needs and desires.[12]

Levitt and Kotler are classics. They are among the most renowned sources for the image of the customer-friendly organization. They summarize the past and define the present – for them, the 1960s and beyond[13]. Two newer, more up-to-date sources for the image of the customer-friendly organization are McIntosh et al. and Baudrillard. They point to developments that are spreading at the moment and, I suspect, will make their stamp on the future even more than at present. As these more recent sources have not yet taken their final shape, let alone become 'classical', I will deal with them in the following section.

The major ingredients of the image of the customer-friendly organization

In the above discussion, we have seen that customer-friendliness is not a fixed concept but has evolved along with general social developments, the primary development being the transformation from a scarcity economy to an affluent society. This section will examine four major ingredients of cus-

---

[11] Kotler, P. Armstrong, G. (1993) *Marketing: an introduction.* Prentice-Hall, Englewood Cliffs.

[12] 'Customer satisfaction engineering' is a concept also referred to by Kotler at a very early stage. Kotler, P. en Levy, S. J. (1969) *Broadening the concept of marketing.* Journal of Marketing 35, January 1969.

[13] A clear summary, which I agree with as far as Levitt and Kotler are concerned, is given by Brown S. (1995) *Postmodern marketing.* Routledge, London, New York. Pg 27–54.

tomer-friendliness. Although customer-friendliness is always closely associated with the well-known customer satisfaction programmes (3.2), I intend to adopt a broader perspective here. I include the constantly further refined approach by customer target groups as a form of customer-friendliness (3.1), together with the phenomenon that companies increasingly want to act as a concerned partner in the (global) society of which they form part (3.3). Finally, I look at Baudrillard's ideas. Even although Baudrillard is seldom cited in connection with the theme of customer-friendliness, his thinking nevertheless includes a view of how customer-friendliness will develop further from the 1990s on (3.4).

Target group approach

As consumers, in their growing affluence, become more selective and more demanding, it becomes more important to target them better. Simply paying attention to manufacturing and distribution – the first phases in Kotler's system as described in section 2.4 – is increasingly unsatisfactory. There has to be real 'marketing'.

From the start, this 'real' marketing is done by thinking more precisely than previously in terms of target groups. The most basic categorization in target groups is the demographic approach. Men's consumption requirements and desires differ from those of women, and young people's from those of older people. And the level of income that consumers have available will influence their desires and purchases. Accordingly, determining demographic target groups and trends forms the basis of marketing.

The goal is of course primarily to get a product to the right man or woman. At the same time, we can also interpret the marketing target group approach as a form of customer-friendliness, since it is an attempt to serve the customer more effectively by providing him with products tailored to his demographic characteristics. This form of customer-friendliness is illustrated even more clearly by the next stage taken by the target group approach.

Particularly in the 1980s, the demographic target group approach forfeited a great deal of its predictive value. It has become increasingly difficult to predict on the basis of the traditional classification by age, sex and income to what extent a product will actually be purchased by the target group. This is because of the increasing affluence and the flood of consumer articles each individual target group has to choose from. The traditional demographic predictors no longer work properly in this context, creating a growing need to know in greater detail what precisely makes a particular article attractive to a particular target group. As a marketing researcher put it in the late eighties: "Social class is just so inadequate. We do a tremendous amount of interviews among doctors. They are all the same demographic group – but crumbs! – you can differentiate between them perfectly in their attitudes towards technology, patients, their attitude towards the profession ..."[14]

This marks the beginning of the age of psychographic or sociographic lifestyle categories. From that point on, segmentation of target groups by lifestyle, occupational mentality, leisure interests etc. grows in importance. It provides much more precise information on the mentality and attitudes of the potential groups of purchasers for a particular product.

This lifestyle segmentation sometimes operates as a supplement and refinement to the traditional demographic categories, and sometimes it replaces them.

As an extension of this, a new post is inaugurated in the advertising agencies – the account planner. The account planner's job is firstly to map out as accurately as possible (often through research) the lifestyle and mentality of the potential target groups for a particular product. Secondly, it is his task to brief the creative people in the advertising agency so that they can produce a commercial message that is as accurately tailored as possible. Thirdly, the account planner has to find the right media channels for the commercial message. What will be most effective, given the potential purchaser's mentality and lifestyle – RTL4 or MTV? In this way, the account planner has to ensure that the intended lifestyle segment is actually exposed to the most exciting, most recognizable, most attractive, in short the most persuasive message. So we might describe the account planner as the customer-friendliness broker at the symbolic/communicative level.

In any case, the target group approach is continuing to evolve. In the 1990s, there is some evidence of fatigue as regards lifestyle segmentation. Not only is it clearly subject to a sort of symbolic inflation – it is constantly delivering the same rather stereotyped images – but also the modern consumer is now so highly individualized that it is argued that each consumer forms his or her own lifestyle category. In this context, a new form of marketing approach is developing: situational marketing.

Situational marketing is not based on a particular demographic/lifestyle target group that has to be served. Situational marketing is based on a particular situation; a particular situation in which innumerable individuals will find themselves at some point in the day, irrespective of their demographic characteristics or lifestyles. For instance, a very large number of people move through the major rail stations every day between 5 p.m. and 6.30 p.m. All (m/f, young/old, shop assistant, civil servant, 'mobile executive') feeling hungry. And situational marketing takes advantage of that feeling. The rail stations have been very successful in expanding to become favourite

---

[14] Gay, Pa du (ed) (1997) *Productions of Culture/Cultures of Productions*. Sage, London. Pg 203.

places for consumers to consume food products, and increasingly to buy other articles too. The same applies to filling stations.[15]

Customer satisfaction

The most visible and most direct representations of the customer satisfaction approach are of course the innumerable customer satisfaction programmes run by many companies. Customer satisfaction stands for the efforts made in all these programmes to provide customers with service as systematically and effectively as possible.

It will be clear that systems of this kind strike a chord in our present times. It is no accident that today's affluent society is sometimes called the stress society. We are working harder than ever in a freelance economy that runs for 24 hours a day. 'Job-hopping' is a term that was not current ten years ago. Nor was 'burnt out'. What matters here is that the customer satisfaction approach is a hit with everyone who is subject to a certain amount of stress, since it meets a real need – a company, a brand, a product that 'thinks for you' and so takes over some worries for you. A company, brand, product that helps to 'de-stress', as the phrase has been for five years or so. Accordingly, customer satisfaction programmes aim to provide their de-stressing qualities in a customized form wherever possible.

Socially responsible business

The 1990s have also witnessed another change in mentality, as regards thinking on the relationship between business and society. Today's consumer expects (or even demands) the companies and organizations where he/she feels 'at home' to be more than just a profit-making machine. Increasingly, a good company is expected to be involved in the society in which it operates and from which it generates its profits. In this thinking, a company not only has shareholders, it also has stakeholders. While the former have shares in the company, and therefore an interest in its prosperity, stakeholders – environmental associations, neighbourhood associations, employees – need not have any shares to have an interest in the company's doings.

Socially involved, socially responsible business is the keyword that best sums up this new thinking. There is absolutely no indication that this keyword will lose its relevance again in the coming years.

A number of socio-cultural factors are working to promote the development towards socially responsible business. First of all, business's role has expanded enormously in the era of globalization and the roll-back in national governments. The world's hundred biggest companies have sales

---

[15] Rohde, C. en Westenberg, M. (1999) *Blurring in snacks en zoetwarenland*. Uitgave Studiecentrum voor Snacks en Zoetwaren, Zeist.

that are larger than the national product of half of the countries on this planet. The incessant global environmental problems also point to the fundamental role that business plays in the world. And in addition, that role is being made obvious to everyone faster than ever before in the information society we now live in. Another factor promoting socially concerned business is that consumers in the affluent part of the world reward socially concerned companies with greater sympathy and greater readiness to purchase than companies that fail to take their wide-ranging global responsibilities seriously enough in any way.[16] This is what Shell found in response to its oil extraction policies in Africa, and Nike in response to its child labour practices in Asia. By contrast, the Body Shop and Third World Coffee have gained their good reputation from their socially involved activities.

By now, there is an impressive range of companies aiming to realize their social involvement – up to a point, of course, because their striving for profit remains primary. Apple is sponsoring disadvantaged schools in London by giving them computers. Levi gives its managers time off to manage projects in poorer districts. Bennetton fights AIDS. Of course, it is easy to take a cynical view of these activities, but at the same time they can also be interpreted as a new, broader form of customer-friendliness. Timberland, the footwear and clothing manufacturer, shows an awareness of the complexity of the situation in which the organization is operating and expresses its social involvement policy in a differentiated way as follows:

> We perceive and deal with social issues in a non-traditional manner. … Timberland doesn't give money to charity. Instead we try to create a return. … We create value for ourselves as a company, our employees, our shareholders, our customers, the community and the non-profit organisations we co-operate with. The traditional notion of philanthropy is not adequate. It is not smart or wise to approach the social problems of society with the financial leftovers of companies. By integrating our social activities into our business strategies, we also provide these social activities with the sustainability that will see them through hard times, and harness business to work in another fashion.[17]

Here, customer-friendliness is deeply embedded in a broad social framework.

The best book on this new approach to customer-friendliness is *Corporate Citizenship: successful strategies for responsible companies* by McIntosh et al. It is a new source for the image of the customer-friendly organization.[18]

---

[16] Miller, D. (ed) (1995) *Acknowledging consumption*. Routledge, London.

[17] McIntosh, M. Leipziger, D. Jones, K. and Coleman, G. (1998) *Corporate Citizenship, Succesful strategies for responsible companies*. Financial Times Management, London. Pg 3.

[18] McIntosh, M. Leipziger, D. Jones, K. and Coleman, G. (1998) *Corporatee Citizenship, Succesful strategies for responsible companies*. Financial Times Management, London.

Providing a narrative with vision

Our age is often characterised as postmodern – a fairly hackneyed term, now that there are postmodern bed throws, postmodern tea sets and postmodern salads on the market. Nevertheless, postmodernism is an appropriate term to characterize our society, also because it points in the direction of a new form of customer-friendliness.

The central feature of our postmodern society is that it lacks any Great Narratives.[19] The great ideologies that inspired and motivated traditional society (Christianity) and modern society (liberalism, nationalism, communism, the belief in technology and progress) have lost much of their grandeur. In the postmodern society, we are all too familiar with the reverse side of the Great Narratives – totalitarianism, genocide, global environmental pollution. So postmodernism means a post-ideological existence. And in it, the focus is on the question how we can still create a meaningful existence, at least at an individual level. On the one hand, the death of the Great Narratives creates freedom: who has the right or authority any longer to prescribe or prohibit anything whatsoever? On the other hand, the death of the Great Narratives has resulted in a post-ideological disorientation that compels us to construct our own little narrative at an individual level, or even to 'zap' one together.

Certainly in their most essential product – brands – companies are responding to this postmodern quest for one's own small (and therefore personal) narrative. After all, in our affluent society consumption no longer takes place from necessity, from utilitarian considerations. Nobody buys a sweater any longer because it's cold; we still have plenty of perfectly good ones in the wardrobe. Consuming in our affluent society is to emphasize who we are, to re-emphasize all the time who we are: it must be a fashionable sweater, or a sweater that suits our personality in some way.[20]

In this context, Baudrillard announces that we have left the 'logic of utility' behind us, and that we are motivated by the 'logic of the sign'. What does this brand of jeans, these shoes, this fashionable suit, this holiday destination, this vegetarian pizza, this car, this net provider say about who I am? What does it 'mean' if I work in the army, in the ICT business, in the meat processing industry? What does it add to or emphasize in my own little personal narrative? That is the question that the postmodern consumer is constantly asking, either consciously or unconsciously, and that gives a direction to his/her purchasing behaviour. "Marketing, purchasing, sales, the acquisition of differentiated commodities and objects/signs – all of these

---

[19] Lyotard, J. F. (1984) *The postmodern condition.* University of Minnesota Press, Minneapolis.
[20] Bocock, R. (1993) *Consumption.* Routlegde, London.

presently constitute our language, a code in which our entire society communicates and speaks about itself", Baudrillard states.[21]

Where identity-constructing signs are provided through products and through marketing communication, it is not usual to designate this as a form of customer-friendliness. And yet this production of signs can in fact be interpreted in that way. Such an interpretation is valid precisely in our present postmodern society, in which the quest for one's own small narrative is both necessary and difficult, and in which the consumer searches for answers even in the signs and symbols that are draped around products, brands and organizations.[22] In that sense, we can characterize Baudrillard's work as a fourth (somewhat wayward) source for the image of the customer-friendly organization.

Functions of the image of the customer-friendly organization

I intended to be brief on the function of the image of the customer-friendly organization. The image fulfils two mutually complementary functions.

Firstly, the image of the customer-friendly organization has a warning effect. Although there is something very self-evident about the image of the customer-friendly organization (what organization wants to be customer-unfriendly?), it is evident, as this article has been intended to show, that customer-friendliness is in fact a complex, multi-layered concept. Accordingly, the first function of the image of the customer-friendly organization must be to warn against an excessively laid-back attitude in the striving for customer-friendliness, to promote alertness in searching for the next innovative implementations of customer-friendliness. An organization that does not do this will sooner or later lose customers.

The second function of the image of the customer-friendly organization is as an inspiration. The scope of the image, the constant new implementations and refinements provided in the literature, make the image a constant source of inspiration to help to increase the organization's efficiency and profitability, its perception and identity.

New developments: e-commerce

In the above, two new developments in the thinking on the customer-friendly organization have already been dealt with. Thinking in terms of socially responsible business has been covered in section 3.3, while section 3.4 has interpreted the provision of symbolic identity ingredients by products,

---

[21] Baudrillard, J. (1988) *Selected writings: Consumer society.* Cambridge, Polity Press. Pg 48.
[22] Jensen, R. (1999) *The dream society.* McGraw-Hill, New York.

brands and organizations as a form of customer-friendliness. But the most radical, even revolutionary development, which will also greatly enrich the image of the customer-friendly organization, is the digital revolution.

In the digital revolution, the image of the customer-friendly organization will quite definitely take new directions and assume new forms. As the digital revolution outgrows its teething troubles – the constant waiting for a connection, the lack of confidence on payment transactions, the disconcerting absence of clear organization – e-commerce will undoubtedly take off in a big way. Virtual shopping streets will be created in addition to the traditional shopping streets, and in these digital shopping streets it will be very easy for consumers to make price and quality comparisons. After all, the competition is always just one mouse click away. This means that the leadership and control in any purchasing process will largely lie with the consumer. We have ended up at the opposite pole from the nineteenth-century situation of the scarcity economy, where manufacturers simply had to produce and distribute to find purchasers. In the digital era, it is precisely the consumer who determines what comes to him and where he chooses to direct his attention – 'permission marketing' is the current phrase.

Competition will adopt new forms in this digital context. In particular, it will be essential to provide the right service, with extremely customized customer-friendliness. The oversupplied customer will demand 'one-to-one marketing'; he/she will only want to be bothered with commercial messages if they are in fact highly relevant to his/her own interests. And the interactive possibilities that the net provides between producer and consumer mean that one-to-one marketing can in fact be achieved. 'Mass customizing' is the advertising term here; mass customizing stands for the ability provided by the digital revolution to market even mass products in a way that is so precisely targeted to the end consumer that the latter perceives them as an extremely personal product.[23] Putting together your own car digitally and then ordering it is one option. Click together your own trainers, your own make-up, your own soft drink – fortified with precisely those minerals and trace elements that you need.

Even though the digital revolution is still in its infancy, it is clear that a kaleidoscope of new forms of customer-friendliness is developing on the net. This is further illustration that the image of the customer-friendly organization has not forfeited any of its importance and inspiring relevance, but that it is constantly looking for and finding new forms.

---

[23] Peppers, D. Rogers, M. (1997) *One to one future*. Piatkus Books, New York.

Differentiating customers: An example

Parallel to the development from an internal product orientation to an external customer-directed orientation, an evolution occurred, in which a generic conception of 'the' customer gradually made way for a more differentiated and sophisticated view of various customer groups. At the same time, there was a transition from segmentation methods, based on socio-demographic characteristics (age, income position, gender, geographic location, education), to types of segmentation based on customers' values. The idea behind this is that all societies are underpinned by values. They provide direction to the choices that people make during their lives, and steer human behaviour. Everyone has certain patterns within himself that determine the way he thinks, and what he does and feels. Given the fact that humans are able to absorb and learn new things in their childhood years far more easily than at any other stage of their lives, most of these patterns are learned during the earliest years of life. When children are about ten years old, their pattern of values has been more or less established. The assumption is that a knowledge of consumers' values is not only important when identifying their needs and behaviour ('what' consumers want and do), but also when making contact with the way they experience their world ('how' groups of consumers think, and the motives they allow themselves to be led by). The latter is particularly important if, in the framework of establishing and maintaining relationships, communication with consumers is to be optimal.

Given the fact that the number of values important to consumers is too large to yield a useful segmentation into customer groups (in her doctoral thesis on the values of Dutch people, Joke Oppenhuizen collected no less than 1376 values), these must be clustered.[24] Although the dimensions used by various researchers quite often differ, they are similar in the sense that they always contain an element of 'the individual' versus the 'social' and of 'freedom' versus 'ties'. Incidentally, this also corresponds to the 'culture theory' dimensions used by the anthropologist Mary Douglas, in which 'group' and 'grid' feature as the central dimensions.[25] I will use the 'individuality' and 'freedom' dimensions mentioned earlier to elaborate consumer orientations. First I will briefly explain the dimensions, and then relate them to each other.

---

[24] J. Oppenhuisen: Een scaah in de bus? Een onderzoek naar waarden van de Nederlander. Amsterdam (SWOCC) 2000.

[25] For an elaboration of the 'culture theory', see M. Douglas: Natural Symbols. Explorations in Cosmology. London (Barrie and Rockliff) 1970. M. Thompson, R. Ellis and A. Wildawsky: Cultural Theory. Boulder (Wetsview Press) 1990.

The individually-oriented versus the socially-oriented dimension

This dimension concerns the extent to which people are inclined to put their own interests first, or to conform to the interests of the group of which they form a part. The 'individual' orientation stands for self-conscious, independent people, who focus on originality, unicity and individual achievements. Examples of associated values are: 'having ambitions', 'achieving', 'enjoying', 'being attractive', 'seeking kicks' and 'being inquisitive'. The 'social' orientation stands for 'we-conscious' people, who subordinate their own interests to the group to which they belong. Involvement, harmony and being of equal value characterise this orientation. Examples of corresponding values are: 'being sympathetic to others', 'listening', 'being helpful', 'being responsible', 'cooperating', 'friendship' and 'kind-heartedness'.

The freedom versus the ties dimension

This dimension concerns the extent to which people are inclined to activate and shape their external environment, or to conform to external influences and rules. The 'freedom' orientation stands for people who are externally oriented, inclined to continually explore their environment, to expand their boundaries and broaden their horizons. Examples of corresponding values are: 'being independent', 'going your own way', 'being carefree', 'being challenging', 'making boundaries shift', 'having your own opinion', 'being broadminded'. The 'ties' orientation stands for people who are focused on their own environment, who are inclined to control and structure external influences as much as possible, or to undergo external influences in a way that is relatively passive. Examples of corresponding values are: 'certainty', 'having your own space', 'safety', 'family life', 'politeness' and 'having authority'.

When related, the two dimensions yield four different orientations:

Consumers' orientations

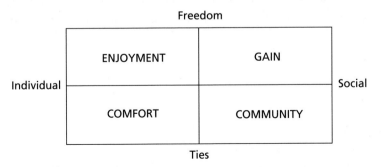

I will now briefly explain the four different orientations.

Enjoyment

The general profile that corresponds with this orientation: contrary, stubborn and actively searching for things that make life exciting. Life is dominated by self-actualisation and self-expression. Accepted norms and values ("suburban bliss") are more or less consciously opposed. The dominant personality characteristics are: independent, active, self-assured, critical, businesslike, adventurous, mobile, innovative, hedonistic, impulsive and impatient. Behaviour is focused on undertaking, discovering, exploring things, on developing and growing, and on kicks. The style of communication is expressive, associative, energetic and emotional. In socio-demographic terms, people with this orientation are young, single, relatively well educated and live in large-urban environments.

Community

The general profile that corresponds with this orientation is: a social disposition and focused on durable and harmonious relationships with family, friends and neighbours. The community type is a 'group animal par excellence'. They have few personal ambitions: group life is of first importance. They define themselves not so much in terms of work, but in terms of their social network. Life is dedicated to harmony and close relationships. The dominant personality characteristics are: honest, sociable, jovial, an interest in others, neat, ordinary, calm, stable, gentle, open, loyal and ethical. Behaviour is focused on sociability, domestic comfort, family activities, domestic environment, community life, striving for 'human standards and a responsible way of life'. Their style of communication is focused on listening to others, demonstrating empathy, and achieving consensus. From a socio-demographic point of view, these are families (often 4 to 5 people) or middle-aged post family people (few young people) with an average family income and an average level of education.

Comfort

The general profile that corresponds with this orientation is: focused on the purposive and efficient combination of various tasks (career, family, free time), the urge to manifest oneself, both at work and in society; life centres around a sort of controlled achievement: on the one hand this is about success and out-performing others; on the other hand, this always occurs within the framework of predictability and reliability. Knowledge is considered important as a way of maintaining control of developments ('knowledge is power'). The dominant personality characteristics are: sober, intelligent, businesslike, assertive, a leader, energetic, well-considered and status-conscious. Behaviour is characterised by functionality, inconspicuousness ('silent luxury' and not 'showing off'), dynamism ('busy, busy, busy') and thoughtfulness. Maintaining relationships with others is not considered particularly important, unless functional (the possibility to 'network'). Their style of communication is factual and sober. From a socio-demographic point of view, this profile concerns co-habitants and families in their thirties and forties, with an above-average income and a higher level of education.

Gain

The general profile that corresponds with this orientation is: focused on personal interests and material survival. The representatives of this orientation regard themselves as the victims of a society in which it is difficult to find one's way, or to hold one's own. The only way to survive, and to prove oneself in respect of others and society, is material success. At the same time, one withdraws to the safe frame of reference formed by one's own group. The dominant personality characteristics are: realistic, direct, reserved and status-oriented. Their behaviour is calculating and result-oriented, while their style of communication is informal, direct and short-tempered. From a socio-demographic point of view, these are groups with a relatively low level of education and below-average incomes. These people often live in areas on the outskirts of a city (older and post-war areas).

The above clustering into customers' orientations not only makes it possible to respond to the emotional factors that play a role in consumers' purchasing decisions, but also to take account of values that play an important role in their daily lives. Knowledge of customers' social environments enables companies and organisations to communicate in a more personal way with their customers, but also to respond better to customers' individual needs and wishes.

Chapter 6

The new manager: idealised image and reality

Willem Koot

Location and origin of the idealised image

When drawing up chronological summaries of academic thinking about top management and research into leadership, organisational scientists usually take the beginning of the twentieth century as their starting point. Reviews on the subject of management and leadership suggest that a great deal has been written on this topic before that time. However, this older body of work lacks the systematic academic approach adopted by Taylor in his theory of Scientific Management. Of course in the centuries prior to 1900 various authors had examined the relationship between people and work and it were these very publications that formed the solid foundations for Taylor's theory (see, for example, the fascinating studies on this subject by Ahrendt 1958, and Casey 1995). Taylor was one of the first to directly investigate management issues using an academic or scientific approach. Taylor felt that, in modern companies, the highest priority must be accorded to effectiveness and efficiency. In his vision, it was the duty of science to help develop techniques for achieving this end. He was presenting his ideas at a time when the repercussions of the industrial revolution were clearly visible. At that time, large-scale companies were in a period of rapid growth. This was accompanied by an increasing specialization of labour and by the differentiation of social classes. Workers had previously not been granted any involvement with the management of their company. Managers, on the other hand, had only very limited control over the company, since they had little influence over how the work was carried out. Taylor wanted to remove the existing contrasts between managers and workers. He therefore conceived an alternative system of rewards, one that he thought would yield benefits both for employers and employees.

In his 1916 publication, Fayol (himself a former top manager) further extended Taylor's instrumental/rational approach. He attempted to develop a general management theory, one that would apply to all types of organisation, both in the private and public sectors. Fayol believed that management can be learned, provided that a good theoretical model is available and that managers keep strictly to the rules that can be derived from the model. His own model consisted of three elements: a summary of management functions and management activities, and a list of what he referred to as the principles of management. For a considerable period of time, many of Fayol's ideas dominated managers' thinking (either implicitly or in the background) about what actually constituted management. Fayol regarded companies as living organisms, with various organs. He considered that all companies have six essential and interdependent functions: technical, commercial, financial, safety, auditing and management. The sixth function binds all the others together and must penetrate each and every 'organ'. It contains five components: *planning, organizing, commanding, coordinating* and *controlling.*

He also felt that managers should have a thorough knowledge of the employees, that they should provide a good example and that they should focus on the larger issues without involving themselves in details. Although Fayol does address the question of how to motivate and stimulate employees, his model is nevertheless markedly top-down and (as we previously indicated) instrumental/rational in nature. After all, the manager is by far the most important directional factor in the organisation, and controlling the perceived significance and meaning of events is based on rational principles and considerations of efficiency.

After Taylor and Fayol, as is well known, the 1930s and 1940s saw the rise of the Human Relations school created by Mayo and others. This increasingly accentuated the promotion of motivation and enhancing the employee's self-image. People became more interested in the importance of the informal organisation (and its leadership) as a means of achieving the organisation's objectives (see, for example, the ethnographic study carried out by Peter Blau in 1955, into interpersonal relationships in two government organisations). As regards to the manager's tasks, this meant that the qualities of being a mentor and communicator came to assume even more pivotal roles. Thus the ideal leader of an organisation should be a process manager with excellent social skills. Nevertheless, the instrumental/rational approach was not abandoned entirely, nor was Fayol's idea that monitoring is an important managerial task (cf. Watson 1994 and 1999; Alvesson and Willmott 1996).

For many decades there was little change in the dominant vision of organisational scientists with regard to the function of managers within organisations. However, the rise of the contingency theory, propounded by Mintzberg (1979) and others, meant a shift of emphasis to flexibility within the organisation and its management. Other work, such as that of Drucker (1954 and 1967) and Bass (1985), placed emphasis on the promotion of decentralization, self-management and empowerment of the employees. The cultural approach adopted by authors such as Peters and Watermann (1982), Schein (1985) and Senge (1990) led to an increased interest in the management of significance and meaning, and to creating a learning, diverse organisation. The theoretical discourse evolved from direction from above to direction from below, and from disciplining employees to self-disciplined employees. Another change was the move from rational, distant management that emphasized unity and stability, to inspirational, intuitive leadership that focused on diversity and change. Or, as Bass (1985) put it: from transactional to transformational leadership. The former is based on an exchange relationship between manager and employee in which mutual efforts and yields cancel one another out, and a contract-type concept governs internal labour relations. The objective is to motivate the employees to perform by creating good conditions (especially in material terms) in exchange for immediate, visible rewards. Transformational leadership is when a leader is capable of expanding and reinforcing the employees' needs, and of aligning these with the objectives of the organisation as a whole. A transformational leader shows confidence in himself and in his subordinates. He is reliable, and is very demanding when it comes to his own achievements and to those of others. He exhibits creative and innovative behaviour, formulates objectives and tasks in ideological terms, and displays marked commitment and conviction.

The theoretical developments outlined above have repercussions in terms of scientific research into the leadership of labour organisations. There are four distinct approaches, each with its own focus and often with its own preferred research method (cf. Bryman 1996). These approaches are set out in chronological order below.

Firstly, there is the *approach* that emphasizes the identification of *leadership qualities* (which dominated this field of research until the end of the 1940s). Researchers mainly focused on the question of what it was that distinguished leaders from non-leaders, generally based on the assumption that good leaders are born and that the right ones must be selected. Research on this approach is directed at three categories of characteristics: physical characteristics; capacities (intelligence, command of the language et cetera) and personality characteristics (such as degree of conservatism, being introverted or extroverted, and possessing self-confidence). At the end of the 1940s, the significance of research into leadership qualities was evaluated (e.g. Stogdill 1948). This made it clear that there were few conclusions capable of standing the test of time. As a result, interest in research into leadership qualities declined sharply. One of the few exceptions was Locke's (1991) research into successful leaders, which concluded that such individuals are characterized by a considerable degree of single-mindedness and a great deal of self-confidence and integrity.

The second is the *leadership style approach;* this reached its zenith between the 1950s and the 1970s. The implicit view is that leadership can be learned, and that emphasis should be given to training. The aim was to investigate certain styles in terms of their effects on the motivation, collaboration, achievements, satisfaction and/or organisational bonding of employees. This research primarily employed the survey method, in which a leader's subordinates were asked to fill in questionnaires about his behaviour. One of the best known research groups within this tradition was that of Stogdill, at Ohio State University in the USA. Among the results of the considerable amount of research work completed here was the provisional conclusion that achieving the organisation's goals could best be guaranteed by a combination of two styles. These were the 'initiating-structuring style' (in which the leader indicates exactly what the employees must do) and a 'companionable style' (which emphasizes being sympathetic towards the employees and winning their trust). However, later research increasingly cast doubt on the degree to which the relationships found could be generalized (by time, place and space). This laid the foundations for the next approach.

The *contingency approach*, which rose to great prominence in the 1970s and attracted a great deal of support. It was oriented towards further specifications of previously identified links between leadership styles and dependent variables such as employee satisfaction, achievements and collaboration, by elaborating situational factors. In this way, relationships were elaborated with the type of organisation and the degree to which a leader exercised control in a given situation. Fiedler (1967) in particular became known for his extensive and systematic research into the relationship between specific variables. These were task structure, the leader-employee relationship and the degree of control exerted by the leader in a given situation. He accumulated increasing 'evidence' to support the view that task-oriented leaders are most effective in extremely highly controlled and extremely poorly controlled situations. Relationship-oriented leaders were, on this evidence, most effective in moderately controlled situations. His method was a further refinement of that used by the Ohio researchers. While it is true that Fiedler also used the survey method, the questions used were often much more indirect and the range of optional answers was also much greater. Nevertheless, his conclusions and methods attracted some criticism. Different researchers were able to show that, in a given situation, the association differed slightly from that indicated by Fiedler. It is actually quite logical that this should happen, since the contingency approach is based on the assumption that the effectiveness of leadership and organisation form is situation-dependent. As a result, it is almost impossible to make universally applicable statements in this connection.

Increasing criticism of the work of researchers such as Fiedler meant that there was less interest in elaborating the associations between the known types of leadership styles and effectiveness. This reduced level of interest coincided with increasing doubts about the value of the rational/instrumental approach to management and organisation, and the rise of new ideas about leadership. This movement led to what became known as:

The new leadership approach. A central feature of this approach is the idea that the leader has an important job to do in terms of generating an organisational identity and a common perception of significance and meaning (or *corporate culture*, to use the jargon). As a *manager of meaning,* he is also responsible for formulating a mission and the associated *corporate values.* This cultural approach to management and organisation derives from the fact that many authors noted the differing levels of success between the contemporary Japanese and Western economies (cf. Koot and Hogema 1990). The difference in success was ascribed to the fact that, unlike their Western counterparts, Japanese managers made every effort to give their organisation a distinct image, to put quality above all else and to convince their employees that they belonged in this unique 'quality organisation'. Following the publication of the Peters and Watermann (1982) best-seller '*In Search of Excellence*', the cultural approach (and the associated new leadership approach) rapidly generated a great deal of hype among organisational scientists and managers. They reported on an analysis of fifty successful American companies, which showed that organisational culture was the single most important factor governing business success or failure. Suddenly everyone wanted to refashion organisational cultures along the lines suggested by authors such as Peters and Watermann.

This changed view of people and organisations was also reflected in the work carried out by researchers into leaders' behaviour. One group of researchers was important in the design of 'the new leadership approach'. Some of the more prominent members of this group were Burns (1978), Bass (1985) and Schein (1985). Following his research into the behaviour of political leaders, Bums introduced the previously mentioned dichotomy of transactional versus transformational leadership. As stated, the first type amounts to a contract being agreed between the leader (or political leader) and their followers. This involves the exchange of various services and types of support, both material and immaterial in nature. The second type of leadership has a much wider domain and a higher objective. It aims to elevate the aspirational and developmental level of the followers. A transformational leader has charisma, he is a visionary who is capable of inspiring and intellectually stimulating people. In the course of his theoretical and empirical research, Bass further elaborated Burn's ideas on this topic. He does not see the two styles as opposite ends of a continuum, but rather as dimensions that can be distinguished by analysis. Together, they encompass the ideal leadership style. Each style contains a number of components, for which quantitative indicators can be designated. Transformational leadership includes 4 components:

1. *charisma*: which expresses itself in the development of a vision and the leader eliciting pride, respect and trust.
2. *inspiration*: this is when the leader motivates people by creating high expectations and appropriate behaviour patterns (and developing symbols that reflect this), as well as providing guidance in the case of inappropriate behaviour.
3. *individual support*: this is the case when the leader gives his employees attention, respect and responsibility.
4. *intellectual stimulation*: this is when the leader continually provides challenges in the form of new ideas and approaches.

Transactional leadership covers the following two components:

1. The *provision of contingent rewards*: providing rewards when previously agreed performance indicators are met.
2. *Using the rule of management by exception*: mainly taking action and providing guidance when an activity related to a given task does not go entirely according to plan.

Bass has done a great deal of empirical research within a variety of organisational settings in the USA. The employees were given questionnaires containing questions relating to the components defined by Bass, and the answers were processed statistically. One of the results of this research was that the components 'charisma' and 'inspiration' greatly increase the chance of achieving the organisation's objectives.

Schein is the third author to give a major intellectual stimulus to the 'new leadership approach'. He concentrated primarily on the leader's role in setting up an organisational culture. According to his vision, the leader is the most important culture 'maker' and culture bearer. This is certainly the case when the leader is also the person who actually founded the organisation in question. The management of culture is one of the leader's core tasks: '*the unique and essential function of leadership is the manipulation of culture*' (1985: 317). Schein sees the organisational culture as the cement of the organisation as it provides cohesion, identification and collaboration. Re rates a culture as 'strong' when the majority of those in the organisation share in the culture, and 'appropriate' when that culture enables the organisation to survive and to achieve success. In other words, the culture in question must have an integrative and adaptive function. These functions contain different elements around which values are developed by the group in question. For the adaptive function, these are: the mission and strategy; the organisational objectives; the means to achieve the objectives; the method of measuring the results; the method of correction.

For the integrative function: these are common language and conceptual categories; group limits and criteria for inclusion and exclusion; power and status; intimacy and friendship; rewarding and punishing; ideology and religion. After a time, these values will not merely form a pattern, they will also lead to a number of basic assumptions about the relationship between people and nature; about the nature of truth and reality; about the essence of human nature; human activities and human relationships (Ibid.: 86). Schein borrowed these basic assumptions from the work of Kluckhohn and Strodtbeck (1961). These authors carried out large-scale cross-cultural research to identify the questions to which each group or culture must formulate a reply. Schein made the major assumption that a culture (or organisational culture) can only be said to exist when the majority of the group members share the explicitly or implicitly agreed values, and where the group has shown stability and continuity. '*If such groups can be defined as stable units with a shared history of experience, they will have developed their own cultures*' (1985: 8). One way in which this stability is expressed is when it has developed answers to the universal questions posed by Kluckhohn and Strodtbeck. The main issue for him is that the leader must create a sense of community and uniformity , as well as a standardization of solutions to the problems posed by the surrounding environment. The visions of cultures can 'age', in which case they will need to be brought up to date. This can be associated with considerable resistance from the employees, since they felt secure with the existing culture. A powerful leader, however, will show them the way in a voyage of discovery to find new values, rituals and symbols. Schein developed his theory on the basis of his years of experience as a consultant. His method of research could be described as qualitative-reflective. Using a systematic series of participational observations, he reflected on the existing understanding of organisational culture. He then used these reflections to develop his own theory. His use of qualitative research methods distinguished Schein from the majority of leadership researchers who, advocated a quantitative, detached approach.

During the past two decades, researchers such as Mintzberg, Bass and Schein have exerted an enormous influence over the debate about organisations and management. Nevertheless, the work done by Peters and Watermann (much of whose work was aimed at a wider public) also had an enormous impact. It generated a great deal of hype among managers and their advisors at the start of the 1980s, primarily in association with themes such as organisational culture, *management of meaning* and transformational leadership. With the publication of their book, and an associated series of lectures, they managed to establish the idea that an organisation's success or failure are largely determined by certain specific factors. One such factor is the possession of a unitary culture characterized by an external orientation, flexibility, innovation and self-direction. The other factors are that this culture must be 'makable' and that the leader is the most important culture bearer and culture maker. Thus the leader even considers the self-directing nature of the organisation to be something that is 'makable'. According to the prevailing view, the leader is the person who has to generate the conditions required for the creation of self-direction. To this end, he provides sufficient space for personal initiative and must be capable of delegating responsibilities. In addition, he must check that delegated tasks have indeed been carried out and that undesirable behaviour is corrected. As a symbolic leader, he can show exemplary self-directing behaviour, by radiating self confidence. In this way, he can make an additional contribution to the process of cultural change (cf. Hartog, Koopman and Muyen 1997).

One of the consequences of the success of '*In Search of Excellence*' was that virtually all organisations attempted to convert to the requisite culture by means of training courses and structural changes. But it did not stop there, they also did everything possible to polish up their own image and that of their leader. It was essential that the outside world should have the impression that the organisation in question was a cohesive unit and that its members operated as a team. Accordingly, considerable attention was devoted to uniformity of appearance (in terms of clothing, for example) and presentation (company logo, for example).

In addition, the organisational science literature (both the serious publications and more popular ones) increasingly circulated stories about successful leaders, some of whom even obtained the status of comic-book heroes. Such stories presented the leader as an almost mythical figure. As a result, there was less interest in middle management.

The majority of publications came to consist of prescriptive, contemplative and rather abstract texts, which devoted little or no attention to the everyday life of the average manager. The road to success is paved with stories about how things should be done, rather than real-life situations such as how managers cope with the exalted expectations generated by the models of successful leaders.

Hypes and trends have not escaped the notice of Dutch managers. In many popular publications (magazines such as Quote, Elan and Management Team) ideas about vision, charisma, empowerment, empathy and the like appear to be gaining in prominence. Trendy news magazines, such as Quote, Elan, Management Team and Dutch, feature articles about successful top managers. These stories reveal boundless adoration and mystification of the leaders of large labour organisations, especially companies involved in the 'new economy'. The Dutch top manager still has an image of being able to make tough business decisions. In addition, as a consequence of the Dutch Polder Model (a type of decision-making by broad consensus), he is also seen as being able to listen effectively to the views held by his employees on a wide range of issues. He is also visualized as an outstanding example of a team player. It may well be that the inconsistencies in these images can be interpreted as an incompletely developed reaction to a period in which the opposite approach (a coldly rational, administrative one) was at centre stage. In other words, this is a type of equilibration. However, management literature is enormously influential and this continues to affect the general image of managers, even in the minds of managers themselves. The images held of managers and presented for them in more popular publications vary from 'cuddly teddy bear' (Kets de Vries 1999) to 'Great Helmsman' and 'hard men'.

How should these conflicting, idealized images be viewed? The answer is to be found by placing the development of these images in the context of modernization processes.

The new manager and the post-modern world

The image of the new manager is a logical response to the social and economic developments that have taken place in recent years as a result of the radicalized ideals of the Enlightenment. The most marked characteristics of this modernization process are greatly enhanced individualization and rationalization, however, these have several paradoxical consequences (Baudrillard 1990 and 1994, and Van der Loo and Van Reyen 1993). The original goal was to liberate the individual and to allow people to come to grips with their social and natural environments. This finally led to the destruction of various hierarchical structures and of some heavy yokes imposed by traditions, kinship networks, local communities and religious ties. At the same time, a new lack of freedom has developed, since individuals must gain control of their own behaviour through self-constraint. In addition, people have become more dependent on specialists. Enormous improvements in technological know-how have given us more power over nature, although one might suppose that nature can strike back ever more aggressively.

We are becoming increasingly aware of these risks of modernization through a process of computerization and globalization (Beck 1992). As a consequence of social fragmentation and in response to it, individuals are increasingly developing lifestyles of their own and are less and less likely to take on permanent commitments. Identities become 'overcoats, that one puts on or takes off as one pleases' (Baumann 1995). This means that the behaviour of other people is less predictable, which increases the uncertainty still further. This appreciation of the risks of modernization and the associated uncertainty explains why, in recent years, so much emphasis has been placed on the concepts of 'trust', 'self-confidence' and 'relationships' (Koot in: Wels, Smets and van Loon, 1999). We have to trust others and to enter into relationships with them if we are to avoid being defeated by doubts and fears. In recent years, various authors on modernization (like Giddens 1991; Maffesoli 1997 and Baumann 1995) have asked themselves how we can best develop trust and self-confidence. Giddens believes that trust involves a lot of hard work: 'Trust on a personal level becomes a project, to be worked at by the parties involved and demands the opening out of the individual to the other' (Ibid.: 121). He feels that this comes down to a mutual process of opening up. In turn, the latter requires self reflection, which should lead to a clear image of one's own identity and insight into one's own successful (and less successful) survival strategies. Maffesoli (1996) is firmly convinced that entering into relationships (albeit temporary ones) with others is an absolute precondition for survival in this fragmented and individualized society. He feels that opening oneself up to others generates life force. In taking this view he is resurrecting Durkheim's concept of the 'conscience collective' as the most primitive form of religion (the Latin word 'religare' actually means to tie up). Maffesoli anticipates that this need to share experiences and interests, intensively but temporarily (he refers to these relationships as the 'new tribes'), win continue to grow. However, he provides little empirical data to support this statement. Baumann also argues strongly in favour of entering more relationships but, unlike Giddens and Maffesoli, he emphasises that these should be not calculative and conditional. The only way to obtain genuine affection and (mutual) commitment is to give yourself fully into a relationship with another person.

Merry (1995) takes an entirely different line. He feels that individuals must develop a 'mutual self', and that they must aspire to 'disidentification'. In his terms this involves casting off all heavy yokes imposed by traditions, loyalties and group identities. Only then can a person be truly free.

The question is, how do Dutch managers handle these new images, especially with regard to their conflicting content (creating flexibility while at the same time introducing bonding and cohesion; giving direction while at the same time encouraging self-direction in others etc.). I will answer this briefly here, using the results of our recent study on how Dutch top managers survive life at the top (Koot and Sabelis 2000).

The image in everyday life: how do Dutch managers deal with the new images (and their paradoxical nature)?

The organisational and management debate is currently focusing on concepts such as trust, self-direction, chaos management, corporate identity and the like. This debate is of a paradoxical nature and there are conflicting elements involved within a broader theoretical, historical context. The same is true of the contrasting ideal images of a top manager. On the one hand, according to the management gurus, they must act decisively, radiate self-confidence, be result-oriented and binding. On the other hand, they must have an eye for diversity and must be culturally sensitive, facilitating and supportive. To put it another way, they must be hot and cold at the same time. Even if they are aware of this paradox, it won't cost them a moment's sleep. Their actual focus is maintaining and extending their position of power. In this endeavour they rely to a large extent on their intuition (as shown by the research carried out by Mintzberg in the 1970s and more recent work by Watson and Harris 1999, and Noordergraaf 2000) and on technical considerations, with associated values such as control, efficiency and linearity. Up front ('front stage'), they often present themselves as a supporter and advocate of the calm, deliberate approach, of self-direction, decentralisation, empowerment, chaos theory and 'the art of letting go'. In their hearts ('backstage'), they rate themselves and one another according to their success in creating the impression of being someone who 'has everything under control'. These individuals have virtually no personal affinity to the soft values, and certainly not in the context of their profession. Oddly, while they are aware that they have not mastered some processes and that they will therefore have to rely on their intuition, they fail to draw the obvious conclusion that the management ideal is nothing less than utopian. They continue to bombard each other with macho demands that they can never hope to fulfil. By increasingly coming into contact with other top managers and by attending symposia on new management and the new manager, they are increasingly reminded of who they are in relation to the ideal image (derived from both their 'front stage' and 'backstage'). The reflectiveness which is a consequence of these 'meetings' extends their self-knowledge, but often their uncertainty as well. This would appear to confirm the assumption by Knights and Willmott (1999: 77) that, 'self-consciousness is a condition of anxiety and insecurity'. It also appears to undermine Giddens' (1991: 21) hypothesis concerning the relationship between reflectiveness about the self, opening up and uncertainty. Giddens assumes that reflectiveness is a good antidote to the increasing uncertainty in western civilization that has been produced by the loss of traditions and 'the disembedding of the social system'.

So, top managers certainly fail to satisfy the requirements of the ideal image. These are not supermen nor are they heroes, they are by no means visionaries and often do not possess the qualities considered essential by the gurus. How then do they maintain their position (in spite of or thanks to this observation) at the top, given all their uncertainties and fears. How do they manage to survive? The most important survival strategies are: the use of bombast and verbal force, the use of specific forms of humour, flaunting know-how, the use of power strategies and coercion strategies, denial, considerable qualification and both mental and physical adaptation. The latter clearly exceeds the strictly formal performance requirements of their profession as a manager. The adaptation has become a habit or, as Bourdieu (1990) put it: an ingrained behaviour pattern of which one is barely aware. This continues in the informal sphere and, sometimes, even in the home environment. This was exemplified by Hannah van der Pas sitting (fully dressed and made up) at her desk at home at five o'clock in the morning, ready for a conference call with people who could not even see her.

Our study provides some insights into how Dutch managers cope with the paradoxical nature of the ideal images. This will nevertheless have to be followed by numerous ethnographical studies if we are to obtain a detailed picture of the various sectors of the Dutch economy. It would, for example, be interesting to obtain data on the group of young 'dot-com' managers. At first glance they appear to be the complete opposite of Koot and Sabelis's target group. They are young, and they were raised in an environment of cultural fragmentation and increasing individualization. They may have considerably fewer problems in dealing with paradoxes and ambiguity. Such intergenerational research should also be capable of showing whether we are at the threshold of a genuine paradigm shift, and whether the western controlling mindset is on its last legs.

Some closing remarks

We have identified various approaches in the theoretical and popular debate on the subject of the ideal manager. There are those that focus on the dimensions of leadership and there is the *managerial behaviour* approach. Especially in the former approach, the knowledge generated on this topic has the following characteristics: prescriptive, model-based, poorly descriptive, decontextualized, displaying pretensions of universal applicability and paying scant attention to perceptions, feelings, emotions, insecurities and fears, social environment, culture and identity of top managers.

Until recently, the studies of Pahl, 1995, and those of Watson and Harris, 1999, carried out on British managers were the major exceptions. Most studies give very little details about the everyday lives of managers as creatures of flesh and blood who, with all their doubts and insecurities, enormous responsibilities for themselves and for the people in their organisations, and a wide variety of 'baggage' (picked up along the way, some of it their professional lives, some in other contexts) have somehow to keep their heads above water.

References

Aken, J. & J. Strikwerda (1997). De onbewuste organisatie. *M&O. Tijdschrift voor organisatiekunde en Sociaal Beleid*, 4, 7–28.

Alvesson, M. & H. Willmott (1996). *Making sense of management, a critical introduction*. London: Sage.

Bass, B.M. (1985). *Leadership and Performance beyond expectations*. New York: Free Press.

Baudrillard, J. (1983). *Les strategies fatales*. Paris: Grasset.

Baudrillard, J. (1988). *Selected Writings*. Oxford: Polity Press.

Baudrillard, J. (1990). *La transparance du mal*. Paris: Galilee.

Baudrillard, J. (1994). *Simulacra and simulation*. Ann Arbor: The University of Michigan Press.

Baumann, Z. (1995). *Life in Fragments*. Oxford: Blackwell.

Beck, U. (1992). *Risk Society*. London: Sage.

Beck, U., A. Giddens & S. Lash (1994). *Reflexive modernization. Politics, tradition and aesthetics in the modem social order*. Cambridge: Polity Press.

Bourdieu, P. (1990). *The logic of practice*. Stanford University Press.

Brymann, A. (1996). Leadership in Organisations. In S. Clegg (Ed.), *Handbook of Organization Studies*. London: Sage.

Bums, J. (1978). *Leadership*. New York: Harper & Row.

Drucker, P. (1954). *The practice of* managemen. New York: Harper & Row.

Drucker, P. (1967). *The effective executive*. New York: Harper & Row.

Giddens, A. (1991). *The consequences of modernity*. London: Sage.

Hartog, D., P. Koopman & J. Muyen (1997). *Inspirerend leiderschap in organisaties*. Schoonhoven: Academic Service.

Pascale, R.T. (1990). *Managing on the edge: how successful companies use conflict to stay ahead*. London: Penguin Books.

Peters, T.J. & Waterman, R.J. (1982). *In search of excellence: lessons from America's best run companies*. New York: Harper & Row.

Kets de Vries, M. (1995). *Life and death in the executive fast lane*. San Francisco: Jossey-Bass.

Luckhohn, F. & F. Strodtbeck (1961). *Variations in value orientations*. New York: Harper and Row.

Koot, W. & I. Hogema (1990). *Organisatiecultuur. Fictie of werkelijkheid?* Bussum: Coutinho.

Koot, W. & I. Sabelis (2000). *Overleven aan de Top, managers in complexe tijden*, Utrecht: Lemma.

Hope, V. & J. Hendry (1996). Corporate cultural change, is it relevant for the organizations of the 1990's? *Human Resource Management Journal*, 5 (4), 61–73.

Loo, van der H. & W. van Reyen (1997). *Paradoxen van modernisering*. Bussum: Coutinho.

Loo, van der H. & M. Giljam (1995). De blinde vlekken van Total Quality Management. *M&O*, 49, 494–506. [The blind spots of Total Quality Management].

Maffesoli (1996). *The new tribes*. London: Sage.

Senge, P. M. (1990). *The fifth discipline: the art and the practice of the learning organization*. New York: Doubleday Currency.

Merry, U. (1995). *Coping with uncertainty*. Westort: Preager.

Mintzberg, H. (1979). *The structuring of organizations*. New York: Prentice Hall.

Pahl, R. (1995). *After Success*. Cambridge: Polity Press.

Perrow, Ch. (1986). *Complex organizations*. New York: Random House.

Peters, T. & R. Watermann (1982). *In search of excellence*. New York: Harper & Row.

Schein, E. (1985). *Organizational culture and leadership*. San Francisco: Jossey Bass.

Senge, P. (1990). *The fifth discipline*. New York: Double day.

Smets, P., H. Wels & J. van Loon (1999). *Trust and Cooperation*. Amsterdam: Het Spinhuis.

Stacey, R. (1996). *Complexity and creativity in organizations*. San Francisco: Berrett-Koehler Press.

Stogdill, R. (1948). Personal factors associated with leadership. *Journal of Psychology*. 25, 35–71.

Taylor, F. (1911). *The Principles of scientific Management*. New York: W. Norton.

Veld in 't, R. (Ed.) (1991). *Autopoiesis and configuration theory: new approaches tot societal steering*. Dordrecht: Kluwer.

Watson, T. (1994). *In search of management. Culture, chaos and control in managerial work*. London: Routledge.

Watson, T. & P. Harris (1999). *The Emergent manager*. London: Sage.

Zegers, R. (1997). Angst en zelfsturing in organisaties. *Management en Organisatie*. 6, 60–91, Alphen aan de Rijn: Samsom.

Chapter 7

The new employee

Ton Korver

The new employee: an elusive concept

The concept of the 'new employee' was born in a period of swift conceptual changes, all relating to an apparently long felt need for making the firm more flexible in its multi-faceted adaptation to an ever more complex and demanding environment. The emphasis on adaptability was accompanied by a strong accent on the redesign of the organizational system. This represented the demand side of the equation, the organizational constraint, while the concept of the 'new employee' pointed to the supply side, the labour constraint.

The concept had a short career only. It came, was popularized – through the media and with some help of the consultant community and a few hesitant echoes within the walls of academic world – and then disappeared to be replaced by the concept of employability. Its disappearance is wellnigh total. In indexes of recently published books, compendiums, periodicals and research reports the entry of the 'new employee' is missing practically without exception – it be then to deny its existence (Fruytier 1998: 37, Halman 1998). One of the authors/consultants who popularized the concept soon after it had made its first appearance in one or two dailies changed his own use of the concept within the year. What had been 'the new employee' in 1994 had become 'employability' in 1995 (Bolweg/De Korte 1994; Bolweg/Maenhout 1995). Why this short and unhappy career?

Every time a new cohort of people enters the labour market speculations emerge as to their demands, expectations and visions *vis-à-vis* work and employment. Given an on average rising educational level and given the picking up of employment during the nineties, the idea was that the rewards of work were destined to grow. Work would have to be attractive, challenging and paying. On the other hand, the recent period not only witnessed a new age cohort in the labour market. Next to youngsters, married women occupy a continually expanding slice of the occupational population (mainly as part-time workers), and the demographic composition of the labour force has changed (relatively few youngsters, relatively many workers of 40 and over). Finally, all projections point to the future dependence on the inflow in the labour market of members from minority categories (SCP 1998, see 'diversity', below).

On the demand side we find a series of deep changes in the make-up of organizations. Sectoral shifts (in particular the growing dominance of the service sector of the economy), international developments (New Industrialising Countries and 'Asian tigers', processes of globalisation and 'glocalisation', the consolidation of regional trade blocs, including the EU), information technology, and customization have reduced and enlarged the scale and scope of organizations at the same time. Firms grow in scale and/or scope, through mergers, joint ventures and 'networks'. Yet, work organizations tend to shrink through decentralization, downsizing, outsourcing, a focus on core activities and competencies. Bridging these intertwined developments in work and employment we find, rather suddenly but with the benefit of hindsight hardly surprising, the concept of the 'new employee'. Apparently, the concept had much ground to cover. Too much ground, I would say.

In 1993 several dailies in the Netherlands noticed that the times had changed. New employment relations had come to the fore (flexible and part-time contracts in particular), the male breadwinner as the typical employee was losing out to double or one-and-a-half careers, work in the market for services fueled the job machine (distributive, producer, social and personal services; see Castells 1996: 203 ff), married women became regulars in the labour market, and the societal process of 'individualization' eroded traditional patterns and bonds of solidarity. The 'calculating citizen' made its appearance and supposedly coloured the image of the 'new employee' (Bolweg/De Korte 1994: 5–7).

On investigation though, the concept of the new employee reflected the disappearance of the presumed role model of the family man (the 'male breadwinner') rather than the emergence of a new typical type of employee. The new employee is the product of a change in the composition of the labour supply. Therefore, new demands on the combination and the division of work, welfare and care appear on the scene, as do new patterns in part-time employment and new articulations of company-time and working times. These new demands and patterns have not led to a new typical employment regime. Rather, heterogeneity rules. Only one factor turns out to be a constant. That is the overarching significance of a focus on the 'primary process', as distinct from support processes and governance processes (Bolweg/De Korte 1994: 55–56, 96). Employees demand demanding jobs, and demanding jobs demand demanding employees. Normatively, then, something has changed.

We end up with two normative parameters, in our preliminary sketch of the concept. One is the changing composition of the labour supply and the norms by which its availability is judged, the second is the normative meaning of the primary process. In the following paragraphs I will explore these parameters. In the concluding paragraph I will return to the concept of the new employee as such. Two dimensions will be offered, one relating the labour supply ('the entrepreneurial employee' and 'diversity and opportunity'), the other to the primary process ('the employee as self-design').

Sectoral changes

From manufacturing to services

Seven out of every ten jobs in the Netherlands are service jobs. Not even two out of ten are in manufacturing. These figures of the year 1995 signal a remarkable shift in the sectoral composition of the Dutch economy in just a few decades. Starting already from a relatively high level, the trend towards services has been accelerating in the second half of the century. In 1960 four out of ten jobs were in the service sector and also four in manufacturing (Van Beek 1998: 49). In 1970 we counted almost three jobs in ten in manufacturing and five and a half in services. Today we have a service sector almost three and a half times as large in employment as the manufacturing sector. And the expectation is a further growth in services (CPB 1992). Within services social services (including health care) during the eighties and producer services (including banking and insurance) during the nineties have been the fastest growing segments. In the distributive services (including wholesale and retail) and the personal services (including hotels and restaurants) the growth has been modest (SCP 1998: 362). Of course, growth of the service sector is not a trend that is unique for the Netherlands. In the US we see the same pattern, as we do in Japan, Germany, France, and the United Kingdom. Canada differs somewhat from the general picture: the rise in social services is very small, the rise in personal services very outspoken (Castells 1996: 282–295, tables 4.1–4.4 and 4.6–4.7). Comparatively, the service sector is rather large in the Netherlands, as it is in the US, Canada and the UK. In Japan the sector is much smaller, although Japan is catching up and moves in the same direction as other highly developed economies. The size of the sector in the Netherlands is historical heritage, partly, (the sector always has been large in the Netherlands, larger in the nineteenth century than agriculture and larger in the twentieth than manufacturing; Van Beek 1998: 48–49), and reflects the very strong international orientation of the Dutch economy, and, of course, it is (or: has been) a salute to a comparatively strong welfare state. If we want to find the new employee we will have to look at services.

From things to people and symbols

If we are to perform our job we need information, we need materials, and usually we need colleagues and supervisors (although the latter category has become a little suspect these days)[1]. We are depending on things, people and symbols. But the degree to which we depend on them differs between industries and sectors. We have grown accustomed to thinking about manufacturing in terms of the transformation of things first, and with information (orders, procedures) and people second and third. Today we are learning to look at manufacturing differently. We now perceive it as work in which the co-operation of workers in teams and the expert handling of information by teams, determine the image. The move in the world of work from working on things to working on people and on symbols is not aloof, then, from the developments within manufacturing. Manufacturing work comes to resemble work in the service sector. Firms hire people whom they deem to be qualified in communicative ('you must be able to communicate your expertise to your colleagues and clients, whether internal or external') and social-normative ('we want you to like to work in a team') competencies. This holds in manufacturing as it does in services and it also holds for lower level jobs (Van Veen/Wielers 1998; Hövels et al. 1999). Producing becomes servicing.

In the service sector proper this is of course quite outspoken. Whether we discuss social services or producer services, the image of work is focused on clients and customers. In social services (dubbed 'in-person services' by Reich 1992) contacts with clients is direct and an integral part of the job. The consequence is that fulfilling the job and its requirements is dependent on the consent and sometimes also the co-operation of the client. Although many of the jobs involved may look like routine jobs just like we find in manufacturing, the simple fact that completion of the job cannot be separated from the acceptance of the client does make a difference. The emphasis on social normative competencies ('service with a smile') and communicative competencies ('helping clients to define and express their needs') is an obvious corollary of this dependence. In the producer services the situation is comparable. It is likely that in part of these services (think of consulting agencies and intermediaries of all kinds and shapes) the communication and the processing of information (the manipulation of symbols in Reich's vocabulary; Reich 1992) looms so large that it seems to overshadow the social-normative competencies. But it should not be forgotten that there, too, communicative competencies are moot without a backing in trust and expectations, and thus in norms and practices of interaction between pro-

---

[1] Due to the introduction of new information technologies and to new forms of work organization supervising as a *function* is becoming everybody's responsibility, to the detriment of supervising as a *position*, i.e. as a specific category of personnel. The waning of 'middle management', a major target in reorganizing and downsizing activities, is the obvious example.

ducer and client. To sum up: not only are we most likely to find the new employee in the service sector, we may also expect the new employee to have a client orientation, based in competencies of a social-normative and communicative vintage.

We cannot infer from the above that these competencies derive from higher educational achievements. The level of education and certification in the working population is certainly rising, as are the educational requirements by employers. On the other hand, these tendencies are not exclusive for the service sector since we meet with them in manufacturing as well (Asselberghs et al. 1998). And again: the tendency of a rising educational level of the working population does not mean that the quality of work is rising along. On that score the developments in the Netherlands over the past twenty five years show a rather mixed picture. The most recent period is characterized by some upgrading of work, accompanied however by a slight tendency of polarization (SCP 1998: 364–365). The latter tendency is underscored by statistics on the occurrence of physically heavy and noisy work: both have been rising in the period between 1974 and 1996 (ibid: 366). We don't need manufacturing for physically heavy work; the health care sector, cleaning, restaurants and hotels and other personal services abound with examples of heavy, and at times noisy, working conditions. Working in services may well mean unsatisfactory working conditions and an underutilization of human capital.

Competitive advantage through people

From personnel to resource

Who is the worker? Is s/he a labourer, a member of the working class, an employee, a unit of human capital or a resource, the rockbed of competencies? The designation of personnel has changed several times in the past decades. Arguably the major rift was established when the economic perception of labour was transformed from *cost* into *investment*. Whether we want to attribute the new perception to the *Sputnik*-effect in the USA, or to a new mood in studying the sources of economic growth, the fact is that the old distinction between capital and labour was replaced by a distinction within the category of capital. Next to physical or material capital we now find human or immaterial capital. In the social sciences the concept of human capital got differentiated as economic capital (education, training, experience), social capital (the company we keep, the people we know) and cultural or symbolic capital (the language we speak, the *habitus* we entertain) (Bourdieu 1989; Gouldner 1979). In a sense this strengthened the economic impact of the capital-concept for it now looked as if the people we have for company and acquaintances, and the languages we live by, are the product of investment decisions just like the choice of one's education. The pivotal importance of one's *curriculum vitae* is just a recent illustration. One's CV gives the image of a stream of investment decisions in a career.

The concept of human *resources* is more lenient than the capital concept. It became popular in the seventies and eighties and pointed to the fact that, unlike capital, the use of human capabilities does not exhaust or use up one's investment but instead adds to it, augments it. The usual economic idea of diminishing returns proved powerless in explaining the increasing returns of human resources (much like the metaphor of the 'new economy'; Kelly 1998, or of 'conducive production'; Karasek 1999)[2]. Today, the concept of human resources is in full force. Its most recent offspring is the image of competencies. Competencies point to the utility of human resources for future, as yet mainly latent, purposes, and the idea is that before the present use of human resources is improved upon by the competition (or simply: gets imitated), new fields of application for the resources of the company should be implemented. Before the learning curve of present uses has run its complete course, a new learning curve must be started. Competencies are capabilities which outpace the present uses of resources. The significance of improving upon your present performance is overshadowed by the significance of inventing new performances (Prahalad 1998).

Employability is the conditional aspect of competence. Like the latter, the concept of employability refers to human resources as a multi-purpose quality that derives its value as much from the uses it *may* be put to as from the actual uses it *is* put to (Gaspersz and Ott 1996; Thijssen 1997). Its focus is on the individual employee and on the responsibility all employees are assumed to carry for *designing* their own careers. The new employee, in conclusion, cannot build the future out of the past. What one did, and did successfully, yesterday holds no credits for tomorrow. Experience is nog longer a fund in which newer achievements add to former ones. Promotions, for example, are no longer a reward for services well rendered. Rather than reflecting proven competence, promotions ar granted on the base of expected competence in the face of new organizational challenges. The past is not so much a *datum* as it is a construction, designed to demonstrate its usefulness for the future. The new employee is under pressure to recreate the past *selectively* through inserting it in the design of her/his own future career. What the new employee wanted yesterday and wants today is determined by

---

[2] Adepts of the 'new economy' like Kelly stress that value does not reside in scarcity but in abundance: the pleasure you derive from your gsm increases with the number of other people using one. The -plausible- idea is that this holds for most of the products and services in the field of communication media. Increasing returns, then, are the result of expanding networks of and opportunities for communication. Likewise, the concept of a 'conducive' economy (Karasek) underscores the fruits of interaction and communication within the processes of production and in the ties that bind producers and consumers. Here too, new technologies like JAVA are among the more prominent examples.

what s/he plans to want tomorrow. We live in a world of expected and discounted, but not yet realized, options on the future. The new employees, mind you, do not own the future. If anything, the reverse holds: the future owns them. We can try and go for any career we think worthwhile but we cannot *not* want a career.

From management to mobilisation

Human resources can not be managed. What we can manage are the *conditions* under which we employ resources. Think of adequate working conditions, a learning environment, attractive payment systems, fair employment contracts and so on. These we can manage and we do so in the expectation that the right conditions will *mobilise* human resources. We can manage conditions, not outcomes. We manage to mobilise, not the other way around (De Sitter 1994; Christis 1998). Mobilisation unleashes ('empowers') productive capability by stimulating the primary process and inviting worker creativity, innovation and autonomous problem-solving. Consequently, managerial authority and prerogative no longer exists in designing operational structures, meant to direct and constrain the behaviour of employees. Managerial authority today is dedicated not to designing work *structures* but to work *systems,* their co-ordination and their fine-tuning (emergent rather than imposed) to organizational strategies. Authority must be systemic, not structural (whether this will lead to a crisis in the employment defining authority relationship, is an interesting point not elaborated upon in the present context. Van der Heijden 1998)[3]. In fact, the decisions to structure employee behaviour are not made beforehand and once-and-for-all. They are spread out in time as much as possible, only to be struck if the situation (for example, the completion of an order) so requires. Moreover, such decisons (who is going to do what with what means and methods and in what sequence) are taken by operational systems (teams, projects, units and so on), not by managerial *fiat.* Think of what Gareth Morgan called the principles of self-organization or holographic design (principles which have been claimed for the design practice of modern sociotechnics): redundancy of functions, minimum critical specification, learning to learn and requisite

---

[3] The employment relationship is, in terms of authority, a promise of the employee to work under the supervision and direction of the employer. But then, what is left of authority, once workers supervise themselves, and direct their own activities in the context of autonomous work teams? This, according to Van der Heijden, is the core of the 'crisis' alluded to. The obvious answer to the 'crisis' is, of course, that authority under these conditions must become a systemic property, that it shifts to the system of which the teams are a part, and with the system made operational through well designed and well monitored forms of renumeration, recruitment (for example: invitations to join project teams), promotion and demotion and so forth. However, realizing these has so far proved a very vexing problem. See: Buitendam 2001, Sanders 2000.

variety (Morgan 1986: 99; Kuipers and Van Amelsvoort 1990: 132–133). The first three principles play down the issue of structure, the fourth principle underscores the importance of adequate and flexible system design. Accordingly, the new employee is not a subordinate taking orders from a boss. S/he is not the product of other-design but of self-design. Non-replicable human resources, i.e. resources that cannot readily be copied by competitors, (the gist of 'competitive advantage through people'; Pfeffer 1994: Gómez-Mejía et al. 1998: xxix):

a. exhibit the redundancy of employability: employees possess and develop a surplus of capabilities in the actual performance of their tasks (redundacy of functions)
b. do not follow pre-specified steps but specify their doings along the way of discharging tasks and assignments including contacts with suppliers and customers (minimum critical specification)
c. learn and get further developed through constant self-monitoring (Sabel 1994) and adjustment of performance and standards (learning to learn) and, finally
d. match the complexity and ambiguity of their environment by means of their own competencies (requisite variety)

This, to be sure, is the normative story of the new world of work and the presumed match of this world with the new supply of labour. The contemporary message (for example: Gibson 1998) is: get bright or get lost.[4] A moment's reflection will tell us that this in itself can hardly be classified as a bright message. Not all of us will get bright – unless we want the word to become meaningless. And those of us who receive the message to get lost will, I hope and expect, refuse to do so. Yet, the message is not rubbish, either. Many are the stories about a threatening two-tier society, with information-winners and -losers divided by an opportunity gap that tends to widen rather than to shrink. Many, again, are the initiatives by governments and private organizations to counter the causes and effects of the divide. That, too, is part and parcel of the world of the new employee.

Employees with less competitive position: equal opportunity and diversity

It is high time, then, to shift our attention to those categories of workers (among whom many women, older workers, the long-term unemployed, the underskilled and – schooled, the ethnic minorities, school-leavers and drop-

---

[4] As we learn from Sennett (1998) the message had better be read as: get bright, even though you will get lost all the same.

outs) for whom the market produces only, to put it mildly, suboptimal effects. In the new, Dutch as well as European, atmosphere of promoting labour market participation and of tying labour market participation to notions of active citizenship, the integration ('inclusion') of these categories is high on the agenda. To be sure, initiatives to correct labour market arrears and discriminations are not new. Yet, the focus on 'inclusion' is. I will now turn to initiatives of diversity.

Diversity

In the realm of politics and the law it is taken for granted that humans differ. The goal is to respect differences, for differences add to the richness of our social and cultural textures. That we are all different is, paradoxically, the one quality we all share, as it defines us as members of the world of humans. Respecting differences means to assign a neutral value to the definitional inequalities associated with them. In politics we have learned to do so: citizenship is a uniform status[5], none can cast more votes than the other and votes all carry the same weight. Respecting differences and neutralizing their effects, also, leads to a politics of equal opportunities and chances, serving as constraints on markets and competitive processes. The constraints have the effect of making differences irrelevant and even invisible: what should count is what people can accomplish, irrespective of where they got their education, where they came from, what their sex, age, colour, religion, sexual preference, life style and so on and so forth is. Difference, in this perspective, is radically different from what today is being hailed as 'diversity'. Diversity and especially diversity *management* are competitive and tied to cherishing distinctions. Distinctions are their *raison d'être*. Diversity is becoming popular, precisely because it acknowledges and even celebrates visibility: the difference makes all the difference[6].

The concept of diversity fits in with multicultural societies, in which dominant and minority cultures all strive for – and should be in a position to count on – equal respect. Equal respect of diverse cultures is not, witness the difficulties surrounding for example the headscarf of Muslim females, an easy accomplishment[7]. And it should not be easy: the Dutch constitution (or, for that matter, the American one) is 'colour-blind', while diversity definitely is colourful and may even claim the image of a 'rainbow'.

In the discussion on equal opportunities in labour markets and employment the concept of diversity has been picked up and has been embraced as

---

[5] Citizenship is the modern form of what Durkheim 1893 calls mechanical solidarity.
[6] This article was written before the 11th of September 2001.
[7] An excellent overview of some the issues is in Parekh 2000: 239–263.

a potential ally in the struggle against structural pockets of unemployment occupied mainly by, indeed, cultural minorities[8].

Diversity emphasizes the positive contribution of different cultures. Instead of quoting cultures as repositories of problems (minority cultures being backward, traditional etc.), cultures are taken as sources of identity, sense-making, active adaptation and solutions to problems of social and economic marketing. Diversity documents the advancement of the co-existence of different cultures from a basic problem to a foundation for a solution. It has the strength of the obvious. A diverse labour force in a diverse world serving diverse markets: what could be more logical? Are, then, the new employees examples of diversity?

Diversity is a relatively new concept; it refers to culturally derived differences[9]. In the field of economics, organization and human resource management the concept is closely connected to the concept of organization culture and the relevance of culture in gaining competitive advantage, both at home and abroad. Diversity, when compared to programmes of equal opportunity, signals a shift in involvement (Hirschman 1982): from the public (and equal opportunity) to the initiative of private organizations (and diversity), including companies and their managements. They have read the writing on the wall: markets were changing, demographics were telling. In the US, the birthland of diversity, the concept killed several birds with one stone. It pronounced a final goodbye to the cherished metaphor of the melting-pot, in which diverse origins would merge into a common and shared identity. Diversity, in contrast, acknowledges new relations of wealth and power, both world wide and at home. Diversity, also, represents a new field of marketing: capturing the newly discovered diversity of markets (of Hispanics, of Afro-Americans and so on) begins with welcoming diversity in the organization's personnel, in its employed labour force. If you want to have a slice of the Hispanic market, better have the way prepared by Hispanics. Moreover, in many critical services – police, medical care, social welfare – the effectivity of the service is simply dependent on the mutual understanding of one another. Diversity, again, is critical in gaining and preserving the legitimacy of social and political arrangements, and in promoting citizen participation in these arrangements. And, finally, diversity cannot be but visible, in the front-offices and in the network of agents out in the field. Diversity underscores visibility and tangibility.

---

[8] A typical Dutch initiative, bridging the public/private distinction is the 'Taskforce Minorities and Labour Market'. The taskforce is directed mainly at the less succesful members of minority categories and it is a good example of the possibility of integrating diversity management and active labour market policy. It is recently very active in promoting diversity ('multicultural' or 'intercultural' HRmanagement).

[9] See Parekh 2000: 142–178.

Female part-time work: from the glass ceiling to the glass door

The policy of equal opportunity for women and men has met with some successes and it has met with a few drawbacks. The major drawback is that it stigmatized the very categories of job-seekers it set out to support (bracketing equality in order to achieve equality; see Bader 1998). A second drawback is that it failed to establish the connection with firm-internal labour markets and the opportunities of advancement within these labour markets. Will diversity fare better in these respects?

How open are internal labour markets for new types of employment relationships, those propelled by diversity included? It is instructive to take female employment, in particular female part-time employment, as a reference. In the case of part-time work, the characteristic Dutch compromise (Visser 1999) of correcting the traditionally low rate of female participation in the labour market, it has been noted time and again that this type of employment is found more at the lower than at the higher rungs of the job ladder, and that it occurs more often in 'female' jobs than in 'male' jobs. Thus, there is a clear correlation between the percentage of female employment in an industry and sector and the occurrence of part-time work (Baaijens 1999; SCP 1998). Also, the average level of female employment is still, despite the progress made in the educational records of girls and women, lower than that of male employment and it offers fewer roads to advancement (Baaijens, o.c.). Part-time employment is somewhere in between the margin and the core of the organization and that conclusion seems to hold also for female employment as a whole.

The limited career chances in female employment have been aptly captured in the image of the 'glass ceiling' (Gallos 1989). You can see the better and more rewarding jobs all right but you can't get at them. Whether it is the old boys' network (i.e. women and minorities not having followed the 'usual route'; Moss Kanter 1977: 136–139) or some other cause that keeps the ceiling intact, the peculiar thing is that top jobs may be held by persons occupying more than one job themselves. Part-time employment does not mean the same thing for all people – as university professors *cum* business consultants *cum* member of one or more boards only know too well.

The point of this short detour on part-time employment is twofold. One aspect concerns the concept of boundary-spanning. Top positions are almost without exceptions *boundary-spanning* positions, bridging the distance between the organization and its diverse environments[10]. These are entre-

---

[10] For the concept, see Thompson 1967. The importance of the concept is that it signals the *bridging* of system and environment, inside and outside, *insiders* and *outsiders*, members and non-members. Boundary-spanning, then, accomplishes the dual task of boundary-maintenance and structural couplings. Hence its critical significance in organizations and organizational activities.

preneurial positions, as distinct from managerial positions within the boundaries of the organization. The 'glass ceiling' retains the majority of these positions for a relatively small segment of employees. On the other hand, the non-entrepreunerial management positions have felt the brunt of the redesigning sweep of the past two decades. Many managerial positions have been transformed from a stepping-stone to the top into dead-ends. In their place we see at all organizational levels the emergence of new boundary-spanning jobs, in touch with suppliers, distributors and customers in a variety of value-adding partnerships and as part of networks that may include competitors (Johnston and Lawrence 1991; Castells o.c.; Hagedoorn and Schakenraad 1989). Diversity, as we saw, is one consequence of the growth in boundary-spanning jobs, tied up to the visibility for customers. Diversity then relates to the dynamics of the principal-agency relationship on the one hand (Milgrom and Roberts 1992) and to the divide between front- and back-office on the on the other. The question is now whether diversity is related to another type of glass border, in this case a 'glass door': do boundary-spanning jobs open up the pathway to the top positions or are they barred and destined to remain at the outer margins of the organization?

The second aspect concerns culture. Female part-time employment has, in conjunction with the general processes of an individualizing society, put the combination work, care and leisure on the agenda. The boundaries around work and the family have to be redrawn, in full recognition of the fact that the once typical 'breadwinner model' is a thing of the past and that new combinations of work, family, partners and friends, self, and the raising and enjoyment of the company of children demand new social arrangements of time. In this respect, again, female employment and the employment of cultural minorities have some resemblance. The critical issue remains the same: will the full organizational and cultural integration of new types of employment be interrupted by a glass door?

We can only pose the question here, not answer it. As far as I am aware, no empirical research has as yet been conducted regarding this question[11]. Diversity, of course, is a relatively new phenomenon and it may well be too early to pronounce any founded generalizations on the subject. We will have to stick to a tentative speculation then: indeed, the chances of glass doors to replace glass ceilings should not be estimated as low. Diversity as an employment strategy is so far predominantly a *HRM* translation of marketing concerns. As such it is an instrumental objective. More equalized opportunities *may* be one of its effects, it is not one of its causes. Its place in society is still

---

[11] But see Baron and Kreps 1999; Benschop et al. 1999, Meerman 1999. These studies indicate that in terms of problem solving diversity will bear fruits, whereas in terms of promoting dialogue and understanding diversity management still has a long road to go. See also Girndt 2000 with new, and hard to interpret, data.

in the open. If the pace of diversity is going to depend on private employing organizations the predictable outcome is a selective (but highly visible) effectivity.

Wrapping it up

Self-design

Self-organization or self-design is a major challenge in organizations today. Above, we quoted Morgan's principles to that effect and implied that such organizations depended on the activity of their employees to self-design their own careers. The truth of the matter is, however, that the demands on the new employee emanating from the new organization are sketched much more easy than the exact characteristics of the labour market. Consider the following list of requirements (Weick and Berlinger 1989; Korver 1995):

a. cultivation of 'spiral' careers. Instead of the habituated linear and vertical career pattern, a career of amassing a variety of personal experiences in which trial and error is "an important source of information" (Weick and Berlinger 1989: 323). In such a career a complex concept of self, incorporating multiple views of self, is a major result and at the same time a precondition for moving ahead. Being left to your own devices, then, is the message and being reflective as to where and what you are at different points in time is in line with a concept of career-conscious employability. Presupposed here is the ability of individuals to synthesize complex information. Also presupposed is their ability to identify distinctive competencies and getting these competencies recognized. In the Netherlands, for example, a growing number of companies and also city administrations is experimenting with 'competence management'. The idea is to create a unified language for all matters relating to the personnel function. At the same time, competence management must lead to consistency in the personnel tool kit, i.e. it must create a unified perspective in processes of recruitment and selection, evaluation, and measurement of performance and development (see for example Fruytier and Timmerhuis 1995, chapter 5). To that end jobs are described in very broad terms only derived from the exigencies of the 'primary process' of producing and servicing (for example, knowledgeability, innovativeness, client sensibility, perception of the environment and so on). These terms span capabilities and competencies with a relatively wide relevance, and they offer possibilities for distinguishing levels of expertness. As a consequence careers assume a variety of shapes, horizontal and lateral rather than traditionally vertical (for cases see Gaspersz and Ott 1996, and Van Sluijs and Hoekstra 1999; for levels of expertise see Benner, 1984, Dreyfus and Dreyfus 1986, and Schön 1983).

b. Career development in the sense just described leads to a second personal requirement: the decoupling of identity from jobs. This requirement entails that employees should not look at themselves in terms of 'positions' but in terms of 'roles'. A job is a position, for example a university professor. A traditional position-bound career concept in this instance spells a progression from assistant to associate to full and tenured professor. A role-bound career concept, on the other hand, spells a university professor as teacher, writer, researcher, and each of these roles with different audiences, statuses and developments. As under (a) it is the 'primary process' that is in charge of the career, and it defines careers as processes of professionalization in which competences are developed and recognized in one and the same process.

c. Preserving discretion is a third, and formidable, requirement. It is related to what Gaspersz and Ott (1996) call 'knowledge of the labour market', i.e. the perception of opportunities for mobility. At the same time it is more demanding and less individualized than mere knowledge since the idea of 'discretion' presupposes the existence of alternative jobs and their heading under more or less broadly defined and formalized communities of professionals. The role-emphasis under (b) returns here, then, for professionalization is a form of identity formation through socializing and by opening up a field of potential job opportunities. The present upsurge of new modes of certification and new credentials finds its place here, as do newer forms of labour provision and mediation (Van Beek 1998: 82–84; Schoemaker 1998: 175). Stating that the viability of self design is extremely dependent on the actuality and visibility of job alternatives may be obvious, but it is far from being realized.

Self design and forging your own career development, in conclusion, go hand in hand. The demands made on the organization and the employee are vexing, however. Actually, although such self design may indicate a direction to the future, it will not be a future for all. Its relevance for network organizations and virtual organizations may be beyond dispute, its relevance for project and matrix organizations is already a litttle more limited and it is dubious what its relevance is for hierarchical and unit organizations (for the distinctions see Schoemaker 1998)[12]. Since we know that network and virtual types of governance are concentrated in customized and knowledge intensive servicing we may infer that the primary processes focusing on self

---

[12] Schoemaker distinguishes between hierarchical, unit, matrix, project, network and virtual organizations. The sequence is dictated by the double influence of 'complexity' and 'dynamics', i.e. by environmental properties. The organization names are dubbed 'operational configurations'; they are related to 'contractual configurations' consisting of industrial relations, employment contracts, employability, pay and development. The distinctions are useful as pointers.

design will be concentrated in that line of work as well, in particular in jobs in which the lines between research, development and boundary spanning activities have become blurred. On the basis of present statistics it is not possible to come up with even an informed *guess* as to the percentage of total employment involved[13]. On the other hand, the conjecture that this concerns no more than a severely limited number of employees is rather likely. The importance of the primary process is on the move all right, but that does not lead to a uniform image of work processes, governance structures and demands on personnel. Many new service jobs (in health care, social and personal services) are of a relatively simple kind. That, to be sure, does not detract from the importance of the primary process. To the extent that services depend on the direct interaction of producer and consumer – which is the case in most health care jobs, as well as in many social services – the primary process is both a visible (and often also a tangible) and an integral aspect of consumer satisfaction. Whether the activities are self- or other designed, then, is from the point of view of the primary process and its effects a secondary matter. When looking for an apt image of the new employee, self design is as useful as it is unrepresentative. Self-design, in conclusion, is not the road post leading us to the new employee. But then, how about the entrepreneurial employee?

The entrepreneurial employee?

Services are in an ever growing demand. Whether discussing care (at home, in the community and the neighbourhood, in institutions) or businesses, on all scores servicing is a growth activity. Although many services cater for a known demand, the idea is that an entrepreneurial spirit is taking hold of service jobs. Entrepreneurial, in the present context, means an emphasis on maintaining one's market share and on developing new markets and new demands in existing markets. The concept of the entrepreneurial employee signals the fact that entrepreneurial activities are no longer the exclusive domain of the top of the organization: these activities are becoming part and parcel of the work of employees (Van Beek 1998). Employees are to a greater or lesser degree on the road to responsibility for their own *portfolio* of assignments. *Getting a job* and *keeping a job* are becoming contingent upon the acquisition of assignments, both within the boundaries of the organization (getting signed on for projects for example) and beyond them.

As a *tendency* this development is undeniable. All the same, we should

---

[13] Jobs in ICT are an often quoted example of the new economy and the new employment. Yet, in recent Dutch studies on work and the information society exact data about how much employment actually is involved in ICT are absent. See Trommel 1999, Van Beek 1998, Weehuizen ed. 2000. Van der Laan 1998 gives a very rough estimate of, all in all, around 5 % of employment in the mid-nineties.

keep two things in mind. One is that the composition of the portfolio in many instances may prove stable over time. Two is that many of these assignments are of necessity either allocated routinely or developed spontaneously as spin-offs from present activities. Both, routines and spin-offs, can of course be made more explicit and conscious and, if so, then most of the activities dubbed entrepreneurial will not be new at all. They are a slice of present activities, and they are activities made articulate and accountable. For example, one may have to account for clients gone away and won, for time budgets and standards of client-evaluated performance, for improvements realized, for exploring new demands and client groups, and so on.

These aspects of entrepreneurialism lead to one conclusion only: anything the entrepreneurial employee does is the product of *choice*. Our usual image of the entrepreneur is as a person making choices and of the employee as a person who executes the choices others have made. The image of the entrepreneurial employee implies, by the same token, a person capable of choosing and a person accountable for the choices s/he made and for their consequences. Needed are employees who are as risk-prone or risk-averse as their employers[14].

Being accountable means being able to present and defend the choices you make as *decisions*. And indeed, *the concept of decision is the only concept unifying the various aspects and worlds of new employees.* Employees are supposed to decide on the career choices they make, they are supposed to decide on how to present themselves in designing a *curriculum vitae*, they are supposed to decide on the distribution of their time between work and care and work and family and, finally, they are supposed to decide on the matter of labour market participation as such. Whether on an individual or on a societal scale, the supply of labour is perceived as the product of a decision[15]. On the other hand all of us know that many decisions come by habits and traditions, by constraints and sanctions, or by hope and fear. Decisions are based, that is, in decision premises[16], and decision premises are needed to reduce (or 'bound', as in 'bounded rationality') the overwhelming informational complexity surrounding each and every decision. Decision premises reduce complexity. Decisions are nothing but applications of decision premises in a variety of situations, routine or non-routine, vital or trivial, predictable or ambiguous, announced or unannounced. They are not 'taken' in a strong sense of that word, so much as they are *selected* according to more or less 'satisficing' criteria. Being responsible for one's decisions means

---

[14] Hence the present upsurge in ideas and practices of financial participation. For a recent overview, see Buitendam 2001a. See also Engelen 2000.

[15] Here we find the connection of labour market participation and the duties of active and individualized citizenship.

[16] See Simon 1976. The importance of the concept of 'decision premises' is underscored by Perrow 1986: 118–140.

in this respect being held individually accountable for one's actually employed criteria of selection.

It stands to reason that such a concept of responsibility must be balanced by a concept of competence, with the latter concept referring to the informational base – and thus to the decision premises – of the decision. Competent decision-making presupposes adequate decision premises. It stands to reason, again, that decision premises cannot be individual in the sense that responsibility is individual. Help, social support, advice, companionship and, above all, *trust*[17], are the indispensable ingredients of acceptable decision premises. This holds for the entrepreneurial employee, for the entrepreneur proper[18], for the traditional employee and for the newcomer on the labour market. The entrepreneurial employee, in conclusion, is no more than a subcategory of the individual as a decision-maker. It does not define the new employee any more than 'self-design' did. Nonetheless, the emphasis on decision-making does point to the necessity of having a viable social network to be able to take accurate decisions. It may be questioned whether such networks are available or rather: are perceived as available by today's employees. To the extent that the answer to this question is in the negative, the new employee is not so much entrepreneurial as s/he is lonely.

Expectations of work

Loneliness is an ominous judgment. Ominous but not unfounded. In a recent research report, based on a representative survey (representative in terms of age, level of education and income) 1600 members of the Dutch population were asked about their expectations and evaluations of future trends in work, care and leisure (Ester and Vinken 2000). The Dutch, now, do not have an optimistic view of the future (the future indicating expectations concerning the first 25 years of the 21st century and the evaluation of the expected trends). Intergenerational solidarity (in particular concerning pensions and superannuation) and solidarity as such are expected to decrease, ethnic and religious strife are expected to increase. On the increase are, also, discrimination (with the major exception of discrimination of women), environmental pollution and criminality. Genetic manipulation is perceived as a development that is certain and unstoppable. Poverty, i.e. a more skewed distribution of income, is expected to become more prominent. Respect for customs, tradition and authority is, again, expected to diminish.

---

[17] See Luhmann 1988; Misztal 1996. Trust is arguably *the* most important mechanism in the upkeep of social interaction in the face of informational uncertainty.

[18] Viz. the talk about 'networks' and networking, and more in general about the social structure of competition, the importance of a balance of 'strong' and 'weak' ties, the pivotal position of a *tertius gaudens* and so on. See Castells, op. cit., Granovetter 1973, 1982, 1985; Burt 1992; Caplow 1968.

These sombre expectations reverberate in the trends concerning work and care. Working in teams is, next to teleworking, on the increase and will remain so. On the other hand, people expect less pleasant contacts with colleagues, they expect more internal competition and, surprisingly, they expect less work that will involve them with people[19]. Moreover, positive evaluations of more responsible tasks, more room for own initiative and a growth in useful and interesting work go hand in hand with negative evaluations of increasing work pressure (and therefore with stress), and a growth in irregular working hours and patterns. Also, the difficulties in combining work and care (in particular care for one's children) are predicted to grow.

No countervaling powers are quoted to reverse these trends. The influence of trade unions, for example, is expected to diminish somewhat, but more conspicuous is the sentiment of the respondents that they are on their own and, consequently, must try and make the best of it on their own accord[20]. You are on your own and must forge your own opportunities. In general the Dutch feel confident about safeguarding their own opportunities, and somewhat less confident about the opportunities others have.

The judgment on loneliness is also a judgment on a powerless *civil society*. It is as if the Dutch are well aware of the fact that participation in the labour market is an option with no real *exits*, with an at best ineffective *voice*, and with a dwindling *loyalty*[21]. Voice, in this connection, is our reminder of social organizations[22] and it has both horizontal (the presence of channels of communication and interaction of like people in like situations) and vertical (the voicing of one's discontent to others) aspects. Voice requires organization and the freedom to organize. If exits are non-existent and voice has been restrained, passivity and resignation are likely to follow (Hirschman 1986: 81).

Passivity and resignation capture, indeed, the mood of the Dutch in the cited report. Many of the expected developments in the next quarter-century are deplored, none is resisted. The grand views of authors like Beck (1999) and Gorz (2000), portraying the possibility of a society in which citizens and citizens' organizations have a determining say in the designation,

---

[19] It may be that people expect more communicative, and less interactive, contacts with other people, both colleagues, suppliers, and consumers. The introduction of more and more ICT in the workplace, then, may lead to a lowering of direct face-to-face contacts. Less work solidarity would be the product of this development.

[20] And of course, they expect that they will succeed better in doing so than the average. Like the automobile driver: accidents will happen but I will manage.

[21] The concepts of exit, voice and loyalty derive from Hirschman 1970. For an application to participation in the labour market see Korver and Wilthagen 2001.

[22] Secondary groups, Durkheim (1893) would call them, while Hegel (1821, par. 182ff.) subsumes them under the concept of the *bürgerliche Gesellschaft*. Sociologically interesting is that Tönnies puts Hegel's contribution on the side of 'community' (as contrasted with 'society'). See Tönnies 1932: 71–85.

design and valuation of social needs and in the activities needed to answer to these needs, are in the Dutch context mere exercises. For these views to materialize one would need both the concept and the practices of a lively and multifaceted civil society and precisely those do not surface at all in the expectations of the Dutch. Nor should this suprise us. For in the first place the Dutch do not have a history of active workplace participation, or 'voice'. The voice actually existing is limited to formal enterprise (works) councils with only a contingent relation to the workplace itself. Teamwork, apparently, is not perceived as an option for effective workplace participation[23]. Horizontal voice is rated low (there is little trust in one's colleagues), vertical voice (combining direct and representative participation) wellnigh absent. And in the second place the reorganization of the Dutch welfare state is based on the ideology of labour market participation which sees participation not just as *conditional* for civil society, but as *identical* with it[24].

References

Asselberghs, K., R. Batenburg, F. Huijgen & M. de Witte (1998). (The qualitative structure of employment in the Netherlands) *De kwalitatieve structuur van de werkgelegenheid in Nederland, deel IV*. Den Haag: OSA.

Baaijens, C. (1999). (Part time labour in the Netherlands) Deeltijdarbeid in Nederland. *Tijdschrift voor Arbeidsvraagstukken, 15* (1), 6–18.

Bader, V.M. (1998). Dilemmas of Ethnic Affirmative Action. *Citizenship Studies, 2* (3), 435–473.

Bader, V.M. (2001). Democratic Institutional Pluralism and Cultural Diversity. Unpublished ms.

Baron, J.N. & D.M. Kreps (1999). *Strategic Human Resources; frameworks for general managers*. New York: Wiley.

Bauman, Z. (1998). *Work, consumerism and the new poor*. Buckingham and Philadelphia: Open University Press.

Beck, U. (1999). *Schöne neue Arbeitswelt*. Frankfurt/New York: Campus.

Benner, P. (1984). *From Novice to Expert; Excellence and Power in Clinical Nursing Practice*. Reading, Mass.: Addison-Wesley Publishing Company.

Benschop, Y., B. van de Berg & F. van Winden (1999). Personeelsmanagement in revisie? (HRM in revision?) *M&O*, 1999/2, 7–20.

Bolweg, J.F. & A.W. De Korte (1994). *De nieuwe werknemer?!* (The new employee?) Assen: Van Gorcum/ Stichting Management Studies.

---

[23] In the EPOC-report (EPOC 1997) on New Forms of Work Organisation (a survey of workers' participation in 10 countries in Europe) the Dutch stand out as having, on the one hand, a high rate of teamworking (surpassed only by Sweden) and, on the other hand, a 'surprisingly' (EPOC 1997: 148) low rate of combining employee representation (f.e. works councils and trade union representation) and direct forms of participation (f.e. consultation and delegation).

[24] See WRR 1990: 7.

Bolweg, J.F. & J.M.M. Maenhout (1995). *Full employability.* In L. Faase, M. Ott & C.J. Vos (Eds.), *Nieuwe breukvlakken in het arbeidsbestel?* (New fractures in the labour system?) (92–99). Utrecht: De Tijdstroom.

Bourdieu, P. (1989). *Opstellen over smaak, habitus en het veldbegrip.* (Essays on taste, habitus and the concept of field) Amsterdam: Van Gennep.

Buitendam, A. (2001). *Een open architectuur voor arbeid en organisatie.* (An open architecture for labour and organisation) Assen: Van Gorcum.

Buitendam, A. (2001a). *Verzilveren en verzekeren; werknemersrisico's en ondernemingsbestuur.* (Cash and insure; worker risks and firm governance) Assen: Van Gorcum.

Burt, R.S. (1992). *Structural Holes; the social structure of competition.* Cambridge Mass. and London: Harvard University Press.

Caplow, T. (1968). *Two against one; coalitions in triads.* Englewood Cliffs NJ: Prentice-Hall.

Castells, M. (1996). *The rise of the network society.* Malden Mass.: Blackwell.

Christis, J. (1998). *Arbeid, organisatie en stress.* (Labour, organisation and stress) Amsterdam: Het Spinhuis.

CPB (1992). *Nederland in Drievoud.* (The Netherlands threefold) Den Haag.

De Sitter, L.U. (1994). *Synergetisch Produceren.* (Synergetic production) Assen: Van Gorcum.

De Vries, G. (1993). *Gerede Twijfel; over de rol van de medische ethiek in Nederland.* (Reasonable doubt: The role of medical ethics) Amsterdam: de Balie.

Dreyfus, H.L. & S.E. Dreyfus (1986). *Mind over Machine; the power of intuition and expertise in the era of the computer.* Boston: Blackwell.

Durkheim, E. (1893). *De la division du travail social.* Paris: Alcan.

Engelen, E. (2000). *Economisch burgerschap in de onderneming.* (Economic citizenship in the firm) Amsterdam: Thela Thesis.

EPOC (1997). *New Forms of Work Organisation; Can Europe Realise its Potential?* Dublin: European Foundation for the Improvement of Living and Working Conditions.

Ester, P. & H. Vinken (2000). *Van later zorg; verwachtingen van Nederlanders over arbeid, zorg en vrijetijd in de 21e eeuw.* (What the Dutch expect: Work, care and spare time) Den Haag: OSA.

Fruytier, B. (1998). *Werknemersmacht in de arbeidsorganisatie; voorwaarde voor het poldermodel.* (Power of workers in the organisation of work) Tilburg: OSA publicatie A 164.

Fruytier, B. & V. Timmerhuis (1995). *Mensen in onderzoek; het mobiliseren van human resources in wetenschapsorganisaties.* (Mobilising HRM in science organisations) Assen, Van Gorcum.

Gallos, J.V. (1989). Exploring women's development. In M.B. Arthur. D.T. Hall & B.S. Lawrence (Eds), *Handbook of career theory* (89–109). Cambridge: Cambridge University Press.

Gaspersz, J. & M. Ott (1996). *Management van Employability.* Assen: Van Gorcum/Stichting Management Studies.

Gibson, R. (Ed.) (1998). *Rethinking the Future.* London: Nicholas Brealey Publishing.

Girndt, T. (2000). *Cultural Diversity and Work-Group Performance: Detecting the Rules.* Tilburg: Center Dissertation Series.

Gómez-Mejía, L.R., D.B. Balkin & R.L. Cardy (1998). *Managing Human Resources*. Upper Saddle River NJ: Prentice Hall.

Gorz, A. (2000). *Arbeit zwischen Misere und Utopie*. Frankfurt am Main: Suhrkamp.

Gouldner, A. (1979). *The future of intellectuals and the rise of the new class*. London: Macmillan.

Granovetter, M. (1973). The Strenght of Weak Ties. *American Journal of Sociology*, *78*, 1360–1380.

Granovetter, M. (1982). The Strength of Weak Ties: A Network Theory Revisited. In P.V. Marsden & N. Lin (Eds.), *Social Structure and Network Analysis* (105–120). Beverly Hills: Sage.

Granovetter, M. (1985). Economic Action and Social Structure. *American Journal of Sociolog*, *91*, 481–510.

Hagedoorn, J. & J. Schakenraad (1989). Strategisch deelgenootschap en technologische samenwerking. (Strategic partnership and technological cooperation) In W.C.L. Zegveld & J.W.A. van Dijk (Eds.) *Technologie en economie: licht op een black box?* (128–155). Assen: Van Gorcum.

Halman, L. (1998). De 'nieuwe werknemer'; fictie of feit? (The new employee: fiction or fact) *Gids voor Personeelsmanagement*, *77* (5), 39–43.

Hare, R.M. (1993). *Essays on Bioethics*. Oxford: Clarendon.

Hegel, G.W.F. (1821). *Grundlinien der Philosophie des* Rechts (reprint 1972). Frankfurt am Main: Ullstein Verlag.

Hirschman, A.O. (1970). *Exit, Voice, and Loyalty*. Cambridge Mass.: Harvard University Press.

Hirschman, A.O. (1982). *Shifting Involvements: Private Interests and Public Action*. Princeton: Princeton University Press.

Hirschman, A.O. (1986). *Rival views of market society; and other recent essays*. New York: Viking.

Hövels, B., P. den Boer & J. Frietman (1999). Formele opleidingskwalificaties en competenties: wat telt voor laagopgeleiden? (Formal educational qualifications and competencies) *Tijdschrift voor Arbeidsvraagstukken*, *15* (2), 124–134.

Johnston, R. & P.R. Lawrence (1991). Beyond vertical integration – the rise of the value-adding partnership. In G. Thompson et al. (Eds), *Markets, Hierarchies and Networks* (193–202). London: Sage.

Kainz, H.P. (1988). *Ethics in context*. Houndmills and London: Macmillan.

Karasek, R. (1999). The new work organization and conducive value. *Sociologische Gids*, *46* (4), 310–330.

Karsten, L. & K. Van Veen (1998). *Managementconcepten in beweging: tussen feit en vluchtigheid*. (Management concepts moving: Fact and superficiality) Assen: Van Gorcum/Stichting Management Studies.

Kelly, K. (1998). The new biology of business. In R. Gibson (Ed.) … 251–267.

Kymlicka, W. & W. Norman (Eds.) (2000). *Citizenship in Diverse Societies*. Oxford: Oxford University Press.

Korver, T. (1995). Sociotechniek en loopbaan. (Sociotechnics and career) In F. Huijgen & F.D. Pot (Eds.) *Verklaren en ontwerpen van produktieprocessen* (265–279). Amsterdam: SISWO.

Korver, T. (eds) (1999). Arbeidspolitiek. (Labour politics) Special issue of the *Sociologische Gids*, *46* (4).

Korver, T. (2000). Arbeid als beslissing. (Work as decision) In R.M. Weehuizen (Ed.) Toekomst@werk.nl; *reflecties op economie, technologie en arbeid* (302–313). Den Haag: STT.

Korver, T. & A. Wilthagen (2001). *Het werkdadig verband tussen arbeidsparticipatie, sociale integratie en sociale cohesie.* (Work relating labour participation, social integration and cohesion) Den Haag: NWO.

Kuipers, H. & P. Van Amelsvoort (1990). *Slagvaardig organiseren.* Deventer: Kluwer Bedrijfswetenschappen.

Leibfried, S. & P. Pierson (1995). *European Social Policy; Between Fragmentation and Integration.* Washington DC: The Brookings Institution.

Lijphart, A. (1976). *Verzuiling, pacificatie en kentering in de Nederlandse politiek.* (Pillarization, pacification and change in Dutch politics) Amsterdam: De Bussy.

Luhmann, N. (1988). Familiarity, Confidence, Trust: Problems and Alternatives. In D. Gambetta (Ed.), *Trust; Making and Breaking Cooperative Relations* (94–107). Oxford: Basil Blackwell.

Luhmann, N. (2000). *Die Politik der Gesellschaft.* Frankfurt am Main: Suhrkamp.

Marshall, T.H. (1950). *Citizenship and Social Class.* New York: Doubleday.

Meerman, M. (1999). *Gebroken Wit; over acceptatie van allochtonen in arbeidsorganisaties.* (Broken white: accepting non-natives in work) Amsterdam: Thela Thesis.

Milgrom, P. & J. Roberts (1992). *Economics, Organization and Management.* Englewood Cliffs NJ: Prentice Hall.

Misztal, B.A. (1996). *Trust in Modern Societies; The Search for the Bases of Social Order.* Cambridge: Polity Press.

Morgan, G. (1986). *Images of Organization.* London: Sage.

Moss Kanter, R. (1977). *Men and Women of the Corporation.* New York: Basic Books.

Parekh, B. (2000). *Rethinking Multiculturalism; Cultural Diversity and Political Theory.* Houndmills and London: Macmillan.

Perrow, C. (1986). *Complex Organizations; A Critical Essay.* New York: Random House.

Pfeffer, J. (1994). *Competitive advantage through people.* Boston: Harvard Business School Press.

Prahalad, C.K. (1998). Strategies for growth. In R. Gibson (Ed.), ... 63–74.

Rawls, J. (1971). *A Theory of Justice.* Cambridge Mass.: Belknap/Harvard.

Reich, R. (1992). *The Work of Nations.* New York: Vintage Books.

Sabel, C.F. (1994). Learning by monitoring: the instituions of economic development. In N.J. Smelser & R. Swedberg (Eds.), *The Handbook of Economic Sociology* (137–165). Princeton NJ & New York: Princeton University Press & Russell Sage Foundation.

Sanders, K. (2000). *Solidair gedrag binnen moderne arbeidsorganisaties.* (Solidary behaviour within modern work organisations) Tilburg: Dutch University Press.

Schmid, G. (2000). Transitional Labour Markets; A New European Employment Strategy. In B. Marin et al. (Eds.), *Innovative Employment Initiatives* (223–254). Aldershot: Ashgate).

Schoemaker, M.J.R. (1998). *Tussen Slavernij en Anarchie.* (Between slavery and anarchy) Deventer: Kluwer Bedrijfsinformatie.

Schön, D.A. (1983). *The reflective practitioner; how professionals think in action*. New York: Basic Books.

SCP (1998). *Sociaal en Cultureel Rapport 1998: 25 jaar sociale verandering*. (25 years social change) Rijswijk/Den Haag: Sociaal en Cultureel Planbureau/Elsevier Bedrijfsinformatie.

Sennett, R (1998). *The corrosion of character*. New York: Norton.

Shklar, J. (1991). *American citizenship: the quest for inclusion*. Cambridge Ma.: Harvard University Press.

Simon, H.A. (1976). *Administrative Behavior; A Study of Decision-Making Processes in Administrative Organization*. New York & London: The Free Press.

Sloterdijk, P. (2000). *Regels voor het mensenpark*. (Rules for the human zoo) Amsterdam: Boom.

Thijssen, J.G.L (1997). *Leren om te overleven*. (Learning to survive) Utrecht: Universiteit Utrecht.

Thompson, J.D. (1967). *Organizations in Action*. New York: Mc Graw-Hill Book Company.

Tönnies, F. (1932). Hegels Naturrecht. *Schmollers Jahrbuch*, 56, 71–85. (reprint in G.W.F. Hegel (1972)). *Grundlinien der Philosophie des Rechts* (779–795). Frankfurt am Main: Ullstein Verlag.

Trommel, W.A. (1999). *ICT en Nieuwe Arbeidspatronen*. (ICT and new patterns of work) Den Haag: Rathenau Instituut.

Van Beek, K. (1998). *De ondernemende samenleving*. (The entrepreneurial society) WRR Voorstudies en Achtergronden V 104. Den Haag: SDU Uitgevers.

Van Doorn, J.A.A. (1986). Classificatie en maatschappij. (Classification and society) In J.W. de Beus & J.A.A. van Doorn (Eds.), *De Geconstrueerde Samenleving* (29–48). Amsterdam/Meppel: Boom.

Van Gunsteren, H.R. (1992). *Eigentijds Burgerschap*. Den Haag: SDU.

Van der Heijden, P.F. (1988). *Grondrechten in de onderneming*. (Basic rights in the firm) Deventer: Kluwer.

Van der Heijden, P.F. (1998). Een nieuwe rechtsorde van de arbeid. *Socialisme en Democratie*, 55 (5), 219–228.

Van der Laan, L. (1998). *Arbeid en de elektronische snelweg*. (Work and the electronic highway) Den Haag: NWO.

Van Sluijs, E. & H.A. Hoekstra (1999). *Management van competenties – het realiseren van HRM*. Assen: Van Gorcum.

Van Steenbergen, B. (Ed.) (1994). *The Condition of Citizenship*. London: Sage.

Van Veen, K. & R. Wielers (1999). Waar zijn de arbeidsplaatsen voor de lager opgeleiden in de industrie gebleven? (Where are the jobs for the lowly educated?) *Tijdschrift voor Arbeidsvraagstukken*, 15 (1), 36–49.

Visser, J. (1999). *Sociologie van het halve werk*. (Sociology of work half done) Amsterdam: Vossiuspers AUP.

Waldron, J. (2000). Cultural Identity and Civic Responsibility. In Kymlicka & Norman (Eds.), ... 155–174.

Weehuizen, R.M. (Ed.) (2000). *Toekomst @ werk.nl*. (Future at work) Den Haag: STT.

Weick, K. & L.R. Berlinger (1989). Career improvisation in self-designing organizations. In M.B. Arthur, D.T. Hall & B.S. Lawrence (Eds.), *Handbook of Career Theory* (313–328). Cambridge: Cambridge University Press.

Williams, M. (2000). The Uneasy Alliance of Group Representation and Deliberative Democracy. In Kymlicka & Norman (Eds.), ... (124–152).

Wilson, W.J. (1987). *The truly disadvantaged: the inner city, the underclass and public policy*. Chicago: Chicago University Press.

WRR (1990). *Een werkend perspectief: arbeidsparticipatie in de jaren negentig.* (Labour participation in the nineties) Den Haag: SDU.

WRR (1994). *Belang en beleid; naar een verantwoorde uitvoering van de werknemersverzekeringen.* (An adequate provision of workers insurance) Den Haag: SDU.

WRR (1996). *Tweedeling in Perspectief.* (Cleavage in perspective) Den Haag: SDU.

WRR (1997). *Van verdelen naar verdienen; afwegingen voor de sociale zekerheid in de 21e eeuw.* (From distributing to earning: social security in the 21 century) Den Haag: SDU.

Chapter 8

The worlds that the concepts of organisation refer to: uses, qualities, origins

Bert van Hees and Paul Verweel

In the previous chapters a number of organisational concepts and images of two central actors have been analysed: learning organisation, self-managing teams, organisation culture, customer friendly organisation, as well as the new images of managers and employees. The authors have shown the framing of these concepts, their embedding in underlying viewpoints, and guidelines for action.

What sort of worlds emerge from these concepts? We will research the tension between the life world of people, that is to say authentic communication, self-determination and courage, and the system world, the instrumental basis of human action. Part of the system world is the so-called stakeholders or 'partisan world'.

We will then discuss the usage of the concepts, their utility and functions in the force fields of organisational networks.

The concepts have various pretensions, but how good is their quality and how ambiguous are they? The quality of concepts is connected to the process of their production: organisation and management science as a mixed industry.

We will round off with a link to the final chapter in which the influence of modernisation on meaning is central. How modern are the worlds indicated by the concepts?

What kinds of worlds: an assessment of the life, system and partisan world in the concepts

To what extent do organisational concepts leave room for both life world and system world? To what extent is the perspective used open to wishes and opinions of individuals and social groups about their way of life, to authentic communication, communal decision-making, and courage?

System and life world criteria

A system and life world can be distinguished by three criteria:

1. Instrumental versus communicative action
In a system world there is a system-functional logic of instrumental action: the treatment of people and groups is instrumental and strategic, that is to say action is an instrument for attaining objectives and action is assessed by its functionality or contribution to the aims of for example the organisation. You could also say: Actions and interactions have a transactional aspect, it is about value-creation, a contribution to an objective of the system or the organisation.

This functionality can also be linked to other units than the organisation and aimed at units like the working group, the category of professionals, single workers, a network, club or clan, or a certain position within the organisation. In such cases we speak of a partisan world, as distinguished from the system world. See below for a more detailed explanation.

This instrumental action can be found intrinsically satisfactory or extrinsically satisfactory, satisfaction can be based on the action itself or on its products. Depending on people's preferences and motivation, value can be attached to involvement in work content, interacting with people, showing oneself, being creative, etc.

Instrumental action that is intrinsically satisfactory is both useful for the individual and aimed at contributing to the organisation. From the point of view of management, that is usually the most desirable form of action.

In a life world there has to be a social logic of authentic communication, the action or the interaction in which people are aims in themselves. This is also referred to as communicative action: (Habermas in: Van Hoof and Ruysseveldt: 302 ff.). Communicative action differs from instrumental and strategic action for three reasons:

1. Truth is of importance (reference to a shared objective reality).
2. Normative validity is of importance (action refers to shared agreements and norms).
3. Sincerity is of importance (action based on the subjective world of the speaker, the subjective validity of the expressions of the communicator: there is no lying, no foul play, no tactical play, no cunning). Sincerity is connected to: Who am I? It asks the question: what is the basis of my actions? Sincere action is also reflexive action, conscious awareness plays a role.

Where in the life world interactions are guided by mutual understanding based on communication, in the system world there are behavioural codes determined by money, formal power etc. (Alvesson en Deetz 1996: 202). In practice it will not always be easy to decide between the sincerity and the instrumentality of behaviour, because much behaviour is a combination of motives.

In summary: social action is authentic communication when and to the extent that people are aims in themselves in the interaction, the action is focused on understanding other people, on being understood and on communicating sincerely. Beside instrumental and social (communicative) action, action in accordance with tradition, and action focused on norms and values can be distinguished. These four aspects are of more or less importance in the actions of an individual.

The distinction between life and system world should not be confused with that of the private and the public sphere. Both instrumental and social action occur in both spheres, for instance in the private sphere in negotiating household chores with a partner.

2. In a life world participants co-create the organisational world they form together and give it meaning
The more strongly participants in an organisational setup collectively determine the meaning of the setup, make it *meaningful and significant* for themselves, the more the life world will be present.

In a consistent form, it is an organisational setup entirely constructed by its members: such an organisation, then, has a) autonomy in task performance, room for fulfilling tasks according to one's own insights, b) autonomy of task design, and in a wider context, of the organisation, including the determination of the aims of the organisation, c) the freedom to distribute the returns. These three elements can also be found in ideas from radical liberalism, anarchism, and company democratisation, and aspects are present in, for instance, modern sociotechnical systems thinking.

When we wish to determine whether there is shared meaning, meaning which is collectively experienced, produced and underwritten, the judgments by the participants themselves should be taken into account. When we do this, it is possible that individuals who positively value existing authority, state and ownership rights, will indicate an authoritarian organisation as meaningful and shared, because this links up with their ideas of social order and community. We should also take into account the process and the initial conditions that are present: Are the participants experienced in making themselves heard, with being heard, with producing shared meaning? Think, for instance, of the position of women in the west before 1900, that of blacks in the USA before 1960, or that of homosexuals before 1970.

3. In a life world there is the courage and the possibility for expressing doubts

Ten Bos (1998) has a discussion of guts, courage and autonomy, an aspect which may well be regarded as the third criterion for a life world. Autonomy or guts of the individual and for example employees. Autonomous people are people who have the self-confidence to express their moral doubt on certain activities (Ten Bos, o.c. p. III), they have the guts to disagree, to express a minority opinion. The possibility of the expression of minority viewpoints and the presence of autonomous behaviour of workers can be regarded as an essential condition for the presence of life world elements. It is dependent upon freedom of speech. It could be construed as a condition of sincerity: the autonomy, or 'having the guts' is about the expression of behaviour which is essential for the individual.

The three criteria for a life world taken together

A life world exists when authentic communication, producing and sharing of meaning, minority viewpoints or autonomy find expression. These three aspects can get in each other's way: In a process of shared production of meaning, minority viewpoints can make the common ground harder to find. At this point a so called partisan world can come into play.

The partisan or stakeholder world as a specification of the system world

Lammers et al. (1997) distinguish between an actor and party model respectively, which, in contrast to the system world mentioned above, refers to the organisation regarded either as a conglomerate of parties, or as a social and cultural system. In the world of a social and cultural system, there is not only instrumental and strategic behaviour, but also normative behaviour relating to norms and values of the system (the organisation), whereas in the party world instrumental and strategic behaviour occurs that goes together with normative behaviour focused on the norms of the actor's own party. Lammers' distinction between party and system world clearly differs from that of system and life world (with authentic communication, co-creation or self-determination and courage). The life world does not enter the picture, neither in the party nor in the system model, although in the party model there may be an aim and a struggle to realise the conditions of a life world. The party world is that of interest groups, subgroups, coalitions, coercion and incentives. The party world is a non-integrated world, it can be opposed to a system world, but at the same time it is based on it. Actions by parties, their forms, aims, culture are to an important degree determined by the organisation, by the division of labour in the organisation, task differentiation and embedding in social surroundings etc. Actions of parties depend on the characteristics and history of the organisation (and members within it). The parties have been developed as a side-effect of technological, organisational and social developments, and they are both intentional and unintentional results of the system (re)design, they are an expression of the struggle of individuals, groups, departments, hierarchical layers, external actors to safeguard interests and secure certain forms of interaction. We will refer to this part model as the 'partisan world', as part of the system world.

The three worlds in the organisational concepts analysed in this book

The system world is found in the concepts through:

- the image of the impartial professional or manager implementing the right objectives and means; a management perspective as in the microcosm for learning and experimenting in learning organisations. This is not based on people's needs and aims resulting from processes of authentic communication on the one hand and negotiation, influence and power on the other, in short, life world and partisan world influences (concepts: Learning organisation, Self-managing teams). Ignoring tensions between aims of production and aims related to quality of work and group aims (Self-managing teams), or paying attention to the individual level, instead of to power and force fields between parties, groups (Learning organisation)
- consensus, integration, monoculture (Organisation culture, Self-managing teams, the Learning organisation); consensus is achieved through values and norms, life in organisations is especially approached through norms and values (Organisation culture)
- meritocracy, hierarchy, autocracy; there may well be criticisms on hierarchy and centralisation, but there is no support for the opposite in the form of democratisation initiatives. Few are supposed to be able to learn (Learning organisation). The content of self-management is limited (Self-managing teams)
- idealised and unnatural image of learning derived from the ideal organisation (Learning organisation)
- No place for courage and the expression of moral doubt (Self-managing teams, Learning organisation, customer friendly organisation)

The life world could be part of the frames of the concepts (but this only takes place in a very limited way):

- there is a tendency of connecting to the life world by paying attention to lifestyles of clients, playing to the so-called small stories of clients through symbols, and through socially responsible entrepreneurship

148

(Customer friendly organisation). But to what extent can sympathising with brands, styles be viewed as a sincere meeting with others?
– Focus on other than material values, such as communication for contact here and now, stress on being, presence, relinquishing, meeting, awareness, experience, and beauty or aesthetics. Possibly post-modern values are at issue here, cf. ecology, holism, feminism.
– Instead of on utility or instrumentality, focus is more and more on emotions and deepest being. Solidarity and connecting to forms of life other than in an instrumental way (Customer friendly organisation).
– Diversity instead of consensus; pluriformity, multiple cultures, allowing for dissidents, marginal figures (Organisation culture).
– Forming consensus through communal production of shared meaning.
– Democracy and representation since they enable collective production of meaning as well as the fair treatment of all sorts of minorities.
– The necessity of freedom of speech for individuals, and the expression of moral misgivings. Connected to this is the enhancement of autonomy in the design of tasks and organisations.
– Viewing learning not as an elite cause, but as a day-to-day process. Management could be more experimental, more dependent on experience, and more open to all sorts of groups within the organisation and society.
– Norms and values are not given and static, but in a process of creation. They can be developed both in authentic dialogue, communication (and of course also by negotiation among parties).

We have seen that the partisan world hardly enters into the concepts and the images of actors. Ten Bos (learning organisation), Leisink (self-managing teams) and Boessenkool (organisational culture) see the concepts framed in an idealistic view of power relations in organisations, there is no place for a partisan world. That would only be the case when:

– There is recognition of the problematic aspects of consensus and loyalty, there is openness to ways of arriving at consensus and shared aims, there is awareness of the unstable and compromising, 'floating' nature of social order.
– There is awareness of parties outside the organisation, of social responsibility.
– There is recognition of the fact that professionals as a party are both professional and party; knowledge and self-interest are interconnected.
– Acknowledgement of tensions within and around management, of exchange and power and of contracting, exchange and negotiations, of ad hoc coalitions and group solidarity.

– Acknowledgement of dependencies and inequalities in spite of, and due to the existence of values like empowerment, fairness, equality etc.

We conclude that these concepts of organisation and management hardly address the tension between life and system world, mostly ignore the partisan world, and do not develop guidelines for managing and balancing these worlds.

A system world constituted by individualistic, ahistorical, utopian thinking

The system world we have seen in the concepts is a world without authentic communication, but also without collective parties and power processes. As we will see below, it is also a world that is individualistic, ahistorical and utopian. First we will focus on the power to define situations. Then we will discuss tendencies which seem to oppose instrumental rationality.

Definitional power

A party view in which the organisation is regarded as an entity of interests (interests, power and force) is hardly to be found. Ten Bos even opines that this is "a withdrawal from reality by higher ranking people". The conceptualisation of organisational problems, according to him is based on decontextualisation (ahistorical) of organisational problems, redefining them in the context of children's rooms. He discusses the problematic status of definitional power. Definitional power rests with managers, members of the organisation in high positions, who try to transfer to employees and clients interpretations of learning, culture, self-managing teams, and customer friendliness, in the name of proper functioning of the organisation. This definitional power is not made into an explicit problem (we might call this 'idealisation'). Leisink makes clear that learning and self-management are conceived within the limits of profits and management control, outside the struggle for definitional power.

Rohde signals a development of customer power whereby managers will be forced to conceptualise organisations on the basis of customer characteristics and customer wishes. The shift of power within organisations from managers to customers is concomitant to a fundamental change in the meaning of products and organisations. Rohde sees a tendency in organisations to move closer to customers and to be more alert to their wishes, and that managers will be forced to increase the autonomy of 'front office' employees. This does not necessarily mean that definitional power of customers and front-office employees will increase where it concerns the setup of the business system and working conditions. Not all categories of employees have equal resources (as to time, imagination, comparative material, labour market position, autonomy) for concerning themselves with the definition of organisational arrangements.

Boessenkool sees most adherents of the organisation culture concept reducing this notion to shared meanings without reflection on diversity, variation, dissension, repression, as factors possibly affecting meaningful situations, so a dominance of integrated system thinking, in which the struggle for the definition of the situation is excluded. The struggle for definitional power is all the more urgent as the giving of meaning plays a greater role in (the formation of) the organisation.

Van Witteloostuijn (2000) does question definitional power when observing in Dutch management a development of the *conflict firm* and macho management. The conflict firm corresponds to the Anglo-Saxon shareholder value models in which a party world is presented where parties react to stimuli from adequately functioning markets. In these models there is no place for historically determined differences in power, abuse of power, for interests over and above individual firms, societal values and institutions.

Instrumental rationality and contrary tendencies: empowerment, logic of sign, fragmentation

The authors signal instrumental rationality as the dominant approach of organisation culture (Boessenkool) and self-managing teams (Leisink). In the eyes of Ten Bos this is reinforced because managers are oriented to concepts that reflect what they like to hear. That orientation is also maintained because managers are conservative and avoid risks (Koot).

We can see some *contrary tendencies* in empowerment, attention to balances between work and private life, spirituality and new (non instrumental) values. This might link up with individualisation and professionals' need for self-management.

The images of the new employee and the new manager show a duality: beside a dominant rational control and production-oriented thinking, there is room for individual, and to a lesser extent collective, issues of identity, binding and experience. However, Koot establishes that managers are still mainly interested in checking and control, and are hardly aware of the paradoxes of modernity caused by the new developments. Isolation and unworldliness are not undermined by the concepts, some concepts offer "a teddy bear for in the nursery" (ten Bos).

Another tendency, brought forward by Rohde, is that of the influence of the *logic of sign* (symbolic aspect), which has a direct influence on both the attractiveness of products and the relationship of customers, employees, and even managers with their own organisation and products. The symbolic aspect of organisation and production and provision of services is increasing, and this requires awareness of emotions and needs of producers and customers, for instance by creating values for, by and with the organisation (co-creation). Boessenkool sees the same aspects as of importance to commitment and loyalty of employees. Increasingly, organisations are becoming providers, or coproducers, of identity for employees and customers.

The use of services or products, then, is becoming less material, more imaginary (less utility value, more symbolic value): 'the meaning to me or to us or to a reference world which we know and aspire to'. Products or services are increasingly becoming experiences made by managers and employees in mutual consultation, and other organisational stakeholders such as customers. The experience is connected to the emotions and values of those stakeholders. Members of the organisations become creators of experiences (Pine and Gilmore 1999). This also means that the instrumental logic is contingent upon the increasing importance of emotional aspects of the service produced. Employees are engaged in creating an experience with and for each other and the customers. This is instrument-driven, but also requires an orientation to values: the value of the customer, of creating and being involved in experiences together. Work becomes a process of forming identity, both for employees and the buyers of products. This identity has a communality based on values, and these values can more or less smoothly combine with different lifestyles.

The customers and the employees, more so than management groups, are *fragmenting*, they have their own lifestyles, and can be subdivided even into (sub-)individual profiles. This development puts pressure on normative integration, the claim of shared values as a condition of production, and makes the search for these values all the more urgent! Shared values are a magic formula for downplaying existing differences, for boosting the search for consensus worlds, in which the tired mind of the manager can find rest and equilibrium, so he feels: here is clarity, here is the light, what appears as chaos is put into perspective.

Individual focus, ahistorical actors, lack of contingency factors

Ten Bos is sceptical about the idealistic and unfounded optimistic content of the concept of learning organisations, where adherents of the concept unwittingly exchange organisational learning for a description of individual learning. This could be called a 'fallacy of the wrong level', that is to say that statements at the individual level are substituted for statements at meso, or higher level. This also occurs in analyses of organisational cultures, for instance of teams: what at one moment is still the sum of the views of individuals, the next moment is the view of the team, an organisation etc. It is clear that such a view makes the organisation into a simple reflection of the sum of opinions, which idea conflicts with ideas of inspiring leadership, leaders that make a difference. In general, in the concepts the connection between micro and macro problems, between the individual and the collective level, is weak. In addition, sweeping changes in society at the local, national or global level, such as the crisis of patriarchy, the nation state, politics (Castells 1996) are not taken into account. In the next chapter we will return to these changes.

In nearly all concepts there is an idealised actor, management, and there is reference to qualities, ethics, and socially responsible entrepreneurship, but managerial responsibility and ethics are not examined and questions of power are not analysed. For the development of communities in organisations and for determining the societal functions of organisations, it is especially the management level that is addressed. Counter-discourses or other stories have little impact, have an existence as sidelines, they are no part of the concept: the Dutch 'polder model' (a representativity discourse and not a meritocratic one), diversity (room for minorities and allowing deviating opinions), the self-management model (work is intrinsically meaningful, what you do is important and satisfying), feminism. As to the question of who is voicing counter-discourses concerning organisation and management, the silence on the part of the labour unions, churches and politics, for instance, is remarkable. Arrangements concerning work and organisation are hardly a public issue at all.

The concepts may focus on the idealized individual, but do not take into account the world of *the acting person*. Actors' personal motives and motivators, knowledge, anchors and grounds for decisions, flesh and blood, are virtually absent. Within the concepts, actors are empty, ahistorical entities, they are managers and employees whose actions are only led by production or service-oriented motives and organisation-related constraints. The concepts appear to be *generally valid*. The organisational concepts in management literature (self-managing teams, learning organisation) leave all sorts of *context and contingency factors unidentified and unproblematic*. There are hardly any indications of the differences between profit and non-profit, professional and non-professional, voluntary or manufacturing etc. Concepts from a production environment – such as units, products, result responsibility, shop floor management etc. – are also found in service environments (De Witte and Van der Zwaan 1998: 53). Every organisational change project is embedded in a social background, but this is hardly problematised or investigated. When a concept is developed to promote a certain view (e.g. Peters and Waterman and their 7 S model, see Boessenkool), the intention is not so much to trace more conditions, but mainly to make a topical point. In order to do this, a limited research database (limited as to periods of time and types of companies) is used to support a particular view. In publications on Business Process Reengineering the message is to start with a specific approach of re-engineering, for example top-down. The choice of an approach is not based on research of the costs/benefits of various approaches in a change situation. In shareholder value models the social or societal costs are absent (Van Veen 1998, Van Witteloostuijn 2000).

Utopia of control

The concepts are based on a utopian belief in the manipulability of the organisation and the idealisation of the possibility of management to direct its course (Ten Bos 2000). The concepts discussed lack the testing which would be expected of scientific theories. While managers need concepts for explanation, they also use organisation concepts for facilitating control and manipulability towards others, for reassuring themselves, for giving legitimacy and direction (Jackall 1988). Because these latter outcomes are at least as important as the informational and explanatory value of a concept, concepts tend to be pictures of a sort of promised land, more than empirically grounded notions. Studies of what managers actually do are scarce, like the study by Mintzberg (1973), which offered a demystification of much of the then current management models, and the study by Jackall (1988). Concepts can be seen as normative programmes, how to get to the promised land, offering rationalisations or *programmes* and a change of focus and direction, as in the concept of the learning organisation. They help to change our perception, to focus on some aspects and neglect others. They are a message and a focus. They can point in a new direction and discuss barriers, for example under the label of resistance. They are not tools for a systematic encompassing diagnosis of problem situation, possible approaches and relevant factors.

Working with concepts. Uses, functions and outcomes

In the analyses of the concepts of organisation and actors and also in the literature on organisational concepts, a number of aspects of their use, application and utility come to the fore:

- They offer the function of playground for designers (Ten Bos).
- Incite managers to be alert to new developments, and they are a source of inspiration (Rohde).
- Offer managers and employees the possibility of activation and participation (Leisink).
- Provide a norm that makes manipulation possible (for instance 'the organisation culture must be strong to increase efficiency'), a social adhesive.
- They posit new tasks, aspirations (for instance, socially responsible marketing), provide new meanings, or other supplementary or competing orientations (Leisink, Boessenkool, Korver). They activate and mobilise (promote new experiences in learning organisations). They provide a working programme (as in the concept of shareholder value). What they give is a programme that is normative rather than empirically or theoretically founded. Concepts therefore have both a socialising, normative,

as well as a critical, creative function (Van Veen 2000), and they offer an orientation in fast-changing societal and organisational conditions.

- They link different terminologies (self managing teams), offer an interpretation of developments to silence older views (in self managing teams, ignoring the tensions between domain of production and domain of community).
- What is remarkable in all concepts is the rhetorical function of the concepts: they are central points of departure for policy, and part of the communication between actors in organisations, they stimulate socialisation in certain points of view or a certain image.
- They can also organise a debate, a knowledge community, function as guidelines for a community. They offer an identity, say 'who I am', creating an in and an out group. They contribute to community building ('we are the managers who think strategically, they are not') and create a self-image that can stimulate socialisation and learning (new manager, new employee).
- They give an image of attractive and motivating working environments, in which elements of play or excitement can be found. Thus they are a sort of image builders. People like work or a work setting not only because of rewards, but also because it has a certain image, e.g. it is a 'problem-solving and creative environment'.
- They reduce anxiety and offer simple images (Koot).

Concepts offer new lines, entail programmes and directions for policymaking, which can inspire and give focus and identity, which can unite and assure. As we have seen, the conceptual worlds tend to be not only instrumental and non-communicative in the sense we have used here, but also utopian in thinking about control, leaving aside definitional power, collective actors and parties, focusing on individuals, lacking historical and institutional contingencies. The concepts are not scientific concepts, and they are fashionable or time-bound. The organisation concepts however have explanatory and programmatic pretensions. At the same time, but more implicitly of course (because it contrasts with the explanatory pretensions), they appeal to a certain normative and value-directed position.

Quality and producers

Quality

In the introductory chapter we indicated that concepts can differ in quality, the way in which they are built and founded on theoretical and empirical arguments, their capacity to deduce clear action guidelines from them, and in the number of elements they comprise, their complexity. In the first chapter we pointed out the interplay between complexity and quality, here we will focus mainly on the quality of concepts.

Concepts can be *badly defined*, like for instance the learning organisation (Ten Bos), sometimes there are different definitions of a concept without rules to decide when to use which one (*ambiguity*). The concepts are not scientific concepts when their theoretical basis is not profound and their empirical basis is limited. They are strongly subject to fashions and there is a big difference between the pretensions of the organisational concepts (what their application promises to bring) and their implementation, what is (or may be) done with them in practice. The underlying assumptions of a concept have not always been thoroughly thought through. The compatibility of concepts, the possibility of linking them to varying theoretical assumptions can be regarded as a strength, because this connects them to various ideas, and as a weakness, because little is excluded and they become empty labels. The possibility of working with different definitions can be confusing, but it also offers freedom. The existence of different ways of framing a concept offers the opportunity for taking up new points of view. Thus, self-management can be approached from a task system, as well as from a constructivist perspective in which dominant actors try to build a dominant image of 'self and management', and in which other actors want to change that image.

The concept of self-management is influenced by both socio-technical systems theory, human resource management as social constructivism, the concept of organisation culture by a system (or integration) model and a conflict or party model, as well as the fragmentation variant of this latter model. Another example is the concept of empowerment that can be linked to a frame of liberation, autonomy and democratisation, but also to performance, group feeling and mental control (Ten Bos 1998, 70).

Concepts with a broad, changing content and range, tend to be relatively vague and undefined. Concepts will be not extensively theoretically founded and empirically tested, especially when they are produced on the borders of the world of science and that of business and management. Scientific criteria like falsification or truth and information content of the theoretical statements, tests of hypotheses, explication of the explanatory and interpretative potential of concepts will not play a dominant role. Views of organisational issues have more journalistic than scientific content, when they are generalisations of experience notions published by leading managers and consultants.

How are concepts built? Organisation or management-science as mixed industries

Organisational concepts as investigated by empirical science are hard to compare with those publicised by the world of consultancy and management sciences. The process of production differs, quality criteria and control of the product differ, as well as the functions of the concept produced. Management science is a varicoloured system in which some parts come very close to empirical science and other parts are far removed from it.

The dividing line between management science and empirical science lies between the *normative accent*, the *lack of theoretical and empirical research*, and the *consumer quality (novelty and media appeal of the 'product')*. We have already pointed out the mostly implicit nature of conditions from the social, political and economic context. Systematic theoretical research would point to these conditions (for example Kieser and Kubicek 1992).

* There is a surplus of *normative discussions* of what a manager and an organisation should be like.

Part of management literature, for instance, is about learning behaviour, attitudes, and methods for dealing with social situations. This literature hardly deals with real social dilemmas between self-interest and social interest, or moral dilemmas that are inevitable consequences of actions in management situations. Much literature on leadership, for instance, leaves undiscussed the traits one has to loose in order to become a leader: humility, willingness to serve, proper perspective on one's own performance. These things can be seen as implicit psychological costs that are incurred when leadership ideas are followed.

There is a lack of an explicit discourse that probes the morality and legitimacy of the story behind a concept. The presentation of a view on how one should tackle society and stakeholders, a *moral programme*, is important, not its questioning. For instance, in the shareholder value concept, shareholder value is to be given more importance, and less importance to other values of interested parties. The concept posits a connection between management action and increased Shareholder Value, even though a concrete programme of management action is not indicated (Froud et al. 2000). Remarkable is that empirical research has shown that there is no connection between raising Shareholder Value and actions undertaken by management (Froud et al. 2000)[1].

* Management science more easily accepts *the unverifiable nature of findings*: in management science, it is common that the names of companies and research units can not be verified or that data are private, so the research is not verifiable or repeatable for third parties and fellow researchers. Manage-

---

[1] The concept is connected to individualism and the "conflict enterprise", and belief in the possibilities of agency control and financial incentives (Van Witteloostuijn, 1999). The shareholder value approach raises the question: who is the firm really for? For clients, workers, management, capital providers etc.? It also raises the question of the affiliations of top management and the degree of involvement of executives with citizens of a nation. In this concept leaders have no touch with people and nation, and can orient themselves to transnational networks (see also Reich 1993, Castells 1996).

ment researchers sometimes claim the rights to research instruments developed by them (as was done in the Netherlands by leading organisation culture researchers), so that replication of testing by others becomes more difficult. Few and far are the studies of management that do not take management as their point of reference, and that is not only because permission is hard to get. There is also a knowledge interest: much more money is available for research that makes a certain policy vision or management remedy saleable, than there is for a description, historical or otherwise, of which the utility is not obvious in advance. Independent empirical research, not bound to interested dominant players, is in a difficult position. There is a *scarcity of empirical historical descriptions* of research that indicates how the social world of organisation and of managers actually works in daily life.

The production and control cycle for a fresh and strategic product, such as an organisation and management concept is different from that of a non-strategic one that is verifiable for academic colleagues (sometimes academic concepts, for instance from *La Distinction* by Bourdieu, or from a writer like Foucault, can gain strong appeal for a management audience). Concepts used by managers, executives, media and political actors are, more so than scientific and empirical research, focused on freshness and originality. If their packaging is too serious (not sexy), or they have not been placed strategically, for instance if their content cannot be linked to leading companies, sectors, or entrepreneurs, they lose their topical and consumer value. They tend to be products of business schools, universities, firms of consultants, publishers, the press and the clients of consultants. Fashion, style, being salient, strategic importance and self-positioning play an important role. They are produced within a 'multi-value regime': They must have value as carriers of knowledge, and value as examples, and value as presenters of successful, sometimes new companies, consultants etc. The industry producing organisational concepts is fashionable and exploring, superficial and sensitive (Ten Bos 2000). Legitimising new relationships and designing new programs intermingle: concepts serve for exploration as well as formation of political projects and moral programmes creating a work field or niche, mobilising parties in the same direction[2].

Production and use circuits as sources of meaning

There is a difference between the framing and the characteristics of concepts as they are developed and used, discussed, consumed by the sector (the circuit of production: business schools, consultants, large companies and entre-

---

[2] The concepts can also be regarded as secundary institutions underpinning new 'conceptions of control' (Fligstein, 1990). In this way concepts can be linked to the rise and fall of powerful companies, consultancies and sectors and announce new coalitions and new hierarchies in the economy.

preneurs, universities, publishers etc.), and the way these concepts are used in organisations (the circuit of use: managers, employees, consultants, politics, the media, interest groups etc.). Within organisations there are other rules of legitimisation than in professional circles, academia and the media. In other words: in organisations entirely different, additional local rules of legitimisation occur, and there is another order of priority for handling these concepts and explaining them.

Sometimes the distance is so great that one could speak of 'doublespeak' (Orwell 1978). When the concepts are ambiguous, for their enactment in the circuit of use, this can be functional because of changing organisational practice, change in actors' wishes, interests, fashions, whims, growth, etc.

In general, the 'life world' is kept out of the concepts by the circuit of production, or placed in a business perspective. The difference between social or public life, and the world within the organisation is ignored. In the latter, individuals are not equal, speech is not free, but there is a production, value creating, and inequality context. In this book (and also in: Ten Bos, 1998, 2000), Ten Bos indicates some of the misrepresentations of the life world within a business perspective (for instance, what learning is and who is learning). The implicit context of inequality makes for a situation where concepts like Total Quality Management can be presented as 'liberating people at work', and in doing so present management as 'liberators'. Whereas there is clearly a situation of 'lie or myth' …, which denies that the relationship between management and worker is a dependency-relationship, a power balance (Alvesson and Willmott 1992: 96–109).

Many of the concepts take a certain morality as given, assuming that it is valid for participants in the organisation, and do not problematise the ambigious situation of management. Management has great difficulty with morality, because of its responsibility for adaptations which have consequences for careers, for happiness at work, for the existence of life worlds (management of meaning). Management, willingly or unwillingly, is an important co-producer of the partisan world in organisations and at the same time managers are the victims of political relations within the organisation. The management layer can well be served by monocultural images. The image of cultural consensus can push reality into the background. Optimism (we can do it) is made possible by simplification. However, the fact that the demand for new management techniques remains buoyant suggests that "the colonization of the life world … is far from complete" (Alvesson and Willmott 1992).

Modern concepts?

There are a number of connections between the concepts, their use and their production (the way in which they are produced) and the modernisation of society and its organisations.

According to Rohde, changes of relationships in organisations and customer relationships are based on the development from an economy of scarcity to an economy of affluence. This development has made customers both more diverse in their wishes, and harder to please. In addition, the digital revolution has led to new concepts such as E-commerce and virtual shopping malls. Because of differentiation and fragmentation in society and organisations, there is a *greater need for identity and binding, as well as for more and new ideologies*. Boessenkool regards the central issues of modernity as individualisation and collectivisation, agency and structure, local and social changes in the organisational culture. The identity of organisations is in need of redefinition on the basis of experience of managers, employees, customers and other actors. In this identity, values and norms as elements of culture play an important role: *the normative side*. At the same time we have seen that the organisational concepts approach the normative side from the instrumental or system world, ahistorical, idealistic and utopian, and the development of norms and values is not represented as a process involving different parties and actors.

There are economic considerations that can lead to increased alertness and quality improvement within organisations. Leisink regards self-managing teams as one of the new *playing fields where a contest takes place of the formulation of economic and social objectives*. Ten Bos sees the inspiration for learning in organisations as based on a loss of belief of certain authors (Senge among others) in the quality of public answers by politicians and officials to changing social situations. Especially managers are regarded as "thoughtful people" who, with their approach, can give more adequate modern answers. *In this way an ideological grip on society by the economic sector* takes shape.

Korver regards the rise of the concept of the new employee as a result of the long-felt need to adapt the organisation to the ever more complex challenges from its social surroundings. The service industry has become ever more dominant, new groups are grappling for position, and the assumption of the traditional breadwinner has become obsolete. *The system of work and labour relations has shifted, and possibly institutions and culture have not managed to keep up*. Koot sees a direct connection between the hybridisation of the image of the manager and the processes of rationalisation and individualisation: the manager is caught *between ideals, (soft) images and hard practices*.

Rationalisation as the increased rationality in the conduct of business leading to enhanced effectivity and efficiency, requires both more attention to integration of values, identity, commitment, community building, shared experiences, as well as an increase in added value and reduction of costs. *Instrumentality* is central in the world in which values and norms and added value are conceived. That is why the issue of *value integration*, the formation of organisational ideals, has a built-in *tension*. How can you yourself, how can groups and units, how can organisations be *instrumentally* involved in values? How deep do values go then?

And what can be expected of the formation of shared values (value integration) on the basis of shared production of meaning when the issue of how shared values and meaning is actually produced does not receive much attention?

In chapter one we referred to societal paradoxes of modernisation:

1. The process of differentiation in structure, the ever-growing specialisation and independence, and greater mutual dependence of separate parts. There have been major changes in the relationships between state, political system, market economy and citizens. This asks for a focus on historical determination, institutions and cultures.
2. The process of rationalisation, the ideal of universal consultation and measurability, and the possibility of individual patterns of choice for actors, and so of pluralism. The accent is strongly on individual patterns of choice, much less on institutions and cultures of rationalisation enabling these patterns. How do institutions and cultures supporting rationalisation evolve? How can integration of values take place based on instrumentality? Or is it based on other institutional and cultural elements?
3. The process of individualisation, the search for identity, and the fact that organisations strongly develop as makers of identity for managers, employees, and customers. The tension between formation of an 'own' identity of individuals and the grip that economic organisations have on this, is underexposed.
4. Domestication, control of natural surroundings, the discussion of the dividing line between nature and humans, increased dependence on technology. The meaning of boundaries between nature and humanity, and the addiction to technology deserve serious thought.

The concepts of organisation either ignore these paradoxes, or formulate simplified answers, thus clinging to an undivided world picture. Hybridisation, differentiation and localisation of answers, which reflect social development in terms of modernisation paradoxes, is found infrequently! The historical contingencies, institutional and cultural embeddedness of rationalisation are under-exposed.

In the following chapter a series of aspects of modernisation of organisation and society will be discussed, showing a background against which the concepts we have examined can be contrasted.

We will also discuss ways of doing justice to the urge for freedom that is behind modernity. We explore forms of organisational liberation.

References

Alvesson, M., H. Willmott (1996). *Making sense of management: a critical introduction*. London: Sage.

Alvesson M. & S. Deetz (1996). *Critical theory and postmodernism approaches to organizational studies*, 191–218 in: Handbook of organization studies. S.R. Clegg, C. Hardy, W.R. Nord (eds). London, Sage.

Bos, R. ten (1998). Merkwaardige moraal. Goed en kwaad in management en organisatie. (Strange morals. Good and bad in management and organisation) *Thema*.

Bos, R. ten (2000). *Fashion and utopia in management thinking*. Amsterdam: John Benjamins.

Bourdieu, P. (1979). *La distinction*. Paris: Minuit.

Castells, M. (1996). *The Rise of the Network Society:* The information age: economy, society and culture, Blackwell, Oxford, 3 volumes.

Fligstein, N. (1990). *The transformation of corporate control*. Cambridge: Harvard University Press.

Froud, J., C. Haslam, S. Johal, & K. Williams (2000). Shareholder value and financialisation: consultancy promises, management moves. *Economy and Society*, 29 (1), 80–110.

Habermas, J. (1981). *Theorie des Kommunikativen Handelns*. Frankfurt am Main: Suhrkamp (2 Teile).

Hoof, J. van & J. van Ruysseveldt (Eds.) (1996). *Sociologie en de moderne samenleving*. (Sociology and modern society) Heerlen: Open Universiteit.

Jackall, R. (1988). Moral mazes. *The world of corporate managers*. Oxford: Oxford University Press.

Kieser, A. & H. Kubicek (1992). *Organisation* (3rd edition). Berlin/New York: Walter de Gruyter.

Lammers, C.J., A.A. Mijs & W.J. van Noort (1997). *Organisaties vergelijkenderwijs. Ontwikkeling en relevantie van het sociologisch denken over organisaties.* (Comparing organisations, sociological thinking about organisations) Utrecht: Spectrum. 7e editie.

Mintzberg, H. (1973). *The nature of managerial work*. New York: Harper & Row.

Orwell, G. (1978). *Homage to Catalonia*. Harmondsworth: Penguin Books.

Peters, T., R. Waterman (1982). *In search of excellence. Lessons from America's best-run companies*. New York: Harper & Row.

Pine II, B.J. & J.H. Gilmore (2000). *De beleveniseconomie.* (The experience economy) Academic service.

Reich, R.B. (1992). *The work of nations*. New York: Vintage Books.

Veen, K. van (1998). Een vergelijking tussen Business Process Redesign en Moderne

SocioTechniek. *Bedrijfskunde, Tijdschrift voor modern management.* (Comparison between BPR and modern sociotechnics), 38–46.

Veen, K. van (2000). Meningen over managementmodes. (Opinions on management fashions) *Tijdschrift voor Management en Organisatie, 5,* 62–86.

Witte, M.C. de, A.H. van der Zwaan, (1998). Nieuwe begrippen voor bestaande concepten? (New concepts instead of existing ones?) – epiloog –. *Bedrijfskunde, Tijdschrift voor modern management,* 51–54.

Witteloostuijn, A. van (1999). *De anorexiastrategie. Over de gevolgen van saneren.* (The anorexia strategy. The consequences of downsizing.) Amsterdam, Antwerpen: Arbeiderspers.

Witteloostuijn, A. van (2000). Après nous la déluge. De economie van egocentrische hebzucht. (Economics of egocentric greed). Preadvies voor de Vereniging van Staathuishoudkunde.

Chapter 9

Modernity and the drive for freedom

Bert van Hees and Paul Verweel

Who hasn't seen it? Modern times, Chaplin's classic film, in which we are shown the rationalisation of industrial production in an existential manner. It is a film that shows us the convergence of the rationalisation of the primary process and the use of management science. In the film, man's alienation within the organisation contrasts sharply with the good fortune that befalls Chaplin outside the factory – only after many adventures, of course.

Today is again a time in which great changes are underway in terms of economic production and organisation, both in a corporate context and in society. What is actually happening at management and organisation level, and in society at large? Using theories developed by Boltanski and Chiapello and by Castells, both of which are based on networking, it is possible to relate these levels to one another. Again the question of the emancipation of humans in terms of their relating to each other, culture and nature (the life world) is being raised, and the question of how to escape instrumentality and rationalisation. Therefore, in the conclusion to this chapter, we will discuss a number of visions of liberation which indicate the routes along which the life world's scope can be enlarged.

Management and work organisation in the information age

The 'Network-project' paradigm of management

A new paradigm of management and social relationships at work is being developed: the *network-project paradigm of management* (Boltanski and Chiapello, 1999, see also: Guilhot, 2000). Boltanski and Chiapello conducted empirical research into shifts in management ideas, between 1960 and the 1990's and published their findings in their extensive work 'Le nouvel esprit du capitalisme' (The new spirit of capitalism), 1999.

Old hierarchical and institutionalised controls are losing their weight, and social and work relationships are becoming more embedded in horizontal networks. Work is becoming a "thick" relationship, in which a number of personality aspects and creativity can be enacted, with a type of freedom that is being linked to self-realisation and self-organisation. The manager that has emerged during the last decade is the leader of an intangible production process that is organised like a project, with a limited timespan, and inspired by a 'vision' shared with 'partners', who contribute in their own, irreducibly personal way. Generic competencies, such as relational and communicative skills, critical and assessment ability, are applied during production; for example, through the coach who mobilises and co-ordinates workers by his intensive symbolic and relational performance. A blurring occurs between production, instrumental action and communication. Within this paradigm, 'being successful' is defined on the basis of the 'activism' principle: being active, the scope of the relations and contacts at work – but also in one's free time – that are useful to the realization of projects. At the level of the self, it is about entering into voluntary relations with others, and about being embedded in steadily expanding contact networks. Constant project changes are accompanied by enthusiasm and heroism. The central asset here is the accumulation of social capital, in particular the ability to integrate separate network structures. This necessitates a charming, autonomous, flexible, communicative, opportunistic and morally light character, and requires a permanent, more or less superficial, mental radar exploration of the environment. The opposite, in terms of character and behaviour, is the demonstration of dislike for an uninterrupted stream of project changes, or an adherence to fundamental values, to specific people, networks, etc. An element such as 'showing solidarity' is ill suited to this paradigm. Showing solidarity can be interpreted as 'being stuck', as not being autonomous, and, therefore, a disadvantage for someone's career.

Boltanski (2000) also signals a trend towards *heterarchisation*: ... the development of forms of organisation characterised by collaborative structures, dispersed authority and ambiguity in respect of assets, that is to say in respect of the answer to the question: what makes that what we are performing well? Within a heterarchy there is a diversity of value creating regimes, due to the active co-existence and rivalry of different evaluation principles or opinions about value and value creation: an organisational unit then works within various cross-networks, each of which has its own value creation regime. If the heterarchisation trend continues, more attention will be required to differences in norms and values, differences in types of value creating regimes and the corresponding types of legitimisation.

The personal and social cost of networks

Networks have their personal and social cost, and, as Boltanski and Chiapello observe, it is striking that these are not indicated in publications on the subject of networks. These costs are twofold; on the one hand, related to the form of exploitation, and, on the other hand, the problems created for the flexible networker.

The network project configuration is a new form of exploitation: the status or the success enjoyed by flexible networkers depends on the inflexibility of the – traditional – inflexible networkers, who do deliver information to their networks, but do not have any contacts or information outside their structural positions, causing the asymmetry of knowledge and contacts to increase. The more flexible units, companies and markets are able to exploit the less flexible and less mobile ones.

The network project paradigm causes a flexible networker to suffer from mental and personal problems. These are the following:

1. the networker's fear of being excluded, of not being involved ("handy mania": I must be connected, have a hand in it, or a way in)
2. exhaustion due to "enforced autonomy or independence"
3. the schism between flexibility and the need for authenticity. The constant need to adapt may affect someone's ability to repeatedly recharge and be enthusiastic, and result in indifference towards what one is working on. Networkers may start to question their true identity and convictions. They do bring their selves into the action, but in a context where this is no longer a choice, but a condition for the successful completion of tasks. This conditionality detracts from the element of choice, spontaneity and empathetic contact. Play-acting may result, where someone acts his own emotions, and in which a more spontaneous enacting of his own personality stays in the background. All this requires an increased amount of control of affect or emotions (cf. the so-called civilisation theory, started by Elias (1939); see also Ultee et al., 1992: 551 et seq)
4. organisations include increasingly more aspects when selecting employees (does the candidate look representative, does he come across well, does he fit in with our company culture) and socialisation pressure is increasing, not only as a result of courses held, but also through group interactions, coaching and tutoring in-company events, 360 degree feedbacks and subjective ratings awarded by group members, superiors and customers. Individualisation may increase hand in hand with disciplining.

We cannot consider these developments in the management and work processes as separate from those occurring in society; this because the image of an individualised society is emerging from behind the image of the network-project paradigm (Bauman, 2001). Especially in Castells' work, changes in economy and society are related to the changed nature and position of management and of social relationships in and around organisations.

Network society and the information age

In his extensive study entitled 'The information age: economy, society and culture', Castells (1997) analyses the transition from an industrial to an *informational and network society,* and the changes occurring to the complex of economy, culture, politics and society under the influence of information technology.

Castells points to decreased central authority (control exerted by the national state) and the reduction of traditional relationships and forms of association (in families, state, politics, etc.).

Castells analyses the emergence of multi-actor networks, which are comprised of increasingly more actors, and in which actors, for example governments, are concerned with more issues – exercise more influence – but, at the same time have less power and less of a grip on results. He also points to the increasing importance of identities and social and cultural communities that are defending their own identity and way of life.

The network enterprise has a flexibility-based production process, and work that is becoming more generic and reflexive, and easier to programme for the individual employee – in which existing career patterns are becoming outdated. The network enterprise is experiencing a change in the nature of capital: it gets global, flash capital. The old class and social structures (including the patriarchate, domination exercised by men) are crumbling: there is an increasing number of employees with their own production means (managers, professionals, engineers) and people without jobs are more likely to miss out. The number of employee collectives is decreasing, and collective identities may shatter or localise (something we have seen in The Netherlands in recent years, in action by employees of the national railways, where employee collectives organised action, when this had always been organised by national or company unions before). Due to the global economy, the national state as a sovereign authority is experiencing a crisis, and, related to this, there is a crisis in terms of democracy: the public sphere is being undermined, traditional institutions and organisational structures are disappearing (research shows that the state, but also the family is getting weaker), political processes and politicians are being *media-tised* more (more subject to determination by the media), are driven less by ideals and ideology, less by an ideal of 'the administrator, and more by survival. The public sphere is becoming less tangible for citizens. Social integration is being undermined due to the decline of the public domain, decreased social homogeneity or increasing diversity, mobility, migration and individualisation. As a consequence, in relative terms and in the citizen's *perception,* the value of contractual relationships, for example at work– in comparison with public and private relationships – is increasing.

Castells shows – and this is in line with Boltanski and Chiapello's analysis – that, in the network enterprise, people are being evaluated more strongly as to:

1. the information and knowledge they have (although this knowledge basis is less stable than in the past, due to permanent changes, the advent of search systems, etc.)
2. their assessment of information and formulation of questions and problem definitions; the formulation of dialogues, answers and policy recommendations
3. network potential: communicative and political talent, language skills

We will now elaborate on five elements of the network society that are of primary importance for the way in which management and organisation changes: subjectivation, mediatisation, diversity, financialisation and the mutual penetration of work and private life.

Subjectivation and soft management

An image of liberation tends to be linked to this: people are called upon to demonstrate their possibilities as a subject, contact becomes more human, there is a more balanced division of power and management increasingly occurs on the basis of mutual adjustment and agreement (cf. the parallel with Castells thinking about the role played by governments: less power, but more influence). The idea that more soft management may result in the liberation of workers has not, incidentally, been substantiated empirically, and is, theoretically, disputable (Foucault, 1981). Control exercised by communities, achievement control, ideological control and perceptual control can replace old forms of control (Alvesson, 1996).

Subjectivation means that more attention is paid to the subject and the usefulness of the subject. The individual can introduce various utility arguments or elements that are valuable to the individual as a subject. De Korte and Bolweg (1994) identify four elements that determine how an individual feels: a need for physiological, psychological and economic safety; the need for appreciation and respect; the need for justice, fair treatment and involvement in decisions; a need to form part of a social community. All these aspects can be incorporated into a psychological contract. Soft management implies that meaning management can be applied to all these elements.

Mediatisation

Management in organisations, business schools and consultancies is becoming more active as co-producers of the truth and ideology about organisations. In the internet economy it is important to continue to work on one's image ('publish or perish'). On the one hand, the increased activity is a result of the blending of the academic world with that of the consultancy, as a result of which the *latest* and hottest insights are important; on the other hand, it is a consequence of the increased dependence and transparency resulting from the information society, which prompts a rapid response and image adjustments. Not only must management inform and 'work' the stock exchange – a media-driven process – information about customer complaints, errors and bad practice in companies also reach the media faster, and information is actively sought and put together by the media and other interested parties, such as competitors, shareholders, pressure groups, consumers (organisations), hackers, etc.

Diversity

The necessity of dealing with diversity is increasing. More different types of lifestyle are developing, and more representatives of different cultures are present. Organisations have to deal with diversity due to their greater customer friendliness and increasing diversity in terms of employees and partners (both suppliers, clients and partners). Alliances between companies from different regions of the world, and also from within the European Community, with business systems that are culturally and institutionally different, also contribute to this.

Financialisation

A greater achievement and performance orientation and their translation into financial data. Van Witteloostuijn (1999, 2001) sees conflict management as a pendant to financialisation, something that is infiltrating the Netherlands particularly from the United States. Conflict management is in line with a business image of a struggle for survival and control. At least the top 1500 companies are embroiled in a global power struggle, expressed in takeovers and mergers amongst other things (Schenk, 1996). What is striking is that the trend towards subjectivation and soft management can go hand in hand with a greater emphasis on results and performance.

Blending Work and Private

The trend for work and private life to merge or become interconnected. Work increasingly requires total commitment from all sides of someone's personality, the contribution of creativity, social skills, communication and sense-making. This may mean increased pressure from work on someone's private life, but it is also possible that work will open up to trends from what we refer to as the life world. For example, many people indicate that their workplace is more exciting, and that friendships there are more intimate than those they have in their private lives (Verweel, 2000). However, Sennett (1998) sees a corrosion of character and observes an erosion of people's social life in the private world. The professional is more sociable, but within a far more instrumentalised context, and the closeness of these social relationships will in actual fact be weak. This may lead to isolation and loneliness and a "quest for meaning" and "ultimate values".

Under the pressure of working life and the demise of such institutions as the family, the national government, etc. as described by Castells, job related social relations may increase in value vis-à-vis an employee's home life. The answer to the question of whether work will have more of a life world, or resemble a real home, depends on an increase of authentic communication, shared producing and sharing of meaning and the courage and opportunity to express doubts (the criteria discussed in Chapter 8).

In respect of the developments described above, one must realise that the new era has different meanings in store for individuals with ample resources and those with fewer resources and that meanings are related to historical background. These differences are worded as such in cultural movements, such as feminism. For example, for 'individuals with ample resources', the world of work is easily seen as: 'work is career and fun'; and shared production of meaning translated as: 'the best should have the greatest say' and having autonomy as: 'to be in control of your career'.

For the average individual, they mean something else. The logic of work means: 'Work is certainly not just fun'; the collective production of meaning is related to protection: 'As long as we are not overruled by the others'; and autonomy is also easily linked to: 'the protection of groups and minorities'. The first group thinks far more in terms of opportunities, the second far more in terms of risks.

Consequences for work: the combination of system world, life world and partisan world in the network economy

How do the changes in work processes and management mentioned above influence the relationship between system world, life world and partisan world, as experienced by employees? To be able to answer this question, we recall the analysis from Chapter 8; see the figure below:

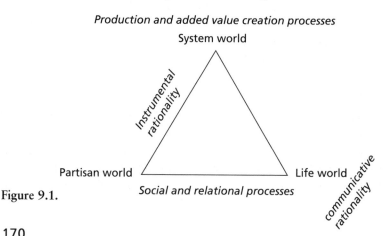

Figure 9.1.

In the last chapter we discerned three worlds, with two continua:

- production and added value creation processes versus social and relational processes (social processes consisting of both influence and communication)
- instrumental rationality (including utility, use-value) versus communicative rationality

Both the world of work and one's private life may consist of aspects from the system world, life world and the partisan world. Work is not a category that overlaps entirely with the system world, nor does one's private life overlap entirely with the life world. Besides instrumental action, work increasingly consists of a social component, due to the change in the nature of work: employees are expected to establish contacts, to maintain networks, to manage a relationship network, to dress for the occasion, to be reachable at home, etc. In private life the instrumentalisation of various social contacts is taking place, such as time-management, the contracting of childcare, etc. De Swaan (1989) has referred to this as the development towards negotiation households. Organisations are becoming places where people are permitted to and can discover identity and appreciation. Thus, instrumental logic continues to dominate, but also increased attention for others *within an instrumental framework*, as apparent, for example, in the roles of coach, tutor, etc. You can imagine that people, led by instrumental motives, start to get more engrossed in others, and that we ought to speak of an *instrumental empathy* of sorts. According to Bauman (1998: 110) amongst others, the latter is a contradiction. In this respect, he cites Giddens, who sees a relationship based on the satisfaction that parties may derive from it as the way to escape the responsibility that each of us has for others. As Lévinas puts it, this responsibility is 'seeing the face of the other, the naked, the helpless, the powerless', separate from any projection.

Networks, cliques and professional or knowledge communities are important for professional development, for the starting of initiatives and for improving one's position. Such networks or communities may support local interests, are suitable for image making, cultural contests between certain groups and help to create subgroup norms. As such, such communities also have a political or partisan world component.

Why so little liberation?

We have not seen a shift from system to life world aspects in organisational practices. This raises the question: why does the system world, or organisation functional logic, dominate? Why is the logic of authentic communication only present to a limited extent? Why is shared production of meaning so limited? Why is there relatively little scope for minority visions, dissen-

171

sion and autonomy of the worker? Why does a life world view, a liberation of system constraints, not dominate the agenda? Does our society and our methods of organisation indeed offer the opportunity to place life world issues on the agenda?

The first line of answering these questions may lie in the nature of modern Western society, with its dominant orientation towards the system world.

The modern, the rationalisable and instrumentalisation are anchored in our culture and ethics: work symbolises self-discipline, a form of civilisation (cf. *civilization theory*), doing your best, being able to put your own small worries to one side is a quality; work and success at work is a symbol of social prestige and a symbol of expression of supra-individual, communal, collective consciousness. There is a tendency towards instrumental and functional logic in all our interactions and communications. Into our thinking about work, usefulness and success, a certain value of working, doing your best, entrepreneurship and task fulfilment, is built in, there is an instrumental work ethic (Landes, 1998). In our society, instrumentalisation is deeply rooted, and the network society builds on this, despite the fact that great shifts are occurring in the institutional and cultural embedding of instrumentality thinking (Castells, 1997). One could refer to this as the individualisation of instrumentality (Bauman, 1998, 2001).

The second approach to these questions is based on the basic difference between the system world and life world, the impossibility of communication between system and life world, for example the impossibility to categorise the life world into ratios. The life world is not about goal-orientedness, but about spontaneity, action, *being there*. By definition, the life world is not rational in the sense of manageable, controllable; nor is it subjected to a logic. The life world needs the discipline of the instrument, the market, utilitarianism, hedonism, authority, etc. in order to become organisable or rational, and will disappear to the extent that this need were to be fulfilled. As such, the demand for a balance between the worlds is a paradox: the determination of a balance is based on the determination of the life world on the basis of system world criteria. This constitutes a fundamental, ontological criticism: they are not compatible, and can only be approached from their own presuppositions.

A third approach is based on hybrid solutions. Organisation is often at odds with democracy, yet does require legitimisation in a democratic environment. Complex organisations show a tendency to break down their own moral order, because they are all about survival, ad hoc changes and political compromises: organisations are hybrids of rational organisation (bureaucracy) and 'fiefdoms'. Therefore, half-hearted solutions are developed for the legitimisation issue. Tension exists between the organisation, democracy, bureaucracy and social relationships (capital, labour, clients, the environment, etc.) and tension exists between clans and classes within and without the organisation (Alvesson and Ouchi, 1980). Management must deal with the tension, both internally and externally, and legitimise developments. Jackall (1988) points to the 'uncertainties within' that ultimately turn the manager into a morally lost figure without commitment. Myths about organisation and management, stories about morality and legitimacy, are a survival element in anyone's career. This third line indicates a prominent role for the political element, the parties world.

Liberation visions: designing space for the life world

There has been a surge of interest in and stories about sensemaking, lifestyles, growth, spirituality, empowerment, and work as a form of liberation. These stories consist of various elements: the wish to increase individual utility (satisfaction, sensations), to further the process of giving meaning, to touch deeper layers, and also the wish to work in a way which takes social responsibility. In a general sense, they express the wish that more scope be allowed for individuals. In the majority of visions about development, the individual world of experience would appear to have a subjective and hedonistic meaning – the good life – instead of one in which the serving of or sacrificing oneself to some form of community, is at the forefront (Schulze speaks of the experience society, 1992). The increased attention for personal development at work is in line with a development in which work (but not all kinds of work) can be regarded as a consumer good or a stimulant (Bauman, 1998). The latter manifests itself in the world of work in the departure from such values as faithfulness, loyalty, love of one's fellow man, and sacrifice (Sennett, 1998). The views in society on how life at work should be given shape go in a number of directions like individual utility and well-being, search for meaning, spirituality and social accountability and responsibility. These aspirations increase but do not go hand in hand.

How, then, could an increase in the number of life world aspects occur in the workplace; how could liberation from the system world in the direction of the life world, look like? And how could it come about?

We offer four lines of thought, each of which contains different principles of liberation, and corresponds to a number of developments in the field.

Two brief comments can be made when elaborating on liberation – from the system world, in the direction of a life world:

Firstly, motivations differ and someone who gains satisfaction from the nature of her work, thus work that is intrinsically satisfying, and does not have a great need for interhuman interaction, could manage well in an instrumental system world, provided it presents her with intrinsic challenges. A condition for the latter is that the individual is able to help design the nature of the work, due to the power she possesses (or her profession like in the surgical profession, for example) or because the organisation offers ample opportunity for adjustment between employees about work. The 'shared production of meaning' aspects of the life world as distinguished by us, incorporates the employee's autonomy, or right, to be involved in decisions about tasks, organisation and aims.

Secondly, we see liberation in the direction of the life world as a threefold process increasing authentic communication or intrinsic social action, shared production of meaning and room for dissent and minorities. There are other life world interpretations, such as an individualistic interpretation, which subordinates the interhuman and collective aspect to the creation of opportunities for the individual, his expression, learning, etc., and there are interpretations particularly based on harmonious collaboration, employees that are at one with each other, sacrificing or contributing to the whole, which of course show an absence of politics.

We identify four lines of thought with which to achieve liberation, and a different relationship between the life world, system world and partisan world, in and at work.

These four lines do not form a blueprint, but give building blocks and directions for scenarios; they also raise useful questions.

The first direction is based on the aim of introducing the life world into the organisation, and to increase an organisation's human quality. We refer to this as the *humanising organisation*.

The second focuses on individuals who wish to achieve liberation from within themselves. The voluntaristic and actor-perspective is strong here: the *individualising organisation*.

The third direction prepares itself to 'live with the evil', that is to say to accept the evil of instrumental work, limited shared creation or production of meaning, limited freedom of minority expression. Here, the emphasis lies on restricting or compensating the evil: the *compensating organisation*.

A fourth development is also imaginable – this does not so much concern design – in the direction of an implosion of the functional and instrumental emphasis in organisation. You could say: the evil is responsible for its own downfall, the instrumental and functional aspects become so strong that the demise of the organisation, its social dynamic is imminent: the *imploding organisation*.

Each type of liberation depends on a number of preconditions. For example, the scope for humanisation in an organisation will depend partly on the competitive and market situations, and the *'slack'* that exists within the organisation, etc. For an overview of contingencies, see Kieser and Kubicek, 1993.

174

The humanising organisation

The first liberation vision 'freedom by means of increasing social life within the organisation' involves the opposite of organisation-functional logic, instrumental action on behalf of the organisation. Here, freedom is the scope for the three aspects that we distinguished in the life world: associating with people as goals in themselves, authenticity, the shared production of meaning in respect of the organisation, and scope for minorities, dissension, being different, showing courage. This type of liberation must represent a counterbalance to a fixation on results, scoring, effectivity and efficiency, and is to ensure that there is room for the employees' own cultures, as well as fragmentation and diversity in them.

Authentic communication may underlie both organisation-oriented and group-oriented actions: people give their time and energy to the shared cause, while the organisation has become a symbol of jointly established meaning, based on the contribution made by those involved. People contribute on the basis of, or because of, their connection with each other. This may be due to a number of motives, amongst others: serving or sacrificing and/or committing oneself to a more all-embracing social whole. Obviously, this is also possible if one's motives are instrumental, but this is something that falls outside the framework of this liberation vision.

Liberation from the instrumental and the functional is possible by appealing to authentic communication between people, by inciting and introducing the power of imagination, by finding alternatives for the organic and machine bureaucracy models from our time. The question is who will be the central driving force behind the humanising organisation: the academic and consultancy worlds, a tight labour market, a social movement of (new) managers, consultants, business schools or, more generally, the professional layer, the 'symbol analysts' as they are called by Reich (1992). Does the social movement have a specific design, or is it more a process of continuous adjustment to increasing individualisation and diversity, increased subjectivation, both in mutual relationships between employees and in contacts with clients, external partners, etc.?

Possible expressions of this liberation

1. Participative management. This may be more or less pluralistic, that is to say there is more or less recognition that different parties exist, each of which must speak for itself. This may concern equipping parties, the facilitation of a 'speak-up habitus' or the empowerment of individuals and parties.
2. The living organisation which seeks or creates 'core values' (De Geus, 1997). This is in line with a missionary or movement organisation (Mintzberg, 1989). Lucent Industries, for example, practises the 'man-

agement of diversity', the aim of which is a pluriform social culture; this, incidentally, within strong shared norms and values in respect of work.

3. The so-called 'modern sociotechnicians' and their predecessors who attempt to link technical and organisational system requirements with social requirements in their programme. In recent years, some Dutch consultancies have been linking the MST to a negotiation process, in order to achieve a better mix of outcomes in social relations and production.

4. Human resource management is being developed based on the idea of different types of people (cf. attention for enneagrams etc.). Quality control, the use of scorecards in a human capital sphere and in the sphere of stakeholders and customer management, diversity management. The promotion of optimal commitment, to which the experience of learning, well-being and coaching is important. Compare the popular 'flow' concept, the 'peak' experience during times at which people are deep in concentration and experiencing intense joy. A new management role may respond to this need for personal development, one concerning personal courage and integrity, team building and dialogue, instead of position, authority and hierarchy (Ramondt, 2000).

5. Democratisation, via dialogue processes, in order to ensure that organisational goals are shared by all, via task democratisation, via formal increased influence and the transfer of ownership (cf. co-operations). Dialogue in which both parties are asked to learn to accept fragmentation and dissension.

6. Conducting business in a way that is socially responsible, developing ethical principles for actions taken by and in the organisation, and attention for openness within and around the organisation.

Sectors in which this process of liberation is expressed, are amongst others the high performance companies in the private sector.

The dynamic of this liberation is that soft management mechanisms are deployed, but also quality instruments and 'scorecards' to measure human aspects and interaction with stakeholders. Actors realise that competitive advantage is based on the opportunities given to growth, knowledge management and creativity besides efficiency, cost and quality control.

Threats

This approach harbours a number of deceptive elements, misleading from liberation. The threats lie in its lapse into a compensation programme, for example how to contribute good things to place next to the 'evil' present: trips for a good cause (supporting a Ronald McDonald house for sick children), or in a development towards a substitute sociable world in which people treat each other in a human way (for as long as a contract lasts), or an environment for re-labelling, in which hierarchical involvement becomes 'being responsible together'.

Also threatening is the build-up of a monoculture: to what extent will it create scope for authentic action?

A more fundamental question is whether you can achieve liberation from an instrumental context, and can you get around coping or living with power? Empirical organisation theory shows that functional system logic and partisan logic (power) appear to be part of all organisational processes, including democratic organisation (there is a long line of thought spanning from Machiavelli and Michels to Mintzberg). For example, in democratic organisations and voluntary organisations too (political parties, for example), leaders and the led, bosses and serfs emerge with the passage of time, as well as dissidents, troublemakers, apathetic volunteers and active members, thinkers and followers. In short, a dynamic of social hierarchies continues to be the case, and inspires both instrumentalisation and power logic. Besides this, organisational processes have a history: organisations in which much is done in respect of shared production of meaning, and where there is much scope for mutual social exchange, may, in time, become very consensual (and dismissive in respect of minority voices). In time, people do not any longer perceive the reality of concrete interactions and communications with each other, but an 'idealised image of what is shared or common'. The political dynamic present behind a common meaning and understanding stays in the background.

The individualising organisation

The *second liberation vision* assumes that **freedom is doing what your heart tells you**. The individual is central. This vision is based on a tendency to subjectivation, fragmentation and diversity and the questioning of the distinction between work and private life. People interpret doing 'what your heart tells you' in different ways, and have different lifestyles and motivations: wanting to excel, experience certain feelings, show something, experience growth, do what is 'right' (such as members of Greenpeace), etc.

Individualisation may take a form where work itself becomes a consumer good, an object of wishes, focusing on variation, being interesting, offering the opportunity for adventure, sensations, excitement and a certain amount of risk (Bauman, 1998): the employee as a consumer. Increased attention for social relationships and the life world, but only if consumption is accompanied by a personal use congruent with this approach. The 'making of sacrifices' and 'serving' are only values for individuals if they see utility for themselves in collective relationships.

To be able to follow one's heart, a number of conditions must be met:

1. the possibility to explore, to examine what your heart tells you
2. to develop and learn in this direction
3. to be able to make propositions concerning how one wants to work, to formulate demands
4. to have some say in the propositions made by the organisation to the employee, about the customers that it seeks/takes, the work that is created, goals, etc.

Some people will want to strive for self-realisation in the form of performance and improved status. This results in a strong meritocratical tendency: you are what you achieve. The shadow side of this is that in an environment where people are assessed on merits, social connections have a secondary basis; virtues such as faithfulness, loyalty, and love of one's fellow man are only functionally appropriate here. Generation differences may play a role in this, as well as different phases of life: ambitious, young professionals have a different perspective (like getting ahead and putting things aside to achieve this) than experienced, older workers who have seen all sorts of situations.

We see the individualising organisation finding expression in the following ways:

1. New companies, pioneers.
2. Internal entrepreneurship.
3. Self-organisation: allow individuals and social groups to indicate it themselves, wherever possible. This can be found in E-commerce, ICT circles, new economy, organisations with continuously learning professionals, and highly changing markets. Radically new, horizontal organisational designs, in which various participants co-create the meaning of organising.
4. Employability.

The dynamic in this is for creating a 'human supportive environment'. The individual need to excel can lead to a house full of primadonnas and to problems in terms of envy amongst individuals. How can conflicts be avoided? At the same time, there is also a need to find like-minded people, to exchange ideas, with whom to experience a feeling of solidarity. There is a need to create a social frame or grip, a certain degree of stability for individual employees, a feeling of 'being at home'. With the growing importance of individual curricula and career paths, friendships at work, a group environment, the shared creation of meaning and leadership are actually becoming more important – however contradictory this might appear. De Korte and Bolweg (1994) point to the importance of the group, the team and the manager as a source of support. It becomes necessary to pay more attention to coaching, and the human process. Paradoxically, this individualisation results in more human resource (human process) management.

Threats

This development carries a number of threats. 'Doing what you want' is no more than a meaningless fiction if it ignores social embedding and the social capital needed to facilitate organisation, both at a micro level and higher levels. Faithfulness, loyalty and love of one's fellow man are virtues that are indispensable in a life world based on people that wish to experience social bonds, who refer to social relationships or groups of which they (wish to) form a part. These virtues are also important in an organisational world, as they contribute to stable expectations, trust, responsibilities and continuity.

The story in which one does what one's heart tells you and where individualism is promoted does not make a distinction between amply equipped and less amply equipped employees, something that we have referred to above. The weakness of this story is that it does not reflect on the consequences that individual differences in position and equipment and motives have for the social dimension. If it did do this, questions would be raised about solidarity, group bonding, inequality and justice. There is a danger that an atomistic idea of life is followed because market relations are shifting towards (certain groups of) employees. Doing what you want may also result in a bottomless search for sensation fulfilment, the search for the sake of searching, a changeable enjoyment (Castells, 1997).

A major challenge for the individualising organisation will be the settlement of intellectual property: if the knowledge possessed by professional becomes the core asset, how do you settle profits based on this knowledge (Handy, 2001)?

The compensating organisation

The third liberation vision: **freedom is living or coping with evil**, with functional and instrumental actions, and with subordination in an organisational context. The 'living with evil' vision accepts organisational functionality, because it creates freedom via the production of goods and services (Landes, 1998). Capitalism ensures prosperity, if the right institutions exist. It is the very separation of institutional spheres (public and private, work and private life) that makes this possible; it provides boundaries and a framework for exchange between spheres.

This 'living with evil' vision is based on the work ethic, an instrumentel attitude to working, giving priority to outcomes more than process of working, a welfare state approach (the state covers the risks of working), intense competition and the view that contract relationships are the basis for economic life, and that it will not be possible to change this to any significant extent.

People can deal with the evil by avoiding it, by passing it on to others, or by restricting or compensating it. Logically, it could also be redefined, but we will not discuss this, as this is included in our vision on the framing of organisational concepts.

This vision can be expressed in a number of ways:

1. The abolition or minimalisation of work. This might be the creation of a basic income by government, the encouragement of small self-supporting economic unit. Cf. the service-barter economy that is valuable as seen by the ecological movement.
2. Giving it to others, outsourcing it, exporting it: 'bad' work might be and is allocated to a certain group, such as dirty work given to outsiders, an 'out-group', or exported.
3. Restrain the evil and/or compensate it by recognising the evil and creating institutions to counteract it, such as the law (in the Netherlands The Working Conditions Act, Works Councils act, etc.), internal and external control by stakeholders and authorities, or countervailing powers (unions, pressure groups), external review boards, social conventions and guarantees for diversity, for civil rights in the business community, amongst other things in respect of expressing complaints, bell-ringing. Engelen (2000) argues the case for economic citizenship, to give rights to the employee, to put right the balance. Various instruments are required to determine the extent to which the interests and commitment of employees and other stakeholders are guarded or realised, such as the quality cards, social audits, labour union reports, etc.

Some of the sectors in which the compensating tendency is to be found are: care, education, and sectors that are generally highly regulated or are (semi) government sectors. In sectors like (health) care and education one finds many professional bureaucracies (Mintzberg, 1979), organisations which are highly regulated by organisational and professional standards, and which have less scope for humanising and individualising strategies. Compensating is an alternative here.

Questions

This vision raises the question of which forces are to restrain the evil. At present, urgency would appear to be absent; it is left to individuals and the business community themselves. There is no movement towards the socialisation of organisations, but there is a movement of responsible entrepreneurship and the formulation of ethical programmes (business ethics). In the Netherlands no explicit political or labour union programme exists – at least in the major parties – in which employees gain more of a grip on the organisations in which they work, in order to increase their freedom of speech and that of minorities. On the other hand, this does not mean to say that there is no potential for a programme such as this within the differentiated categories of the working population. Apart from this, there is a long term development towards European participation underway (cf. European works council and European labour unions, labour and work laws).

This vision is based on the distinction between production and reproduction, working hours versus free time, which is also recovery time. The more work is regarded as a consumption article, the less relevant this distinction is becoming.

The imploding organisation

A *fourth liberation vision* is not so much concerned with a design as with a process that negates the instrumental, because the evil undermines itself: the **implosion of the evil**. This is not a liberation in which a part is played by visionary actors.

Increased instrumental action, from purely contractual social relationships and experiencing the organisation as a contract world, result in negative consequences that are out of control. In some companies, managers change every few months because of career opportunities, and this makes it virtually impossible to build up trust and stable expectations. The working environment is permanently incomplete. Reward components are used or deployed that can no longer be linked to achievement, as the person has already left before results become evident.

The instrumental may go too far when, in the homecare sector for example, an elderly client has to be 'finished' in a space of just several minutes, and work appears a pointless action (mechanical work). An underlying factor is the auctioning of work on an increasingly large scale (globalisation), accompanied by the deterioration of the welfare state (Castells, 1997).

The dynamic in this development is increasing work pressure, rationalisation and the disappearance of stabilising positions, such as middle management or tutor hours at schools; responsibilities for contracts and organisations are no longer monitored together, continually, systematically or on the basis of a vision. This results in the devolution of control, fragmentation of the social system and social cohesion. The organisation sinks under the weight of overrationalisation and the neglect of social cohesion. The organisation implodes due to the decreasing learning (adaptive) ability of the internal, once so successful, formula of functional rationalisation. Van Witteloostuijn (2001) relates this to the anorexia-strategy of management and to macho-management tendencies.

These are developments that can be found in call-centres, sectors with illegal labour, parts of the care and education sectors.

Threats

As long as rich countries continue to dispose of low-value work to social fringe groups with no political significance within the rich countries and elsewhere in the world without political repercussions, an implosion of the evil will not be possible.

Concluding remarks

Organisation concepts which claim to surpass the limitations presented by the rational and functionalistic models are put into practices full of rationalisation and functionalisation.

It is no question that new concepts, like the network-project paradigm, will face psychological and social problems for employees, organisation and society, based on the contradictions of rationalisation and modernity. The network-project concept covers a segment of the labour market and a specific set of forms of work organisation. Liberation is part of such a new concept, but dilemmas, paradoxes, conflicts and compromises are also found in practice.

We have indicated four different types of liberation based on the possibility of gradual evolutions, adaptation and collapse. It is possible that these developments, differing in various sectors, types of organisation and contexts, will occur at the same time, so that patches of emancipation and liberation may show an incoherent and patchwork-break away from the practical and intellectual chains of rationalisation.

We hope that our de-framing of concepts will provide an opportunity for intellectual and practical re-framing, a re-framing that does justice to both old questions put by such pioneers as Weber about value rationality besides mechanical rationality, and (post) modern questions about the importance of the life world for both the functioning of organisations and for the development of man and social man.

References

Alvesson, M. (1996). *Communication, power and organization.* Berlin/New York: Walter de Gruyter.

Alvesson, M. (1998). Social identity and the problem of loyalty in knowledge-intensive companies. Paper for the WESWA-congress, Rotterdam.

Bauman, Z. (1998). *Leven met veranderlijkheid, verscheidenheid en onzekerheid.* (Living with change, diversity and uncertainty). Amsterdam: Boom.

Bauman, Z. (2001). *The individualized society.* Cambridge UK: Polity Press.

Boltanski, L., E. Chiapello (1999). *Le nouvel esprit du capitalisme.* Paris: Gallimard.

Boltanski, L., L. Thévenot (1999). The sociology of critical capacity. *European Journal of social theory,* 2 (3), 359–377.

Boltanski, L. (2000). Judgements and regimes of justification, part of the seminar on heterarchies, organizational innovation, organized by the Columbia university USA.

Castells, M. (1997). The information age: economy, society and culture 3 vol. Blackwell, Massachusetts.

Dijk, A. van & P. Verweel (Eds.) (1997). *De ladder op omlaag, een psychologie van besturen.* (Climbing the ladder downwards. A psychology of governance. Assen: van Gorcum.

Elias, N. (1982). *Het beschavingsproces.* (The civilization process). Utrecht: Het Spectrum.

Engelen, E. (2000). Nieuw burgerschap van de werknemer. (New citizenship of the worker). Paper Universiteit van Amsterdam.

Foucault, M. (1981). Themanummer over macht. (On power). *Te Elfder ure, 25* (3).

Foucault, M. (1984). De wil tot weten. Geschiedenis van de seksualiteit I, (The will to know. A history of sexuality). Nijmegen: SUN.

Geus, A. de (1997). De levende onderneming. (The living firm). Schiedam: Scriptum management.

Guilhot, N. (2000). Review essay of L. Boltanski, E. Chiapello Le nouvel esprit du capitalisme. *European Journal of Social Theory, 3* (3), 355–379.

Handy, C. (2001). *The elephant and the flea.* London: Hutchinson.

Hees, G.B. van (1993). Bedrijfsmatige effecten van vakbonden en ondernemings-raden 1993, Leuven: Garant. (Organizational effects of labour unions and work councils).

Jackall, R. (1988). *Moral mazes.* Oxford: Oxford University Press.

Korte, A.W. de & J.F. Bolweg (1994). *De nieuwe werknemer?!* (The new employee?). Assen: Van Gorcum.

Kieser, A. & H. Kubicek (1993). Organisation. Berlin, New York: Walter de Gruijter.

Lammers, C.J., A.A. Mijs, & W.J. van Noort (1997). *Organisaties vergelijkender-wijs.* (Comparing organisations). Utrecht: Spectrum.

Landes, D.S. (1998). *The wealth and poverty of nations.* New York: Norton.

Mintzberg, H. (1979). The structuring of organizations. Englewood Cliffs, N.J: Prentice Hall.

Mintzberg, H. (1989). *Mintzberg on management.* New York: Free Press.

Ouchi, W.G. (1980). Markets, bureaucracies and clans. *Administrative Science Quarterley, 25,* 129–141.

Ramondt, J.J. (2000). Bedolven macht. (Flooded power. The anchoring of power in contemporary organisations). De verankering van de machtsrol in hedendaagse organisaties. *Management en Organisatie, 54* (4), juli–augustus.

Reich, R.B. (1992). *The Work of Nations: Preparing Ourselves for 21st Century Capitalism.* New York: Vintage Books.

Schenk, H. (1998). Thema: fusies. (Theme: mergers). *Zeggenschap, jaargang 9, nummer 3.*

Schenk, H. (Ed.) (2001). Herpositionering van ondernemingen. (Repositioning firms). Utrecht: Lemma.

Schulze, G. (1992). *Die Erlebnisgesellschaft. Kultursoziologie der Gegenwart.* Frankfurt, New York: Campus.

Sennett, R. (1998). *The corrosion of character.* New York: Norton.

Swaan, A. de (1988). *Zorg en de staat. Welzijn, onderwijs en gezondheidszorg in Europa en de Verenigde Staten in de nieuwe tijd.* (Care and the state. Welfare, education and health care in Europe and USA in the new time). Amsterdam: Bert Bakker.

Ultee, W., W. Arts, & H. Flap (1992). *Sociologie.* Wolters Noordhoff: Groningen.

Verweel, P. (2000). Betekenisgeving in organisatiestudies. De mechanisering van het sociale. (Giving meaning in organisation studies. Mechanising the social). Oratie Universiteit Utrecht.

Wanrooy, S.A.G. van (1999). *Diversity management: theoretische droom of organisatorische realiteit.* (Diversity management: theoretical dream or organisational reality). Universiteit Nijmegen.

Watson, T. (1994). *In search of management. Culture, chaos and control in managerial work.* London/New York: Routledge.

Witteloostuijn, A. van (2001). Après nous la déluge. De economie van egocentrische hebzucht. (The economics of egocentric greed). In H. Schenk (Ed.), *Herpositionering van ondernemingen.* (Repositioning firms) (1–31). Utrecht: Lemma.

About the authors

Jan Boessenkool is senior lecturer and researcher at the Utrecht School of Governance, Utrecht University, the Netherlands. As an organisational anthropologist he combines an interest in organisational culture, management and organisation of sport clubs with organisational research in South Africa.

René ten Bos is a philosopher and consultant who works for Schouten & Nelissen, one of the biggest institutes of management training and education in the Netherlands, and a professor in 'Philosophy and organizational theory' at Nijmegen Management School, University of Nijmegen, the Netherlands. He is the author of several books and many articles on various topics including strategy, ethics, philosophy as well as consultancy. His current research interests are poststructuralism and organization, organizational hygiene, ethics and globalization.

Cary L. Cooper, CBE is BUPA Professor of Organizational Psychology and Health at the Manchester School of Management, UMIST, England. President of the British Academy of Management; Member of the Board of Governors of the Academy of Management; Fellow of the British Psychological Society, Royal Society of Medicine, Royal Society of Arts, Royal Society of Health, and Academy of Management.

Bert van Hees, organisation sociologist, works at the Free University of Amsterdam (department economics and business science) and at the Baak, management centre of the Dutch employers association VNO-NCW. Interests: meaning of work, leadership, buddhism, karate. Published a number of books and articles on work, labour and industrial relations. Editor of Work, organisation and labour in Dutch society (with G. Evers, J. Schippers), Kluwer Academic publishers, 1998.

Willem Koot is Professor of Organisational Culture at the Department of Culture, Organisation and Management at the Free University of Amsterdam, the Netherlands. He has published extensively about topics such as organisational culture and theory, insecurity and management. Recent papers appeared in books edited by Sackman, *Cultural Complexity in Organisations* (Sage, 1997) and by Jeffcutt, *The Foundations of Management Knowledge* (Routledge, 2002).

Ton Korver economist, senior researcher/consultant at TNO Work and Employment, Hoofddorp, the Netherlands. Author of four books and numerous articles on work, employment and organisation. His current research areas are the European Employment Strategy, and Transitional Labour Markets (life time careers). Recent publications (in English): Regulating Labour: Employment Policy in Europe (pp. 58–86 in: The European Journal of Social Quality, 2/2, 2000) Social Quality and the Policy Domain of Employment, Joint project report VS/2000/0777, April 2002 (with D. Gordon, J. Hamilton and others); Amsterdam, European Foundation on Social Quality

Peter Leisink is Professor of Public Administration and Organisation Studies at the Utrecht School of Governance. His teaching and research are in the fields of work, organisation and management. He (co-) edited several publications including *Work and Citizenship in the New Europe* (Edward Elgar, 1993*)*, *The Challenges to Trade Unions in Europe* (Edward Elgar, 1996) and *Globalisation and Labour Relations* (Edward Elgar, 1999).

Hans van der Loo read Sociology at Utrecht University. He worked as a lecturer and researcher for the Institute of General Social Sciences and also as a researcher and lecturer for the Center of Policy and Management. He was published on topics such as paradoxes of modernity, the welfare state, customer-friendly organisations and issues of customer-related services. Currently he is an independent management consultant and publicist after having worked for &Samhouds (consultancy for customer-related services).

Carl Rohde lectures at the University of Utrecht, Department of Mass Communication and General Social Sciences. Next to that he leads *Signs of the Time*, a virtual network of trend- and market researchers worldwide. Rohde conducts research on the movements in the social-cultural climate of Europe. At the university Rohde conducts academic research. At *Signs of the Time* these academic research are translated to their both practical and strategic meaning for business and government.

Paul Verweel is Professor in Organisation and Management from a Multicultural Perspective at the Utrecht School of Governance, Utrecht University, the Netherlands. He has published widely on topics such as diversity in organisations, mergers, strategic management, organisational culture and the construction of meaning in sport organisations.